THIS IS ME:

One hell of a path to happiness

Lis Cashin

liscashin.com
@liscashintalks
She Who Shines: facebook.com/groups/shewhoshines
@liscashin
@liscashin

Dedication

This book is dedicated to Samantha Atherton, my lifelong friend and guide along the path we have walked side by side.

And to all the Atherton family whose love, compassion and support was an incredible act of selflessness in your time of deepest grief. My heart-felt thanks to you all.

Acknowledgements

There are so many people to thank who have contributed (knowingly or unknowingly) in the creation of this book. There are too many of you to mention all of you by name here, but please do know that my heartfelt thanks go to each and every one of you.

My biggest thanks go to my mum and dad, without whom I would not be here and could not have lived my life or written this book. I love you both very much. Next come my sisters Sarah Carrington (who has always been a rock on whom I can depend), Emma Gregory and Lucy Cashin, along with their partners Tom Gregory and John Carrington, and my gorgeous nephews James and Jack Gregory. Thank you all for the laughs, the love, the tears and the shoulders to cry on. And to Grandma Ida and Kath Johnston, you really were (and are) angels in my life.

To all my Mcgrath cousins, aunties, uncles and extended families who I grew up around and who were big influences in my early life, especially in memory of Jeanette Carless, Aunty Sheila and Aunty Angela. To Louise, Arron, Alfie and Charlie – thank you for making Christmas's more special. Special mention to David, Sarah and all the extended Potter family, to Yvonne and all the (extended) Cashin family, and to Emma Sidney and all the Australian Cashins.

I have been blessed with many friends over the years, but there are some in particular who have helped me to see myself more clearly, laugh more loudly and to pick me up when I was down. They are (in no particular order) Judith (Jude) Davis, Sanja Djeric, Jayne Robinson, Tracy Grafton, Siobhan Jones, Cathy Berry, Toby Walsh, Michael Mooney, Marc Cameron, Fordy, Siobhan Harding, Mary Daniels, Sally May, Paul Lomax, Jane Tyson, Mary-Lys Carberry, Dympna Mc Namee, Kate Peel, Sarah from Kent, Juliette Guest, Karen Santamouris, Jayke Branson-Thom, Louise Hawkins, Lisa Rigby, Joanne Embleton, Sally Fernley, Amanda,

Liz Crisp, Steve James and the very gorgeous Ella James.

To all my lovely fellow volunteers, participants and leaders from the Essence Process, Alternatives, Nilambe meditation centre, the Youth Mindfulness training (there are too many of you to mention everyone by name but thanks to each and every one of you and especially my London group Vidya, Anne, Kate, Caroline and Denise), Swami-ji, Bhagawati and the team at Parmarth Niketan ashram, The Esalen Community, Asa Schill, Jesper Juul and the teachings of Familylab and to Lucy Sicks, Cathy Wood and all the team at LIFEbeat.

Thanks to Elsa and Amelie Lobet for the fun times we shared and to Mary Smith for the wonderful years staying in your home. Big thanks to Gordon Jessiman, Dave Lee, Ray Butler, Nichola Ure, Kelly Quinn, Gill Stanyard, Vaz Sriharan and Stuart Kerslake for supporting me and helping me to grow in different ways. For being a fantastic manager in my early career my heartfelt thanks to David Taylor. And thank you to Hannah Power for helping me realise I needed to get a PTSD diagnosis.

Special mention to the Solanki family for their kindness in connecting me to the Parmarth Niketan ashram.

To those wonderful people I met travelling (and their families); Heather McShannon (Paul and Anna), Adinda BentzVa DenBerg, Juliet Anson (Nasia and Kathleen), Rebecca, Sushila and Pradeep Varma, Vita Levchenko, Amit, Nicky and Sandeap and Jean-Benoît.

And a massive thanks to those kind and willing souls (and great friends) who were the first to read this book and to give me feedback and encouragement to get it published; Kate Edwards, Jacky Hems, Kate Peel, Lorna Jacques, Penny Power, Sally May and Cassandra Farren. And to my amazing publisher Sean Patrick and That Guy's House publishing, Lisa Carden for professionally editing the book and James Muller for the wonderful front cover photograph.

Last but by no means least to the very patient and supportive therapists and healers Marie Adams, Sean Carroll, Upchar, Dr. Menis Yousry, Merry Gibbons, Judy Ban Greenman, Kora Dierichs and Emilia Grabczewska, Annie McIntyre, Dr. Lyndsay Lunan, Will and Michael Schwammberger.

Thank you all for holding me to become the happiest and most integrated version of myself.

'Your task is not to seek for love, but merely to seek and find all the barriers within yourself that you have built against it'

Rumi

Introduction

As you read this book, I am going to take you on a journey: my life's journey.

Some people are born and their lives appear to be filled with joy and ease from the beginning. They seem to coast through life; happy childhood, good progressive career, 2.4 children and coping with everything life throws at them. I am not one of those people.

For a long time growing up I thought that life was suffering. It felt like it was all that I knew. Happiness, for me, has been hard won but ultimately worth every step of the way. The joy of the discoveries and the journey I have been on have been the adventure of realising who I am, along with the people I have met and the lessons I have learned.

In outlining the very unhappy childhood I experienced, I then walk you through the steps I have taken which ultimately have led to me discovering inner peace, happiness and personal freedom. Unknowingly I began writing this book in my diaries, from which I have taken much of the content of the book (through keeping a journal as I progressed through the different stages of my life). I then began to put the pieces together in book form whilst travelling in India in 2009.

So why did it take me a further 10 years to complete? I realised that there were still some missing pieces that I needed to live and to learn before I could finish writing it. In the past two years I have had a diagnosis of and treatment for Post-Traumatic Stress Disorder (PTSD) that has given me insights that have enabled me to put a lot of my life into context. So now the book is ready to be shared.

The way the book has been structured is that there is a thread throughout of the beliefs that I formed throughout my personal journey, which you will read in bold letters. This is to enable you, the reader, to reflect on your own journey and what beliefs you may have created about yourself from your own childhood that may be impacting your life today.

This is a story of hope and of triumph of the human spirit. Despite feeling like all the odds were stacked against me as a child, I have found a way to navigate through the pain and suffering, to become happier and to live a fulfilling life. I have found a way to step more fully into my personal power and integrity and to let my light shine.

Please do take care of yourself as you read through the first few chapters of the book where I highlight the emotional abuse and major trauma that I experienced as a child. If you feel you need to get extra professional support and are in the UK I have listed some organisations at the back of the book that you can contact and ask for their advice.

Not just for people who have themselves experienced abuse or trauma, this book is also for those people who are on a journey of personal and spiritual growth; who may be feeling confused or not sure which is the right way to go or the right choice to make. Or they may just need a little inspiration, motivation and encouragement to keep taking the next steps.

Looking back on my own path to happiness I would have loved someone to have been there for me as a guide, to point me in the right direction. This book is that guide.

From my heart to yours.

Lis x

July 15th, 1983

'The force of the shock was so intense that my whole body froze completely. Then I felt the life force drain from my body and I collapsed onto my knees with my head in my hands, saying, 'Oh my god, oh my god, oh my god!'

The sight was horrific. It was too much to absorb. What the hell had just happened? My brain couldn't process the detail and make any sense of it. This couldn't be happening. It was so at odds with the hopes I had had just a moment before. This was like a scene from some sort of horror film. I saw lots of people running over to help.

Then panic and terror overwhelmed me, and I wanted to run to telephone for an ambulance, to get some medical help, to make sure that she was OK. I tried to get up to run for help but my legs were giving way and I was stumbling in a daze. I was trying to get people's attention to tell them what had happened, but my words couldn't come out properly.

This was the day my life changed forever.

But before we get to that, let's go back to the very beginning.

CHAPTER 1
The Early Years

"I can't say this strongly enough, but our feelings about ourselves are actually the most important barometer for determining the condition of our lives!"

Anita Moorjani[1],

'This child is not hungry. This child is not thirsty. This child is just bloody minded!' These were the words the midwife said to my mum about me.

It was 18 minutes past 6am on Wednesday 3rd September 1969 at Nether Edge hospital in Sheffield when I came screaming into this world – and according to my mum, I didn't stop screaming for a long time afterwards!

Who knows why I cried so much as a baby? Maybe I was very sensitive to something in my environment? Maybe I was picking up on tension in our house? Maybe it was one of many other things. But no, the midwife insisted that she knew, and so there I was, labelled right from the start as being 'bloody minded'.

An astrologer once told me that as I was being born, on the eastern horizon, the sun was minutes away from sunrise and just about ready to crest. It was literally the dawning of a new day. We joke in our family that this was probably one of the only few sunrises mum was awake for, as she is definitely not an early riser!

I was the second child in our family born with an older sister (Sarah) who was 2½ years older than me. Like me, Sarah had curly hair. Unlike me, she was apparently always smiling.

We were a very typical middle-class family in most respects. Mum was a teacher and Dad was a sales representative. Mum was 5ft 4' tall and Dad 6ft 4' (I ended up somewhere in the middle). They both had curly hair and so my sister and I inherited curls on both sides of the family. Although when he was growing up on The Wirral Dad had a soft Liverpool accent, my grandma had sent him to elocution lessons and so he then sounded (as Scousers – people from Liverpool – would say) 'dead posh'. Mum's specialist teaching subject was English and so my sister and I grew up being constantly corrected for our grammar and pronunciation, much to our frustration!

Mum had been brought up as a practising Catholic (the middle one of seven sisters!) and Dad a Protestant which caused some tension in the respective families when they announced they were to wed. My dad's mum, Ida, refused to go to their wedding as it was to be held in a Catholic church. Despite the challenges, Mum and Dad married and moved away from The Wirral, where they had both been raised, to Sheffield.

Married for a few years, and with Sarah growing up, my parents decided to try for another child. They had been experiencing some additional challenges in their marriage but had decided to really make a go of it and to have a new baby. That baby was me. Unfortunately, once I arrived they still couldn't find a way to make it work and they divorced when I was just 18 months old.

Hearing this is what had happened when I was growing up, it had seemed to me as though I had been born in a way to help to bring them back together as a couple. This had obviously failed – *I* had failed, I thought – and so the story I told myself was that I had not been good enough, right from the start.

The seed was planted in my mind.

'I am not good enough.'

All the first references I remember hearing about myself were negative. 'Your sister was so angelic… and you just would not stop screaming.' It seemed like Sarah was the good child and I was the bad child, although I never really understood why as I didn't know what I was doing wrong. No matter how hard I tried I never really felt accepted as I was (and I tried really hard!).

'There is something wrong with me.'

More seeds were being planted in my mind about who I was very early on in life. Growing up I would find what I considered to be more and more 'evidence' to reinforce these ideas until they would become the foundational beliefs I held to be true about me.

And yet paradoxically, and at the same time, I felt that deep inside myself I was also a good person. I always wanted people to like me and I wanted their approval and felt I was doing all I could to achieve that. How other people responded to me seemed at odds with how I really felt about myself inside. And so I came to create the negative beliefs about myself based on what I perceived to be other peoples' opinions of me, not on who I really felt myself to be deep down inside. I trusted other peoples' opinions, more than I trusted my own. This would become a very difficult habit to break as I got older.

I remember feeling anxious as a child and like I didn't fit in. I would observe other people seemingly finding it easy to connect and wonder what was wrong with me. My sister, Sarah, was someone whom everybody (including me) loved (and loves) dearly. She had such a sunny disposition and always seemed to be giggling and laughing. I always felt inferior next to her and that I had to be better, to try harder so that other people might come to love me as they seemed to love her.

'I must be better. I must try harder.'

Sarah and I would often have running races with each other, as children do. As she was older than me she would invariably win the race. 'I've won!' she would exclaim. 'Yes, but I was first next!' I would protest.

I was born on a Wednesday and according to the children's rhyme, *Monday's Child*, 'Wednesday's child is full of woe', so even the children's nursery rhymes I was reading were reinforcing the messages I was beginning to believe about myself.

After my parents' divorce, Sarah and I stayed with Mum and we moved back to The Wirral to be nearer to her family (with Dad staying in Sheffield). Initially we lived with another one of my mum's (six) sisters for a while, Aunty Angela and her son Dave and I loved spending time playing with my him.

Then we moved into our own home. Being a single parent of two small children, with the stigma of being a divorced Catholic, was very hard on Mum. As well as continuing her profession as a teacher, she also worked some evenings in a bar to make ends meet.

This meant that a lot of the time I was placed in the hands of different childminders while she was at work, and once one of the childminders, who came to live with us, was only 17 herself. We also moved home quite regularly during this period and Mum had a couple of boyfriends around this time. Moving home regularly became a pattern in my life (I have moved 36 times to date). I think the fact that Mum was so busy, and that I spent time with different childminders, culminated in me feeling unsafe and insecure.

'The world is unsafe. I must not become too attached to anyone as they move on.'

On the occasions when Mum was home from her two jobs, she would be busy catching up with schoolwork, housework, chores, phone calls etc. I always seemed to want more attention and time than she could give to me, leading to an empty feeling inside and a longing to be seen, to be heard and to know that I mattered. I thought that she did love me, but I really craved more time together, just the two of us, and to feel more secure.

I remember feeling very lonely during this time, even though I had an older sister to play with and other adults around me. This empty feeling just would not go away. There was a growing feeling of anxiety within me and I used to bite my nails constantly and was always being told to stop it. One day my poor mum, in desperation, painted some liquid onto them that was called 'Stop and Grow'. It was designed to taste horrible to prevent children from biting their nails. I vividly remember how disgusting it tasted but was so determined to bite my nails that I held my nose, licked it all off and continued to bite my nails anyway. Now that's determination!

A very sensitive child, I was often sick with one thing or another. I used to get attention from Mum when I was unwell and so I think that unconsciously I created sickness to get the attention I craved. Most ailments were something to do with the mouth, throat or stomach. I had lots of problems with teeth and infections, tonsillitis, bronchitis, and later as a teenager with glandular fever. Seeing my dad always seemed to make me feel nervous on some level and I would often become unwell just before he was coming or come out in a rash.

Dad would visit me and my sister a few times a year. He worked in management for a well-known sweets manufacturer and so he would arrive with a boot full of chocolate and sweets that he had bought for us from work – enough to share with friends and family. I think they looked forward to his visits as much as we did (although for obviously different reasons!).

I loved spending time with Dad. He would take us to visit his mum, Grandma Ida, and other relatives that lived on The Wirral. Going to stay with Grandma Ida was always a special time for me. Despite her initial qualms about the marriage between my (Catholic) mum and (Protestant) dad, as far back as I can remember, Grandma always gave my sister and myself lots of unconditional love.

Whatever we did was perfect in her eyes. Any achievement that we made, anything we told her that we had done was always met with 'oh, that's wonderful, dear'. It felt so fantastic to be really seen, heard and acknowledged by her. As bad as my life got at times, I could go and see Grandma Ida and pretend that we were in a different world, a different life than the one I left at her front door and collected again as I left.

Her mum (my great grandma) had run a shop selling savoury pies in Liverpool when my grandma was young. Apparently, her pies were legendary, and people used to come from miles around to buy them. My grandma had learned from her how to bake the most amazing steak and kidney pies. The pastry would just melt in your mouth. My sister and I would always hope that Grandma would make a steak and kidney pie whenever we went to visit.

When we arrived at her house, we would ring her front doorbell and then stand below her front step waiting in great anticipation for her to come and open the door. When she opened it with her wide beaming smile we would rush in to give her a big hug, and at the same time we would take in a deep breath, to see if we could smell the pie cooking or not! I think she was secretly delighted that we loved her cooking so much. She took great pleasure in cooking for us and we took great pleasure in demolishing what she'd made.

Going to stay with Grandma was always a lovely experience. She obviously doted on my sister and me and we could spend the time easily together. Nothing bad seemed to happen whilst I was with Grandma, although we did have some fun adventures together over the years - one of which I'll describe shortly! It felt like a safe space to be with Grandma and here was somebody in my life whom I could tell loved me and Sarah both equally. She was never annoyed with me and she always had time for me. I feel blessed to have had her in my life.

She was an incredible lady. I remember once when we went to stay with her and she was baking some cakes. At this point in time she was around 75 years of age. When I asked her who she was making cakes for, she replied 'Oh, I'm making them for the old people at the lunch club'. I couldn't help but smile. Despite her advancing years, she was still helping others less able than herself.

She used to take Sarah and me out on trips whenever we went to stay. Once, when I was around four years old, she took us on a river boat trip which travelled up and down the River Mersey and there was music on board and children could dance and have fun. When the boat eventually pulled back into Liverpool dock, I had lost sight of both Sarah and Grandma and so feeling a little panicked I ran to the side of the boat and ran down the wooden plank to the harbour side.

The plank was then taken back on board the boat and it sailed away to Birkenhead on the opposite side of the river. Unfortunately, Grandma and Sarah were still on the boat. When they went to disembark they realised I was missing. What a fright I must have given poor Grandma! Incredibly, a lady who lived in her road just happened to be on the dockside in Liverpool and ensured I was taken to safety and eventually re-united with Grandma and Sarah.

Dad and I never had the close bond you might get with a parent when you live with them from birth as I was so young when he and mum divorced, but I loved him dearly and looked forward with great anticipation (as well as nervousness) to his visits. He remarried when I was aged five to my step-mum Lisa and they had two more children, Emma and Lucy, whom I enjoyed seeing a couple of times a year whilst growing up. When they first married, Lisa was very loving and supportive of both Sarah and myself and we even went on their honeymoon to the Isle of Man. But when Emma and Lucy came along, Dad and Lisa moved to another part of the country and Lisa, Sarah and myself became more and more distant over time (until much later in my life when we reconnected with Lisa once more).

Although we didn't see him very often, Dad did always telephone regularly. Unfortunately, he usually called us from work and sounded distracted when he called, which I found very frustrating. I wanted his attention, his whole attention but, just like with mum, I never seemed to get the one thing I longed for.

Mum also got married again to my step-dad, whom I will call Robert, when I was six years old. At first, everything seemed to go well. Robert was a sales representative for a children's toy company and so he would often give me toys as a gift. That would be enough to get any six-year-old child on side!

The first year or so of their marriage went smoothly, as I recall. We moved in with Robert and his son from his first marriage, and my sister and I both went to the same school where Mum was a teacher. We also gained a step-sister. I really liked both my step-siblings. They were a lot older than me and treated me kindly.

Slowly everything started to change. Robert was a jazz singer in his spare time and always liked to drink and be the life and soul of the party. People seemed to love having him around.

Now remarried, working full-time, and being the mother of two children plus having two step-children meant Mum had even less energy or time to devote to me individually than before, and it was affecting me more and more deeply as time went on.

I loved to escape my feelings of loneliness by reading as much as I could. I was an avid reader and would often ask for book tokens or books for my birthday or Christmas presents. I loved getting lost in the fantasy of whatever book I was reading and often didn't want to finish the book as I wanted the illusion to continue for as long as it could. My favourite books at that time were the *Mallory Towers*² series, *The Wickedest Witch in the World*³ and *The Rescuers*⁴. I loved writing stories as much as I enjoyed reading them and was often lost in the escapism of the storyline or poem that I was creating.

When I was nine years old, one of my poems was selected for inclusion in the local newspaper. I was thrilled to see my name and poem in print. I also loved to sing and to act, so regularly took part in our end-of-year shows and choir performances which I really enjoyed. I dreamed of being a famous author or an actor as they both sounded very glamorous and far removed from the reality of my life at the time.

Gradually it became apparent that Robert was taking up more and more of Mum's time and focus. He also began to criticise us all and to have aggressive mood swings. One minute he would appear calm and then the next he would explode with rage and start to say nasty things to me, my mum and my sister. He resented my relationship with Mum and would often try to turn her against me.

He became more and more emotionally abusive towards me over time. It started slowly, with the odd aggressive comment thrown in my direction, which progressively grew worse over the years to the point where I could do nothing right in his eyes. He would question every move I made and constantly criticise and berate me. He loved to say a particularly hurtful comment to me, leave the room and then one minute later put his head around the door so that he could laugh at seeing me cry. He would also make rude comments about my appearance whenever he could. It got so bad that if I heard his car coming up the driveway or his key begin to turn in the front door lock I would feel my whole body tense up, then I would bolt upstairs and shut myself away in my bedroom so that I didn't have to see or speak to him (I spent a lot of my later childhood and teenage years shut away alone in my bedroom).

I tried to suppress my emotions, to avoid feeling shame and humiliation from his comments but it never worked, and to my frustration, I would always end up in tears. It wasn't always over anything big, Robert would just argue for argument's sake. He loved to be in control. If I said I wanted to watch a TV programme he would start to watch it, then suddenly turn the channel over halfway through to put sport on. If I got sick, he would suddenly 'become' sick to get the attention back on him. If I wanted to go somewhere or do something he would automatically say no. I felt stifled and trapped and his behaviour became more controlling as the years went by.

I have a particularly painful memory from when I was 10 years old. I loved to look after Bobo, the class guinea pig at school. I would feed him and clean his cage and take him out and cuddle him. Previously I had been allowed to have two gerbils, Bubble and Squeak, at home. One day I came home from school and they had both died. I was very upset. So, when a teacher at school, who bred guinea pigs, asked if anyone at school would like one, I was so excited. I couldn't wait to get home to ask Mum if I could have one. She agreed in principle but said we would need to check with Robert.

When I asked him, I got his usual initial response of 'NO'. He then proceeded to tell me it was my fault the gerbils had died because I didn't look after them properly – which wasn't true. Mum tried to talk him around and eventually it was agreed that I would have the mother guinea pig and her baby for the summer holidays, and if I looked after them properly I could keep the baby. I was overjoyed! I loved these guinea pigs and made sure that I did everything I could to treat them well. I named the baby guinea pig 'Pickles'. At the end of the holidays it was time to go back to school and I was sure I would be allowed to keep Pickles as I had done everything I could to look after him.

Robert, however, had other ideas, and point blank refused to let me keep Pickles. He would not be swayed no matter how hard I tried. He smiled and laughed as he told me I was not responsible enough to look after it. It was as though he had allowed me to get my hopes up just so that he could dash them. It seemed so cruel.

I had to give both guinea pigs back. I was heartbroken and devastated. I remember lying on the floor and beating my fists in utter frustration. I had really grown to love Pickles and here was something in my life that was just for me and that I could love.

Robert's mood worsened with the increase in his alcohol consumption. Sometimes he would wake up and take paracetamol and Bell's Whisky for breakfast.

I intuitively knew that the family environment I was growing up in was not OK, but as a child you put up with what the adults in your life tell you to do as you don't believe that have a choice.

If I tried to say something about not being happy or to complain about the way things were, I was often told to stop being so negative and to just do my best to get on with things, which I really struggled to do in these difficult circumstances. I felt infuriated as I tried and tried to please my step-dad and yet he still undermined me at every opportunity. Slowly but surely, he systematically attacked my self-esteem.

I stopped asking friends to come around as he would be rude to them too. If we were watching tv, for example, he would come into the room and tell them to get out of his chair and then he would sit down and switch over to another side. He would also say insulting things to me in front of them. I felt so embarrassed.

I would try and tell my real dad when he rang how unhappy I was, but I never seemed to be able to get him to understand how difficult it all seemed and how desperately unhappy I was becoming. And he was busy with his new life and marriage, with the arrival of my two half-sisters, Emma and Lucy, who naturally took a lot of his time and attention. I loved the fact that I now had two more sisters, but I was also envious that they got to have Dad all to themselves and living with them. A lot of the time I felt invisible and unimportant to the key adults in my life.

Every parents' evening or school play that I was in, I would secretly hold out a hope that Dad would surprise me and come to watch. I would daydream about it and how happy I would be and how proud he would be of me. But each time I felt a pang of disappointment when the event would begin and Dad wasn't there.

One thing that was working well for me at that time was the junior school that I went to. I had a great group of friends and we all got on well and were often at each other's houses or being invited to birthday parties, etc. My best friend at that time was Jayne. I remember Jayne and I would have lots of fun playing together out in nature. We would make plans for when we were older and how much fun it was going to be. I felt a real sense of belonging and stability at this school and with these friends that I had not felt before.

Mum had the prose poem from Max Ehrmann entitled 'Desiderata⁵' (meaning desired things) propped up on the side in the kitchen when I was growing up. Its opening line is "Go Placidly amid the noise and the haste and remember what peace there may be in silence". Throughout the chaos that we sometimes lived in I would take great comfort from reading the words at times when I really needed support.

When I was nine years old, Mum wanted my sister to take the entrance exam to a good standard state-run grammar school. Unfortunately, to be able to attend the school, you had to live within a certain catchment area and we didn't live there at that time. Once we found out that my sister had passed the exam we then had to move home to be in the catchment area so that she could start school in the September.

Moving home meant I also had to change junior schools, leaving behind the great friends I had made and to start again in another new area.

This was tough on me, and it took me a while to feel like I had been accepted at the new school as most of the pupils there had known each other since nursery school and had formed very strong bonds of friendship.

Home life with Robert was becoming harder for me to cope with and now I was also feeling like an outsider at school. I didn't realise until I left my previous school just what a source of comfort and security these former friends had been for me.

At my new school I would try and hide how I was really feeling, which was anxious a lot of the time. I started to eat sweets in secret in the cloakrooms at school. In the morning I would take some money from my mum's purse and I would stop at the sweet shop on the way to school and buy lots of sweets. In the break times I would keep eating the sweets until I felt better. And then I would feel guilty and hope no-one would find out what I was doing.

It was the start of an addictive tendency that would surface time and time again throughout my life in various forms. It was also the start of relating the food that I ate to how I felt about myself. I used food as a means of control and also as a way of feeling bad about myself for many, many years.

At such a young age I began to reject myself. I thought there must be something wrong with me and that I had to put on a mask to try and please other people and get them to like me. Because Robert's moods were so unpredictable I began to try to anticipate both his and other people's moods and to try to please them in order to feel loved and to avoid feeling rejected; but it never worked.

I was having trouble sleeping at night. My bedroom was above the living room in our house and Robert had one of those loud voices that boomed when he spoke. This meant I would constantly hear him shouting and complaining to my mum every night while I was in bed, trying to get to sleep. Often, I would hear him shouting my name and complaining about some thing or another that had annoyed him about me that day. Even when I wasn't in the room I still managed to somehow provoke his anger towards me.

To try to block out the sound of his voice I used to fall asleep with my fingers in my ears. It never totally blocked out the noise, but it helped a little and it moved my focus to inside my head where I would try and comfort myself. It became such a habit that I came to the point where I could no longer sleep unless I had my fingers blocking out external noise (and I still do this to this day).

It got to the point where even just hearing his voice my body would tense up in anticipation that I would be accused of having done something wrong. I would always feel I had to think ahead to justify my actions to avoid getting into trouble, which fuelled my inner feelings of anxiety.

I would often feel anger and frustration building inside me but also felt powerless to do anything about it. Robert was so intimidating that I was too afraid to speak up about the injustice of what I felt was happening in our home. I did try a few times but realised that it only made things worse. Mum was constantly trying to calm him down and make things more harmonious, which may have worked for a short time but would quickly escalate again. Mum remembers that I did answer him back and did stand up to him as I got older. I only remember how much trapped rage I felt inside and the frustration of having to live with this man whom I hated so much.

I wished that he would go away and leave us alone. I never wanted him to die - I just wanted him to disappear.

Sometimes when the pain was too much for me and I was unable to sleep, I would sit on my windowsill and stare out at the moon in the night sky. I didn't know why, but I found this to be incredibly comforting. I would sometimes imagine that I was being drawn out of my home in a tunnel of light right up to the moon itself. Like reading my books and writing stories, this was another way for me to escape the feelings of loneliness and anxiety that were growing inside me.

I regularly planned to run away – I felt more powerful somehow in thinking that someday I could escape from this place. There was a motorway near to where I lived and every time we drove along it I would notice a copse of trees along its side. I thought that would be a perfect place to run away and hide in, where nobody would find me. I never found the courage to run away and I would beat myself up about this too. Because I was being bullied at home and was feeling so low, I was now a prime target for some bullies at school.

When I was 10 years old, a group of boys started picking on me and this affected me quite badly. One of these boys had wanted to kiss me and I had refused (he was a year older than me). Because he probably felt rejected and a little humiliated, he decided to humiliate me. He started to call me names and would get his gang of friends to do the same. I was absolutely horrified and felt completely powerless to do anything about it. These boys would follow me home from school, taunting me and calling me names. I really felt afraid.

'The world is unsafe. Men are unsafe. I am unsafe.'

One day, one of them threw a stone at me and it cut just above my eye. While they did get into trouble for that, I continued to be afraid walking home from school each day. Fortunately, being a year older than me, they left school and went onto secondary school at the end of the school year.

Coming back in my final year of junior school I felt excited as I got to take the 11+ exam. This was the same entrance exam to go to the grammar school that my sister went to. I thought that going to a new school would be a fresh start and I felt safer knowing that my sister would be around too as she had become my rock of stability and someone I could always turn to for support. She also stood up for me and I loved having her as my sister.

I passed the entrance exam but wasn't prepared for the effect that it was to then have on my friendships at junior school. My best friend there, Sally, did not pass the exam. She then stopped being friends with me and started to gang up with other girls who hadn't passed the exam and they too started to taunt me and call me names. I couldn't understand why we still all couldn't be friends – to me it was just an exam and we were all still the same people, but to them I think it must have been painful that they hadn't passed and so to regain some control they rejected me.

It was at this point I began to realise that me being intelligent and getting good exam grades was something some other children might not like and could tease and bully me for. It was a pattern that would re-emerge once I got to secondary school.

'I must not be successful as people will reject me.'

All around me were the examples and the evidence I needed to reinforce the negative beliefs that I had embedded in my unconscious mind during those early years of life. They began to develop into my identity, who I believed myself to be, and the world around me reflected the image that I had developed of myself.

'I am worthless. I am powerless. The world is unsafe. I am alone.'

I had developed a very negative image of myself and had internalised everything bad that happened as somehow being my fault (as I was often blamed for things that I hadn't done by my step-dad). Sometimes I began to question myself and wondered if I had missed something and that maybe he was right – maybe there was something wrong with me? I didn't know who I was supposed to be, but I just knew that who I was just really did not seem good enough.

I started to wonder if I was a bad person for all these painful things to keep happening to me.

Somehow, I thought, I had to do everything I could now to be a good girl and to try to please everyone around me, no matter what the consequences were to myself. I tried hard to be as perfect as I could so that people would finally love and accept me. When this didn't seem to work, I would try even harder.

The world overall felt like a very lonely, frightening, frustrating and sad place to live.

CHAPTER 2
The Accident

"There's no tragedy in life like the death of a child.
Things never get back to the way they were."

Dwight D. Eisenhower[6]

Moving onto grammar school felt in some ways like the fresh start I wanted. New people, new start. Everything began well. Still craving recognition and to feel of value, I thrived on receiving positive praise from teachers. I paid great attention in lessons, did my homework on time and got great exam results. This was one area of my life where I knew that if

I did well, I got immediate praise and I felt better about myself. It was as simple as that. I always did the best that I could.

I did well in the first set of exams we did at the Grammar School and it was quite a shock to me afterwards when girls who had been quite friendly to me before the exams started to make snide comments about my results. I could feel the panic starting to rise in me again, familiar with this feeling from when I had been bullied for passing the 11+ exam. I didn't want to lose friends again.

Once again, in my mind it was confirmation from the outside world that excelling in my exam results was not something that was a safe thing for me to do, not if I wanted to be accepted and to fit in, which is what I wanted more than anything else in the world at that time.

I just wanted to be like everyone else but seemed to be alienating myself further. Other girls did well at exams and they seemed to be accepted for it. Not me; for me it seemed a good reason for others to pick on me again. 'What is wrong with me?', the question would resurface in my mind.

I felt very confused. On the one hand I really wanted to do well because it gave me the only real positive attention I was getting in my life from the teachers, and on the other I didn't want to do too well because I felt it would just lead to more misery (from being picked on again). I made an unconscious decision then to continue to do just well enough (to get the positive attention I craved) but not so well that I drew unnecessary negative attention to me. Unconsciously I decided to believe that it was not OK for me to excel in my life as it would only bring me pain and lead to separation from others.

'Excelling in life brings me pain.'

Sometimes I would help classmates with their homework if they were stuck on an aspect that they couldn't understand. I remember one day a friend whom I had known from my junior school) asked if I would help her with some maths homework that she was struggling with. I had already finished my own and so I readily agreed to help her with hers. I told her that I couldn't do the work for her but that I would help her to understand the formula and then she could work it out for herself, which I did.

Several days later we received our maths homework back which had been marked by the maths teacher. I had received full marks for my homework, but my friend had received a bad mark as she had not finished the work correctly.

She then told everyone in my class that it was my fault that she had got such a bad mark and that I had deliberately wanted her to do badly. They all decided, as a class, to send me to Coventry (to refuse to speak to me).

I was so hurt that she could a) think that I would deliberately set out to make her fail, b) not appreciate that I had tried to help her and c) turn the class against me. After the class had left to go to the next lesson I sat in the cloakroom at school, almost beside myself with what had just happened. I sat there crying and planning that I was going to run away right there and then as I could not take any more being blamed for something I had not done, especially when I had been trying to help. It all seemed so unfair at 12 years of age.

'Life is unfair.'

Another classmate, Nicky, was also late for class and she saw me crying and came to talk to me. She said that she felt bad over what had happened and that she didn't blame me at all and wanted to carry on speaking to me. I told her I was going to run away, and she sat and talked to me and made me feel like I at least had one person on my side and she talked me into staying at school. I will always remember her kindness that day.

To avoid being in the limelight and to try to stay under the radar of the girls who picked on me I started to not work quite so hard at my homework and in exams.

Overall, the experience of being at a new school was only adding to my feelings of insecurity and isolation and the situation at home was becoming more and more difficult too.

'I must try harder', was my repeated thought, 'I must try and keep out of everyone's way and do my best to please everyone'. It was exhausting to live like this, not knowing how to act, or the right things to say.

Another way of me getting positive attention had been through doing well at sports. I had always been picked for the sports teams in junior school and this had started well in my secondary school.

To other girls, it was probably just something that they enjoyed doing; something they had fun doing with their friends. To me it was a way of getting attention, of getting praise and because of this it mattered a lot to me.

I loved playing netball and had often been one of the best players in my team in junior school. Now I started to be picked less and less to play for the netball team and I was becoming more and more disheartened as a result. It felt like yet another rejection in my life and so I tried harder and harder to be better at it. The more I tried, the worse I became at the game, or so it seemed. Other girls were always picked and seemed to be having fun.

I played tennis too and would be successful up to a point, but then suddenly my game would worsen, and I would end up losing. No matter what I did, I would always fail in the end. The winning was so important for me to gain recognition but I unconsciously worried about the rejection if I excelled and so I spoiled my game by trying too hard. Then I would berate myself for having failed again and so the cycle would continue.

'I am a failure.'

But I never gave up trying.

One day, during a summer school sports lesson we learned how to throw the javelin. Compared to the other girls in my class I was good at throwing and my throws were often measured longer than my classmates. So good, in fact, that my PE teacher asked me whether I would take part in external matches competing in the javelin events against other schools in the area.

I was overjoyed! Here, at last, was something that I could excel at that other girls didn't. Throwing the javelin was not considered as 'high profile' as netball, but to me it didn't matter in the least. I had finally been chosen. This was my chance to shine. And I felt excited about it.

In February 1983, when I was 13 years old, I joined the javelin club and attended every Wednesday night after school. It was a very supportive group and there was no animosity from any of the other girls in the club. We all got on well together. Some of us would travel to other schools to compete in competitions between the schools.

I remember that Friday 15th July 1983 was a warm day.

The day started like any other. I had breakfast, as usual, and went off to school. I was looking forward to going to school that day as it was our school sports day. In our school we were divided up into four houses (Tudor, Hanover, Windsor and Stuart). The idea of having the different houses was that on days such as the school sports day, each house could compete in events against each other.

I had been selected to represent my school house (Stuart) in the long jump, high jump and the javelin event. I was therefore feeling excited and looking forward to the day ahead.

During our class registration that morning our form teacher had asked if anybody would be willing to assist with the various events at the sports day that afternoon. Because I was already competing in three events I didn't have time to volunteer as well, but some of the other girls who weren't competing put their names forward.

There were several girls willing to help as I recall; Sammy, Sarah and Sara, amongst others. Sammy was someone who was always laughing and joking. She was very playful at school and didn't take life too seriously. I remember one evening at school open night when Sammy brought her mum and dad to our classroom and introduced us all around the piano. We all then started singing songs and having a laugh – it was very funny. She was best friends with a girl called Sarah. We would often all go to the same parties with our classmates. I always got on well with Sammy. She never picked on me like some of the other girls. Sammy, Sarah and Sara were all happy to help out in the afternoon's events.

We had normal school classes in the morning and then, when afternoon came it was time to start the various sporting events. At lunchtime, Sammy had been called in to see the Headmistress. I didn't know what their meeting was about, but I think she was upset about the conversation that took place.

Walking across the school field towards the sports events, I felt a growing sense of excitement, and determination that I wanted to win a medal for my house and to gain some recognition for myself. Maybe then the bullies would stop taunting me and Mum and Dad would give me some attention. I was full of hope and optimism as the afternoon's events began.

Firstly, I participated in the long jump event. I did my best but didn't get a medal. Next to the high jump and the same result. I was frustrated but not massively surprised as some of the other girls were very good and regularly competed in external competitions.

All my hopes were therefore pinned on to the javelin event. I was very excited and also a little nervous as I couldn't bear the thought of not doing well in this event too. I knew there was a chance I might be able to win a medal, so I was determined to do my very best when it was my turn to throw.

Sara and Sarah were standing in the field to mark the javelin throws. A history teacher and an English teacher were overseeing the event, as they had done in previous years. Sara decided she wanted to go and get a drink and so Sammy stepped in to replace her measuring the throws until Sara returned.

During the competition the throw that was measured to be the furthest distance from the starting line (and in the throw area) would be judged the winner and each girl got two chances to throw in each round.

Sammy was standing ahead of the throw area and to the right, and Sarah was standing behind her and a little further back. Sammy was standing just outside white painted lines that showed the designated throw area. A throw that landed between these two lines would be counted as a good throw and the distance entered for the thrower into the competition. Anything that fell outside of these lines would be considered a foul throw and would not be counted. Sara was just returning with her drink to stand behind Sammy when it was my turn to throw.

Around five girls had already been called to throw before I heard my name called. I felt nerves rising inside me as I walked into the designated throwing area. I wanted so badly to win a medal in this event. Focusing on winning, I lifted the javelin in my right hand, took a few deep breaths, ran a few steps and threw as hard as I could.

All my hopes flew with the javelin.

There was a tense moment as I waited to see how far I had managed to throw with my first attempt – willing it to be good enough. At first, the javelin looked to be flying in a straight line and then, at the very last moment, it seemed to swerve off to the right, almost as if the wind had taken it and blown it off course.

For some reason, Sammy did not see the javelin coming towards her. Some other girls and I screamed her name when we saw it veer off course and at the last minute she ducked her head, and, for a very brief moment, I began to breathe a sigh of relief, thinking 'oh my goodness, that was a close call'.

That is until I saw the javelin strike her in the head. The force of the shock was so intense that my whole body froze completely. Then I felt the life force drain from my body and I just collapsed onto my knees with my head in my hands, saying, 'Oh my god, oh my god, oh my god!'

It looked as if the javelin had flown straight into Sammy's left eye and she staggered forwards with her hands moving up towards her head trying to pull it out and I could see blood pouring out of her head.

The sight was horrific. It was too much to absorb. What the hell had just happened? My brain couldn't process the detail and make any sense. This couldn't be happening. It was so at odds with the hopes I had pinned on the throw. This was like a scene from some sort of horror film. I saw lots of people running over to help Sammy.

Then panic and terror overwhelmed me, and I wanted to run to telephone for an ambulance, to get Sammy some medical help, to make sure that she was OK. I tried to get up to run for help and my legs were giving way and I was stumbling in a daze. I was trying to get people's attention to tell them what had happened, but my words couldn't come out properly. Later I was told that I was running around in circles on the field speaking incoherently until another teacher realised I needed help. My memory becomes hazy after that. I know that I was taken into the school buildings at some point and given tea with lots of sugar. I remember my body physically shaking and I couldn't get it to stop. Someone had to lift a cup up to my mouth as I couldn't hold it myself I was shaking so violently. In the distance I could hear the siren signalling that the ambulance was arriving onto the school site, but I had no idea what was happening to Sammy or how badly she was hurt.

Some teachers tried to reassure me that everything was OK, that Sammy would be OK. But they hadn't been there and had not seen what had happened. I knew. I had seen what had happened and I knew in my heart that she was not OK.

At the very least I believed that Sammy would be blinded in one eye by what had happened, because it had seemed as though the javelin had gone straight into her left eye. And that thought alone was terrifying. That was devastating to the 13-year-old me. I was desperate to see Sammy and to tell her that I was sorry, that I didn't mean it, that it was an accident. I had to make her believe me and to know that she didn't blame me.

I don't remember what happened next, but my mum said that the deputy headteacher at my school called her at the school where she was a teacher to tell her that I needed to go home, that I had been involved in an accident during sports day but that it wasn't anything too serious. The school then put me on the phone to speak to her, but I didn't say a word and that was when Mum started to worry that it was all a lot more serious than she was being told by the deputy head.

The school told Mum that someone was going to take me home. Mum then rang my step-dad to let him know I was coming home and that I was not to go to sleep as I was in shock after what happened, and she knew from her first aid training that shock could be very serious and that going to sleep could be dangerous.

Robert however didn't say anything to me when I arrived back at the house and so when mum got home I was upstairs in bed. I was shaking so violently, however, that sleep was not possible. I was wrapped tightly in my duvet, still shaking and I was very cold. I couldn't seem to get warm.

Mum came in to see how I was and she came to give me a hug. I couldn't feel it. I felt numb, like a zombie. From that moment I would feel like I was here physically, but not here emotionally. I felt as though separate from the world and locked in the shell of my body; alive but not living, just functioning in survival mode.

At this point I still had a glimmer of hope that Sammy might be OK and that the doctors would be able to save her sight.

'I really want to go and see Sammy,' I said to Mum, 'and take her some chocolates and tell her I am sorry'. Mum agreed to take me to the hospital, but we would first go and visit Sammy to see how she was before we bought her any gifts.

I was so relieved that I would be able to tell Sammy how sorry I was. I was still desperate for her to know that it was an accident and that I hadn't meant to cause her any harm. I couldn't wait to get to the hospital and have the chance to talk to her.

Mum and I set off in the car, with me still wrapped up in the duvet trying to get warm. I felt a bit of control coming back that I would be able to try and make things right again.

I just remember this feeling of needing everybody to know that it was an accident, and how I had just done what I was told to do, and that I never meant to cause any harm. And please could someone make sure that Sammy would be OK.

I was so used to getting the blame for things that I hadn't done, what on earth would people have to say to me about this?

Mum and I arrived at the hospital and we asked the receptionist if we could see Sammy. She looked up Sammy's name on the computer and asked us if we were related to Sammy (which is standard hospital procedure). Mum explained to her what had happened and who I was, and the lady said that Sammy had been transferred to Walton Hospital in Liverpool because her injuries needed more specialist support.

I felt my whole body go weak again.

I knew then, for definite, that something was seriously wrong. I didn't know much about Walton Hospital except that sometimes I had seen ambulances going there on the motorway and had been told that people only went there when the regular hospitals couldn't deal with an injury as it was so severe and life-threatening.

The feeling of dread was growing stronger and stronger inside me. My stomach felt completely tied up in knots. I could hardly breathe for the pressure on my chest. 'This cannot be happening. This cannot be happening,' I kept repeating and wishing that this would all just be another one of my nightmares, and that I would wake up.

Mum then decided that she would go and try and speak to a doctor to find out more information. She left me in the A & E waiting room. I think she was gone for about 30–45 minutes, but it seemed like forever.

I became more and more agitated as every minute went by. My mind was racing and the fear inside was getting stronger and stronger. People were coming into the A & E department with cuts and broken bones and ambulances were bringing people in on stretchers.

'Please be OK, Sammy, please be OK, please be OK. I am sorry. I am sorry. I am sorry.'

By the time Mum eventually returned, I could barely speak, and my mind was in a state of panic and confusion. Everything seemed so surreal.

She asked me to go outside with her. I remember it was still warm outside and I sat for a moment on a plastic chair near to the back entrance to the A&E department. Mum spoke quietly to confirm that Sammy's injuries were very serious and that she had been transferred to the other hospital to see if the doctors there could help her, although the prognosis was not good.

I heard a quiet voice from inside me ask, 'Is she going to die?'

I knew the answer instinctively before she said it.

'Yes, I think so,' Mum replied.

The pressure on my chest became immense. I was struggling to breathe now. My head was spinning out of control.

How could this have happened? How could this be happening to me? None of it made any sense. My mind was racing, trying to grasp at something that would make sense of all this turmoil. I felt as though I had fallen through a gap in reality and entered some alternate universe.

Why had Sammy not seen the javelin coming towards her? Why had it veered off to the right at the last minute? Why was Sammy not able to move away in time? Why had this been allowed to happen? Why why why why WHY?!

I had so many questions and no answers.

Going home from the hospital I was in a complete daze. This couldn't be real. It couldn't be happening. Before long, the accident was being reported on the local (then national) radio, television and newspapers. Fortunately, my name was not allowed to be mentioned, but the details of the accident and Sammy's current state of health were being reported. Everybody would know what had happened. I would definitely be seen now, but not in a way that I could ever have envisaged or wanted.

Not like this. Not like *this*.

Part of me wondered whether the police would come. It was all so serious, and I was terrified. I was convinced that I would be sent to prison.

Sammy's parents were amazing, right from the start. They wanted me to be protected and out of the media. Now that Sammy was in Walton hospital it became more important in my mind to be able to go and visit Sammy. Her parents said that it was my choice whether to go but advised me not to as Sammy was hooked up to various machines and she had bandages around her head from the operation she'd just had. They thought that seeing her like that would be very traumatic for me. After talking it through with Mum I decided not to go. I still wanted so desperately though to tell Sammy that I was sorry for what had happened.

Unfortunately, I never got the chance. Four days later, Sammy died in hospital from her injuries.

My life was torn apart that day. What once were the boundaries of what was and wasn't possible had now been blasted wide open.

My life would never be the same again. How could it possibly be?

Terrifying things were possible. I knew because I had seen them happen that day on the school field; right out of the blue with no warning at all. 'Normal' rules no longer applied. The world, already feeling unsafe to me, was now a terrifying place to live.

'I must live life on full alert to be ready to stop anything like this from happening again.'

Events like this only happened to other people. Things like this were on the evening news on TV. And so it was that I became one of those people; one of those people that other people talked about. 'I am friends with someone who knows the girl who killed her friend with a javelin,' someone boasted to me in my twenties once at a party (not knowing who I was).

Sammy's parents Ian and Yvonne always seemed to understand that it had been a terrible accident. I am eternally grateful to them for their kindness. They really wanted to get to understand what had happened that day and why it had been allowed to happen by the school. That was what they were interested in – getting to the bottom of what had happened and ensuring that it never happened again to anyone else.

Even in their time of deepest grief, their concern was for me. They asked to see me at their house. Mum was worried that I might not want to go as I was feeling so much guilt, and so she told me that we were going to visit my aunty. When I realised we were driving in a different direction, she admitted to where we were going. I was terrified. The guilt was overwhelming for me. I felt totally responsible for what had happened and being in Sammy's house, with photos of her everywhere was devastating. I dread to think however, looking back, what might have happened to me if Sammy's parents (and family) hadn't been so incredible and supportive towards me at the time.

Once Sammy had died, we got a call that I had to go up to the school to talk to the police and to give a statement. 'This is it', I thought. 'Now I will be arrested and sent to prison'. As I arrived into the school entrance I could see that the rest of my year group were in the school hall being informed about what had happened. Everybody would now know.

I felt numb as I walked slowly into the headmistress's office and sat down in a complete daze. I had been in this office on several occasions, but it was still a daunting place to be. The headmistress's desk was higher than the chairs on the other side, where we now sat. I think it was set up like that so that the headmistress could tower over students seated on the other side of the desk and be more imposing and it worked.

Mum was with me now. There was a policeman and woman who had come to take my statement. They began to ask me questions about what had happened. At one point I was asked 'so were you friends with

Sammy?', 'yes' I replied. 'Had you argued with her that morning?' they continued. I froze.

Oh my god, I thought, they really do think that I did it on purpose. 'No,' I stuttered 'we were friends'. I stumbled through the rest of the interview with their accusatory question ringing through my ears. This question reinforced my fear that other people would blame me. 'I didn't mean it.' I heard myself repeat the words trying to convince them it was true. At the end of the interview I wasn't in fact arrested but was allowed to go home. I was surprised as I felt so much responsibility for what had happened, even though I knew that I had not been messing around or done anything on purpose. I felt that I was definitely going to have to be punished for Sammy's death.

The following week was the funeral. This was the saddest day of my whole life. Seeing the pain and suffering of Sammy's grieving family and friends and feeling totally responsible for all of it was almost too much for the young me to bear.

As I stood and watched the hearse bringing the small coffin into the crematorium, I was convulsing with tears. The coffin was so small, and Sammy was inside it.

'This is all my fault.'

Sammy's family were incredible. On probably the most painful day of their lives too, they came to find me, to make sure I was OK and to invite me to sit with them at the front of the chapel. They showed so much care and compassion towards me.

I sat holding my sister's hand tightly and cried my way through the whole service. The crematorium was packed with people, and they were all there because of me, I thought. Looking back I honestly don't know how I managed to get through the day and, without the support of Sammy's family, I am not sure that I would have.

Being brought up in a Catholic family (although mum's divorce meant that my sister and I weren't brought up as practising Catholics), I was terrified at the idea that there might be a God; a God who would want to punish me for what I had done. Isn't one of the Ten Commandments in the bible, 'Thou shalt not kill'? It doesn't specify whether that killing is done by accident or not. It just says 'Thou shalt not kill'. That statement was not clear enough to put my 13-year-old mind at ease.

Although I felt that I deserved to be punished and even to die for what I had done, I was at the same time terrified of dying because I believed I might go straight to hell and be stuck there forever.

I therefore felt stuck from that point forwards – living, but not living, like a walking dead person straddling two worlds (life and death).

Sammy's grandma at the funeral came to find me to give me a doll that she had made for me. I treasured that doll and kept it close to me. I slept with it for many years until it fell apart, and still I keep it to this day. And later on Sammy's parents bought me a necklace that I wore all day every day for many years.

These acts of compassion towards me seemed in so much conflict to the guilt I was feeling. I am sorry now that I was not able to take the compassion and kindness that all Sammy's family showed to me to heart back then. But the traumatised me just thought that they obviously could not see what a bad person I really must be inside.

On the way back home from the funeral my step-dad told us in the car that that was it now, we were never to mention what had happened, or Sammy's name again in our house.' It is all in the past' he said, and we were to leave it there.

I think he just couldn't handle the fact that I was getting so much attention from everything that was happening, and he wanted the spotlight back onto him once more.

This meant that, even in my own house, I couldn't talk about how I was feeling. It also meant that the beliefs I was creating about myself had a chance to become deeply embedded in my unconscious mind and began to impact every aspect of how I lived my life.

'I am evil. I deserve to be punished.'

How could I ever come to terms with The Accident? When I truly believed that I deserved to be punished for having done something so terrible that even God would not forgive me? And with no help at all to process what had happened?

CHAPTER 3
The Teenage Years

"There are wounds that never show on the body that are deeper and more hurtful than anything that bleeds."

Laurell K. Hamilton[7]

In today's modern world, counselling and psychotherapy are accepted terms that we hear all the time. It is commonplace for someone who is going through a difficult time emotionally to go and seek help from a therapist. There is also a widespread use of antidepressants.

In 1983, when The Accident happened, there was no such help readily available. Mum went to speak to our local GP and he said that I didn't need to go and see him and that it didn't even need to go on my medical record! I remember my mum asking me whether I wanted to talk to a psychiatrist. I panicked. As a 13-year-old child I thought that only people who were crazy went to see psychiatrists. I thought that if I went to talk with a psychiatrist that this would go on my medical record and that nobody would ever want to employ me in the future. Children often form distorted opinions based on limited knowledge and experience in life.

For this reason, I turned down the offer. I also thought I needed to try and pretend I was OK because otherwise I might be sent to see a psychiatrist anyway.

'I must pretend that I am OK.'

So, I never got to talk to anybody about what had just happened and bottled everything up inside. Can you imagine what that was like for the 13-year-old me? Badly traumatised, I had to try and hide the exploding volcano of emotions erupting inside of me. It was tough, beyond anything you can imagine and took a huge amount of energy each day just to keep functioning.

The Accident happened just before the school summer holidays and so

I didn't have to go back to class until September, giving me a couple of months break from school. I felt like I was in a daze the whole summer.

Going back to school I remember clearly the day that I walked into the classroom and saw the empty desk and chair where Sammy would have sat. Being in the same school environment there were so many reminders of Sammy and of that tragic day. Every time I walked past the school sports storage area where I could see the javelins piled high, every time I was out on the girls' playing field I could see through to the boys' sports field in the corner where The Accident had taken place. Every time I saw Sammy's best friend Sarah I felt guilt around having taken her best friend away from her.

And I had nobody to talk to about any of it. To be able to say to Sammy what I really wanted to say to her I began to write letters to her (which a therapist later in life told me was the best thing I could have done). I poured my heart out in those letters. I asked Sammy lots of questions about her life and about the dreams she would have had that would now no longer come true. I expressed my deepest sadness and regret for what had happened and asked for her forgiveness. I thanked her family for having treated me with such kindness in their own time of sorrow. I would of course never be able to post those letters or to receive a response to them from Sammy but just writing them helped me to feel closer to her somehow. Although I would never be able to tell her face to face how sorry I was at least she would be able to know it through my writing, I thought. I felt great comfort in writing them.

The headteacher was in regular contact with my mum and told her that all the teachers were keeping an eye on me to check if I was OK at school. That felt very strange to me – as if all eyes were on me, but no-one was saying anything. This only heightened my own feelings of guilt and shame and not wanting anyone to see me, for fear of what they might discover. I had this double bind now inside; part of me still desperately wanted to be seen but another part was terrified of what people might see if they looked too closely.

The girls who had been picking on me about getting good exam grades before The Accident now stopped belittling me. In fact, they seemed to be trying to be friendlier towards me, which was good in one sense but felt very strange and surreal at the same time. I didn't know if I could trust them.

The inquest into Sammy's death took place in October 1983. I really wanted to be at the coroner's hearing. Up until that point I only had my version of the events that day in my mind and I wanted to hear what other people had remembered and to hear whether they thought I was to blame in any way.

The police, however, spoke to my mum and advised her that there would be a lot of press at the hearing and that it may be better to keep me away and out of the media spotlight. There had been an incident not long before when my sister had been walking down the road and a boy had shouted 'murderer' towards her, which had obviously been very upsetting for our whole family. The police were worried that there may be other incidents like this if I was to go to the inquest.

At the end of the inquest, the coroner recorded a verdict of 'Death by misadventure'. This is all I was told at the time. Many years later, I learned that he said that, if the jury felt that the school had properly organised the javelin event in every respect, a verdict of 'Accidental death' could be recorded but if not then they needed to record a verdict of misadventure, which they did. It was determined that two 13-year-old girls should never have been allowed to mark javelin throws and that a warning sign that the next person was about to throw (like a claxon or a siren) would be safer in future to allow the people marking the throws to pay attention that the next javelin was about to be thrown.

Not being allowed to attend the coroner's hearing I heard the verdict of 'death by misadventure' and thought that it related to me. I thought that somehow the coroner thought that I had 'misadventured' in some way – I didn't know what the word really meant but I heard it to be more evidence that I had done something wrong. I think if I had heard the word 'accidental' I would have felt much better and less responsible.

I wanted to read the coroner's report that came out after the inquest but was told that it contained explicit details about the injuries Sammy had sustained and that it was better that I didn't read it. I felt powerless and not in control again. I had really wanted to see Sammy in hospital and had been advised it was better not to see her, then I was told it was better for me not to be at the inquest and finally it would be better if I didn't read the inquest report.

I was left alone again with just my version of events in my mind and the conviction that somehow, in some way I was to blame for what had happened and that there was something inherently wrong with me.

I would get flashbacks for decades of that day and the horrors of what I had seen and experienced. They became tattooed on my mind. I just needed to make sense of something that made no sense at all. And so the only thing that seemed to make any 'sense' was that somehow it was my fault.

I managed to get up every day and go through the motions of survival; eating and drinking, getting dressed and going to school. Sleep was not something that I was getting enough of. My already disrupted sleep got worse and some nights I would not sleep at all before having to get up again for school the next morning. I was exhausted and running on empty the whole time. It was often 3-4am by the time I fell asleep and then had to get up for school the next day.

I had a deep rage inside and I also felt trapped in fear. Part of me was frozen in time, still stumbling around the playing field reeling in shock. The next few years at school went by very slowly and extremely painfully. To try and escape the overwhelming pain I was feeling inside, I threw myself into my studies. I wanted to do well in exams in memory of Sammy – I thought I owed her that much at least. Her parents had been so adamant that they didn't want another life ruined by what had happened on the school field that day and I didn't want to let them down. It was very difficult at times to concentrate, with everything else I had going on, but the memory of Sammy spurred me on to do the best that I could.

Life at home got progressively worse as Robert's drinking increased and his moods became more unpredictable and erratic. Most afternoons he would go to the pub before he came home. As before, I would hear his car pulling into the drive or hear his key about to turn in the front door lock and I would bolt upstairs and lock myself in my room with music turned up so that I couldn't hear him – although his voice was so loud that I could always still hear him booming, no matter how I tried. In the end I got headphones and turned up the music so loud that it probably damaged my ears but much better than having to hear his voice any more.

Not surprisingly, I became very depressed. As I was so young – by now just 14 – Mum was worried about me and so she made an appointment for me to see her doctor. We now had a different doctor from the previous one who had said that The Accident didn't need to go on my medical record and whilst at the appointment with this new doctor, he asked me what was wrong. I told him that my mum thought that I was depressed.

'Depression, my dear, is a serious clinical condition,' he chastised, and added, 'I don't think you're depressed.' He then dismissed me without helping at all and without really asking me about what had happened when I was 13.

This comment and dismissal by the doctor were incredibly damaging to me. They prevented me from going to seek any more medical help for the next six years. It also reinforced the idea that I didn't matter, and that no-one wanted to hear what I had to say, that I should try and pretend that I was OK because even the doctor had dismissed me without listening to what I was going through.

'I am worthless. I must pretend that I am OK.'

Whichever way I turned for help I seemed to come to a dead end. No-one seemed to be there for me, except my sister Sarah, my cousin Kathryn and Grandma Ida. They all seemed to see good in me and were always there as a shoulder for me to cry on.

Kathryn was nine months older than me and we had lived around the corner from each other growing up. She became like an additional sister to me and I loved spending time with her. Kathryn is one of those special people in life whom everybody loves. She is always giving to everyone else and I am very grateful for the happy moments we shared that helped me to survive those difficult times. We would often walk to school together and Sarah and I would call around to my Aunty Ro's house to collect Kathryn on the way. There would always be a mountain of toast waiting for us as Kath also has two brothers and poor Aunty Ro would have to toast and butter the lot!

I tried to push my emotions deeper and deeper inside where no-one would ever see them. But the rage was building because of how oppressed I was feeling at home. I felt squashed and insignificant and completely powerless to change.

'I am powerless to change. I am a victim.'

On many occasions I wanted to end my life to stop the chronic emotional pain I was living through every day. But how could I take my own life when I knew how precious life was? And if I did, would I go straight to hell? Would Sammy be waiting to take revenge on me? One day I did start to swallow paracetamols but only got to around 10 before I panicked and stopped. I never told anyone about what I had done. The fear of going to hell was worse than the pain of living, I decided. I carried on surviving somehow, day after day, not realising that I didn't need to die to go to hell. I was already living in it within my own mind.

I was terrified of going into churches. On the rare occasion that I did, I would feel so guilty and so undeserving of love that I would run out in tears.

I felt alone, isolated, disconnected from everybody, including myself. I hated life and I hated myself. And it was becoming unbearable to live in our house.

Even the girls at school who were supposed to be my friends were now rejecting me. If I left the room and later returned, I would see them whispering together in groups, and immediately shut up when they saw me. I knew that they were talking about me. They would invite each other around to their houses and exclude me, and then I would hear about it at school the next week.

Then when I was 15-years-old, my sister had her 18th birthday. There was a local nightclub which gave free tickets to people reaching this milestone, and so Sarah had got some and was going to celebrate there with all her friends.

Because of the situation being so difficult at home, Mum agreed that I could go along too. I was excited! It felt very grown up and I felt that I was creating my own social life, without having to rely on the girls at school.

This was the start of me going out a lot at night to pubs and clubs – anything to get away from my step-dad. It was such a relief to be leaving the house and him behind. I was so grateful to my sister for letting me go along with her (and my mum who let me go). I was lucky enough to look a lot older than my age and I was tall which helped me looked 18. I remember, once, a bouncer stopped Sarah's friend from getting into a bar and demanded to see her ID and she really was 18. Meanwhile, the 15-year-old me just smiled and walked straight in behind my sister. I felt accepted into this new world.

Exam pressure was growing at school and aged 16 I took my 'O' level exams (these were national exams that all schoolchildren took at that age, which have now been replaced by GCSEs). I did exceptionally well and got 12 'O' levels, of which 8 were Grade A. I am incredibly proud of this achievement. It shows that even despite all the pain I was feeling, I was resilient enough to focus on passing my exams. Throughout this time there was a deep inner strength I can see I was drawing on, even though I couldn't feel it at the time. Part of me knew that getting good exams and going to university would mean that I could get away from my step-dad and I also felt that Sammy's memory had been honoured, which was so important to me.

Meanwhile, Robert's drinking and his behaviour got progressively worse.

Sarah passed her A levels and then left home to go to Coventry Polytechnic to study Business Studies when she was 18. Although I was already the main focus for Robert's anger before she left home, this became increasingly worse once Sarah had left and I was the only remaining child to target with his aggressive behaviour.

Things got so bad that I couldn't bear to be in the house with him. In fact, I couldn't even bear to be in the same room as him. If he came anywhere near me I would instinctively back away and I tried to stay locked in my room as much as I possibly could. My bedroom had become my 'safe place'. I would put my headphones on and try and imagine I was somewhere else, anywhere else but there.

Mum was finding it increasingly difficult to cope too. The toll of living in such a challenging and abusive environment was negatively affecting her self-esteem and she ended up having a mental and emotional breakdown around this time. Watching her slowly descend into turmoil was terrifying.

She was finding it ever more challenging to cope with my step-dad's excessive demands along with the stresses of a full-time teaching job. Part of me desperately wanted Mum to leave Robert and to take me with her, but she really loved him and wanted to stay to try and make it work. I hated him for what he had done to our family. And I was so angry with mum for not standing up for us.

In my sixth form at school, I really started to enjoy life a bit more. I asked to change classes from the girls who were making my life miserable and I made some great new friends who I used to go out with a lot at night. One classmate, Cathy, lived in the same road as me and although we had up until then been in separate classes from each other, we had often walked to school or caught the bus together. She was always really nice to me and our friendship meant a lot, so I asked my form teacher at school if I could be transferred into Cathy's class, which is what happened. It was such a relief to be around nice people again.

Siobhan and Stacey were also two new classmates. I had been in Siobhan's class earlier in school and had seen Stacey around but we started hanging about together and going out at night. We always had a good laugh together at school and very often I would go out with them or my other friend Joanne to the pub in the evenings to escape life at home. I had passed my driving test now and Mum let me borrow her car. I wasn't drinking alcohol, but just the release of getting out of the house at night was fantastic. I didn't have to be stuck inside any more, dreaming of running away, and it felt so liberating.

Robert, though, didn't like this at all. He couldn't control me if I was out of the house. Even though I was not physically at home, he would still be constantly criticising me to Mum and trying to brainwash her with all sorts of ideas about what I was getting up to every night. When I was 15, he told her he was convinced that I would come home and announce I was pregnant one day and that if I did that he would leave straightaway. When Mum told me this I did seriously consider getting pregnant, I was so desperate to try anything to get him away from us, but at that point I had not even kissed a boy!

Eventually, after turning 17, it all became too much for me.

After one particularly loud and heated argument with Robert I'd had enough. He was going on and on and on and on about what a terrible person I was. I wanted to scream out loud.

Instead I stole Mum's car keys and took her car. I knew that this was irresponsible, but I had come to the end of my tether and I didn't know what else I could do. I ended up staying out all night talking with my ex-boyfriend to try to decide what I should do because I knew that I just couldn't live with Robert any longer. I couldn't take any more of his abusive behaviour.

I didn't come back home until the early hours of the morning. Mum was really worried that I had gone off to hurt myself. She had tried calling my friends but no-one had seen me that night and so she became more and more anxious about what I might have done to myself. She left me a letter that I read when I came back home in which she apologised for not having sided with me the night before and acknowledging how difficult life at home had become.

The next day I told Mum I was going to see Citizens' Advice Bureau (CAB) to take advice on what my options might be around moving out. She said that she wanted to come to the appointment with me. So, we went to see an advisor and I told them how unbearable life had become living with my step-dad.

I wanted Mum to listen to what I was saying in the meeting and to want to protect me by leaving Robert. I wanted her to tell me that I was more important to her than he was. I wanted her to tell me that she was going to leave him now and to take me with her to somewhere safe without him. But she didn't.

The lady from the CAB asked both me and my mum a lot of questions about my step-dad and his behaviour. She took what I was saying seriously. Then she agreed to find me some sheltered housing that was available to young people who had been living in abusive home environments.

A short time later, I was told that they had found me somewhere to live. I was to be moved into a council flat in a very rough part of Birkenhead, the largest town to us, which was quite a distance from my family and school. I didn't care! I was so delighted at the thought of being away from my step-dad that you could have stuck me anywhere else and I would have been happy as I would be free and away from him at last.

As an adult I look back and see that, even though I was desperate to leave, it still took a lot of courage and strength to leave home at the age of 17.

This move felt like the first real inner victory in my life. For the first time, I felt I had really taken control of my own life and was moving myself to a place of safety. I no longer had to do what the adults in my life said I had to do. I felt so empowered at the thought of being on my own and away from the emotional abuse and control I had had to endure all these years.

My extended family were not so sure about my move. I vividly remember a party I was at with Mum's sisters and their families. One of my uncles came and took me to one side. He wanted to tell me, he said, on behalf of the family how disappointed they were in me because I was moving into this flat to have parties every night. And he was being serious! I couldn't believe what I was hearing. I was distraught that during this time of struggle they could judge me so harshly and believe that wanting to have parties was my primary reason for leaving home. But my step-dad was very manipulative and was very charming to them – so they just saw me as being moody and believed Robert when he said that I was the real problem.

Not long before I was due to move out into the flat my real dad appeared at the house one day unexpectedly having driven up from London to talk to me (a three-hour drive). All those years as a child of hoping that my dad would come and surprise me with a visit (at parents evening, etc) and here he was. I was thrilled to see him, especially as I was feeling particularly vulnerable at that point and assumed that he had come to give me some support. 'Finally, he understands and has come!' I thought. I was so happy.

He sat me down and said that he had come to see me to convince me not to move into the council flat. I was initially confused. And then I mistakenly thought that he had come to give me an alternative solution that would be even better. 'Are you going to pay for a private flat for me?' I asked hopefully (and excited) as this seemed to be the only other solution I could think of. 'No,' he replied. 'I want you to stay here with Mum and Robert. I don't want you living in a council flat.'

I was absolutely devastated. It seemed cruel somehow to have come all this way to see me and when, for a brief moment, I had felt that I was really being seen, heard and that I DID matter, to pull the rug from under me and advise me to stay in such an abusive and unhealthy environment. I felt crushed.

Not long after that visit I moved out, and Dad did not come to visit me while I lived in the flat. I developed a lot of anger towards him for not being there for me at the time when I felt that I needed him most.

Although Robert had been emotionally abusive towards me, I had also lived a fairly sheltered life in other respects and was not streetwise at all when I moved out. I became so quickly though!

I went from living in a house in a suburban neighbourhood to a flat in one of the roughest parts of a big town, with a drug dealer living in the flat below me. It was quite a shock at first, but I also didn't mind at all. The flat itself was part of a bigger block of council flats on the junction of two very busy roads in the centre of town. It was noisy due to the traffic noise outside, and there was lots of people activity day and night, but to me it felt like the best place in the world.

I was sharing with a flatmate who had some mental health problems and severe eczema. She was on steroid medication for the eczema and used to stand there constantly scratching and making herself bleed in front of me. She had a boyfriend (who was a massive *Dr Who* fan and who used to dress like him!) and they would pretty much keep themselves to themselves.

I loved the newfound freedom that I had. Even though my flatmate acted strangely, and even though the flat was less than ideal, it still felt better and safer than where I had just come from. There was no-one controlling me, no-one belittling me and no-one telling me what to do. It felt liberating.

I didn't have a telephone in the flat and, as this was in the days before mobile telephones (or computers) had been invented and/or in general use,

I didn't have any means of communication with the outside world unless people came to visit me.

Grandma Ida would have been really upset to learn that I was living in a flat with a stranger and so I didn't tell her that I had moved out of mum's house. Mum and I developed a system whereby whenever Grandma would call my mum's house to speak to me, my mum would tell her that I was in the shower, or that I had just gone out and then Mum would drive to my flat and tell me to call Grandma, which I did from the pay telephone kiosk which was located over the road from the flat! This was quite a distance for Mum to drive and I am very grateful to her for doing this, and for lending me her car sometimes too so that I could continue to go out with my new friends.

I preferred Grandma Ida not to know. That way, when I saw her, we could just have a lovely time together and I could forget all about my troubles for a little while. Her home was such a special, safe place for me growing up and I loved going to stay with her, which Sarah and I continued to do every few months or so.

CHAPTER 4
The Great Escape

"Reality is just a crutch for people who can't handle drugs."

Robin Williams[8]

Studying for my 'A' levels whilst living in the council flat was not easy. Unlike my classmates at school, I had to do my food shopping, cook my own meals and look after myself and study at the same time. I didn't feel prepared to take on so much responsibility, especially still having had no support to process anything that I had been through.

Mum was still living with Robert but she helped me out at the flat as much as she could, and she lent me her car at times so that I could still go out and visit my friends. I was still angry with her for not leaving home with me (but looking back I am grateful that she gave me what she could during what was a very difficult time for her).

Despite all the challenges, I passed the 4 'A' levels at school that I needed to get to university. I was so proud of myself for this achievement and was delighted to have passed the exams at all, in the circumstances. I had done it! Despite everything, I had worked as hard as I possibly could, and was offered a place at Hull University to study French and Business Studies – which meant I would be spending my third year in France, either studying or working. And Hull was located on the other side of the country from The Wirral which made it even better in my opinion. I wanted to get as far away as possible.

Before I went away to university, I had a summer break. I had had a Saturday job working in the department store Littlewoods from the age of 15 and had been putting some money into savings since I moved into the flat. After I got my 'A' level results I spent my savings by going on holiday to Ibiza with some friends from school.

We had a great time! 18-years-old and let loose in the bars and clubs of

Ibiza, we had such a laugh together and I felt free. A different kind of seed was planted in my mind.

'When I travel to other countries I feel free.'

Arriving back from my holiday I felt different in some way. Feeling so liberated on holiday had opened up something in me that I had not felt before. In travelling to a different country, I somehow felt I could be more 'me' without the pain and suffering I was carrying. It was as if for the time away I could leave it behind and pretend to be someone else; the someone I had known at times before the accident. It was as though I didn't feel that I had the right to experience any happiness when living in the UK, but whilst abroad that seemed to change for a brief time. It felt as if the time abroad was like living in a dream and then I came back to the reality of life at home.

Coming back to the UK, I knew that a whole new chapter of my life was about to begin at university. With the help of Mum, I moved all my stuff over to Hull in time for the start of term in October 1988.

During my first year at Hull something started to change inside me. I think I had been holding on to pain for such a long time without being able to release it, that once I was finally both away from my step-dad and living in a different part of the country I began to realise just how much emotional and mental pain I really was carrying inside.

I started missing lectures and staying in bed a lot. I just wanted to hide away from the world. I was tired of having to struggle through every day and pretend I was OK. I just kind of gave up, I think. Eventually one of my French lecturers called me in to see her to chastise me for missing lectures. I just broke down and cried and told her my whole life story.

She was so kind and really listened to what I had to say. She suggested that I go to see the doctor at our university health centre, which I did. He referred me to a clinical psychologist who came to see patients at the centre (usually for eating disorders). Part of me was so happy. It seemed that I was finally being taken seriously by a medical professional. Finally, somebody had listened to what I had been through and agreed that I did need some help to release the emotion trapped deep inside me (unlike the doctor who had dismissed me aged 14).

When I arrived at the appointment with the psychologist I was like a dam ready to burst. Almost as soon as I walked through the door I started to cry, and to tell him what I was feeling and what I had been through. He stopped me quite abruptly and told me that he was going to be making notes and could I please slow down and just tell him everything one sentence at a time, so he could write it down. His tone appeared to be one of disapproval and agitation.

I couldn't believe it. I couldn't speak slowly! Everything just wanted to come gushing forth and he was telling me to somehow stop it, to slow it down so that *he* could make his notes.

I only went to one session and once more I tried to push my feelings back into the box where they had been shut so tightly all these years. It would be several years before I would have the courage to try and speak to somebody again.

I decided I felt I needed to put on a mask again to pretend to the world that I was OK, when inside me the pain was growing and growing and growing, gnawing away at me.

During my first year away, Mum finally found the strength to leave my step-dad. I was relieved as I thought I would now be able to get my mum back. She moved out of the house she shared with him and was renting a flat in the town where my own flat had been. Although I was still carrying a lot of anger at this point towards Mum, I loved her too and wanted to support her decision to leave him and so agreed to go and stay with her during my Christmas holidays.

At the end of term, I got an earlier train home to surprise Mum but when I arrived at her flat, Robert was sitting there. I got such a shock to see him. He was so charming towards me and pretended how pleased he was to see me. I felt like my world shattered again. I couldn't understand how Mum had put me through everything with Robert and had not protected me. And now, when I was so happy and racing back to spend time with her, here he was sitting in her flat when she told me she had left him.

I lost a lot of trust in Mum at that point and so, even though I never saw him with her again, I never trusted that she was telling me the truth if she said that she hadn't seen him. I would have nightmares that they were back together again even many years later, and I would wake up shaking and in tears.

I behaved badly towards Mum after this. I think I was trying to punish her in some way for all the hurt I was feeling. I spoke down to her and was quite rude at times. I had lost respect for her and wanted her to hurt as I was hurting so badly.

Going back to university, I continued my first year and passed my exams. In the summer holidays I went abroad on a holiday to Greece with Stacey from school and another friend of ours, Laura, and once again this felt like freedom for me.

We went out every night to various pubs and clubs and in the daytime, we sunbathed on beautiful white sandy beaches. We met some lads from Manchester who we would take the mickey out of, and them us. It was a lot of fun. Then it was time to return to 'reality' and back to university once more.

My second year at university passed by with nothing major to report. That said, I was finding it increasingly difficult to cope in stressful situations and particularly around exam time. It was as if exam pressure was tipping me over into a level of internal chaos that was harder and harder to contain. I didn't talk to anyone about it. I just kept wearing my 'I'm OK mask' and did the best I could to get away with pretending that I was OK. I was living in a university hall of residence with at least 100 other students and so life was never dull or lonely. There was always something happening that I could be a part of or to distract myself with. And there was lots happening at the university too.

I didn't have high self-esteem, although I could appear confident on the outside. Although I found some of the guys attractive at university, they didn't feel the same way towards me in the first couple of years and so I felt a lot of shame with regard to the way I looked. Ever since I was small and smuggling sweets during breaks at school, I had used food as a way of beating myself up and this happened a lot whilst I was at university. I would think to myself 'if only I were thinner, boys would like me'. For every mouthful of food I ate, my internal voice would berate me and punish me by calling me all sorts of names: 'You fat cow, you should be ashamed, how could anyone find you attractive.' The ironic thing looking back at photographs of me around that time is that I wasn't fat; I created a physical and mental image of myself that wasn't true and beat myself up about it consistently. It was a way to keep punishing myself, as I could not avoid eating food.

Much later on I discovered the difference between confidence and self-esteem. Confidence is a measure of what we are capable of doing – what we are good and clever at doing, or what we find difficult or are not good at doing. Self-confidence is about what we can achieve. It is more of an external, acquired quality. Because I had passed my exams and had done well at school academically, I did have a level of confidence.

Self-esteem, however, is our knowledge about, and experience of, who we are being. It could be envisaged as a kind of inner pillar, centre or core. People who have a healthy, well developed sense of self-esteem feel self-contained and at ease within themselves. I really didn't have good self-esteem. When I learned the difference I could understand why some people think that I have always appeared to be confident, when the reality in my mind about how I have viewed myself has been very different.

At the end of my second year at university, one of my cousins got married. At the wedding, my mum started chatting to the father of the bride, David. They got on well and soon after formed a firm friendship that has lasted to this day. It felt too soon for me to be allowing another man back into our lives, in whatever form that took. I panicked, and I strongly resisted their friendship in the early stages, afraid of the possibility of another abusive man coming into our world. I was rude about him to Mum and I didn't want to be in our home if he came to stay when I was there. Sarah was living back at home at the time, and she really struggled to accept him as well.

Bit by bit, David showed us how different a man he was to Robert. He would always tell us his honest opinion, even if he knew that it might be difficult for us to hear. So, we always know where we stand with him – even if we don't like it.

This was like a breath of fresh air for the whole of our family. Here was someone on whom we could depend. He helped Mum to regain her self-respect and has been a great support to her (and us) over the years. He also helped my sister Sarah, when she bought her first house, with odd jobs that needed doing and so slowly he also gained her trust and her respect.

I am very grateful to him for coming into our lives when he did, even if I did anything but welcome him in the beginning (sorry, David). Along with David came his two daughters, Sarah and Louise, and over time their partners and children too. Our families have become close, which has meant a lot to me.

My third year at university was fantastic. This was the year I got to spend in France as a part of my degree course. Because I had previously shared my background story with my French lecturer at Hull University and she had a lot of sympathy for my situation, she managed to find me a work placement in Paris (one of only two that the university placed - everybody else had to find their own placements in France). I was incredibly lucky and extremely grateful to her for giving me this opportunity.

My work placement was in a Patent and Trademark Attorney's office in Paris. I was to work principally for the managing director, but also for the other engineers and their secretaries. I was translating and teaching English and giving administrative support. It was a well-respected role within the company and it paid well for the type of role that it was.

I remember my first day at work there vividly as it was the day of my 21st birthday. Mum surprised me by sending me a birthday helium balloon to the office and I was touched to receive this connection to home.

The first three months living in Paris I found to be challenging. Learning French in the UK and living and working in France are two separate things. I couldn't initially understand what people were saying, due to the speed with which they talked. When lots of people were talking together it just sounded like a lot of noise and it was exhausting trying to concentrate all the time to try and understand what people were saying.

I hadn't been working there for long when one of the engineers came into my office and said 'Vous l'avez fait exprès?' and looked around the room. I had no idea what he meant and so I just replied 'Oui'. 'Oui?' He repeated and looked puzzled, shrugged his shoulders and walked back out again. I quickly grabbed my dictionary as I had grown accustomed to doing and looked up what he had said. 'Have you done it on purpose?' was what he had asked me, and I realised that I was sitting in a dark office without the lights on. He had obviously been asking whether I really meant to be sitting in the dark – and I had said yes! Then I thought that I had to sit there without the lights on, feeling like a bit of an idiot. I made the decision then that I would not reply yes or no to a question, unless I knew what I was being asked!

This, however, wasn't the only or the biggest blunder that I made linguistically whilst I was there. One day I came into the office and (thought I) said that I had been sitting next to two people who were kissing non-stop on the Metro (tube) on the way to work. My colleagues looked really shocked, a little bit too shocked for liberal French people I thought. They repeated the word I had used for kissing just to confirm that that was actually what I meant to say. I grabbed my dictionary and looked up the word I had used. I had taken the noun for 'a kiss' and turned it into a verb to make 'kissing' (which was often a good way to guess a verb in translation from English to French) To my extreme embarrassment the word I had used as the verb was something far more intimate and shocking than just kissing and if the couple had been doing it would probably have resulted in them being arrested! Fortunately my colleagues and I were able to laugh about it, which we did for quite a while afterwards.

My office was located near Gare St Lazare in the 8th arrondissement of Paris and I lived in the 7th. Being so central for work and home was fantastic. I lived in a very small 'chambre de bonne' which had a view of the Eiffel Tower from the window. A chambre de bonne (maid's room) is a type of French apartment consisting of a single room in a middle-class house or apartment building. It is generally found on the top floor and only accessible by a staircase, sometimes a separate "service staircase". My bathroom was shared with several other people living on the same floor.

I didn't have much space in my room, but the location was perfect, and I felt safe walking back from the metro station at night as I was in the area called 'Les Invalides'. This is a complex of buildings containing museums and monuments, all relating to the military history of France, as well as a hospital and a retirement home for war veterans, the building's original purpose. There was always a military presence there with soldiers patrolling the streets.

I was happy to discover that a friend of mine from school, Anna, was also in Paris and she lived just a couple of Metro stops (French underground train system) away from me. She had several of her University friends also working in Paris so we all went around and socialised together as a group.

We had great fun! There was something again about being away from the UK that gave me a tremendous sense of freedom. Although Anna knew about the accident with Sammy, she had only joined our school after The Accident had happened, so apart from being told about it by other people she didn't really know what I had been through or what that had entailed.

So, I was free to be me without all the stigma I has been carrying around about The Accident. I was respected at work by my colleagues and I made some lovely friends there too. I was eating healthily. I looked and felt self-assured for the first time in my life. I attracted a lot of attention from the French boys and I started dating a lovely French guy called Jean-Benoît. He was very good looking with brown hair, brown eyes and was also quite shy. Madly into *The Doors*, Jean-Benoît couldn't speak English and it was interesting trying to translate song lyrics such as 'Break on through to the other side' into French... and with his French accent it sounded like 'Bweak on fwoo to zee Uzer side!'. I loved this time in my life.

Dad flew out for a weekend to try and resolve the issues between us but he ended up going home earlier than planned as we argued a lot. Looking back I can see that I was still holding a lot of blame at that time towards

Dad for not coming to rescue me in my younger years.

The rest of the year was spent working and socialising and having a great time.

There was no social media in those days, so I'd just kept in touch with my mum by phone and letter. At the end of the year and upon my return to the UK, my mum picked me up from the airport. I had lost weight, my appearance had changed, and I was wearing my hair in a different style. So much so that when I walked through the doors, she didn't recognise me and looked straight past me! I was looking forward to bringing my new-found confidence back to university life.

Back in my fourth year at university in Hull, it became apparent very quickly that we were in our final year and that exams were looming large. From the very first day back, we were constantly hearing about final exams, final exams, final exams. There was a lot of pressure put on us and our study workload increased tremendously from what it had been in the previous years.

With this increased pressure, I felt that the cracks were really starting to show internally for me. Although I had always done well in exams when I had applied myself before, my core beliefs about feeling worthless would rear up whenever exams loomed large. I was convinced each time that I would fail which would create a lot of fear and anxiety in me, and yet somehow, I still seemed to do well each time. My final year, however, was taking me to a new level of anxiety that I was finding much harder to contain. When I felt anxious the feelings of deeper trauma were triggered, making it very difficult for me to function well.

During this time, Stacey, my best friend from school back at home on The Wirral told me that whilst I had been away she had been to a rave and had taken the drug Ecstasy. I was shocked. I had always been anti-drugs growing up and even strongly berated my mum when I was growing up for her heavy cigarette smoking. Stacey told me that, contrary to what we had been told before, taking Ecstasy was an amazing experience and that it was nothing to be afraid of. In fact, she enthused, I would love it. I told her that I was too scared about what might happen to me if I took it, but that I would like to come to the rave any way to experience what that was like (rave was a term used to talk about dance music events from the late 1980s to the end 1990s where people would go to a club or a venue or even a field to dance to house music and, invariably, take drugs).

So, one night whilst I was on a visit back home from university, Stacey and I decided to go to a rave. I had no intention of taking any drugs and had told her that before we set off. As she was driving to the club a police car appeared to be following Stacey's car. She reached down, took a white pill that I hadn't seen resting in the ashtray, split it in two and said, 'eat that quickly in case the police stop us.' I was so taken by surprise that I swallowed the ½ pill straightaway.

Suddenly realising what I had done, I started to panic and I said a prayer. I asked that I be protected from any harm coming to me. How strange, on reflection, that I prayed to a God I didn't even know that I wanted to believe in, just as I had done after The Accident, dropping to my knees in shock, saying 'Oh my God, oh my God, oh my God.' Here I was again praying to a God whom I feared might want to punish me. I really didn't know if I would survive the night!

Once I had swallowed the ½ white pill (called a Dove because of the birdlike marking on both sides) I resigned myself to the fact that anything could happen and that it was too late to do anything about it now.

I didn't have to wait long for the intensity of positive feelings that soon followed. Extremely quickly after taking the Dove, I felt the physical 'rush' of a feeling of ecstasy coursing through my entire body. It was quite overwhelming, and I found it difficult to catch my breath for a while. You would say that you were 'coming up' on the drug at this point.

I had never felt anything like this before. Every bit of me was rushing with feelings of bliss. And it was coming in waves and waves and waves. We got to the rave and I couldn't wait to get in. I wanted to hug everybody. My friends and I were constantly hugging each other too.

My feelings of fear and anxiety disappeared completely.

No longer feeling separate from other people, complete strangers looked like long-lost friends and loved ones, and barriers were instantly broken down that had been there before. Nobody thought twice about going up and talking to each other, sharing with each other, laughing together, hugging each other. I felt as though I had entered an alternate universe.

I was hooked on taking drugs from that very first night. Ecstasy is not a physically addictive drug, like heroin or cocaine, but to me it was *mentally* addictive from the very first time that I took it. I had no idea that I could feel so alive! I never wanted that feeling to end.

When taking the drugs, I acquired greater feelings of confidence that I had never felt before, even when I was living in Paris. I also felt like I was part of something very 'cool' and exciting – the new rave movement that was spreading across the UK at that time.

When on Ecstasy, my mind became much more open and expansive and the critical inner judgements I had towards myself stopped completely. The pain I was feeling would completely disappear.

This was taking the feeling of freedom to a whole other level of reality. I had a sense that there was a lot more to 'reality' than we can currently understand. It's difficult to explain unless you experience it, but it was like a total feeling of euphoria and connection to everyone and everything.

I used to have amazing conversations with complete strangers that would last for hours, and very often you would both think that you had reached some incredible insights into the meaning of life and then five minutes later you had no idea what you had been talking about. And then you would laugh and repeat the same thing over and over again.

I loved the messages in the songs back then too, like 'You got the love' by Candy Statton, 'Moving on up' by M-People, 'The Key, The Secret' by the Urban Cookie Collective and 'Things can only get better' by D-ream.

It was unfortunate timing, however, to discover this whole new rave scene in the final year of University. Because I was already feeling the strain of final exams and cracking under the pressure, taking drugs at the weekends became a welcome relief and something I started to depend upon to escape the increasing anxiety, and - with the benefit of hindsight - underlying trauma, that I was feeling.

Sometimes I would go back to The Wirral to go out clubbing with Stacey but I also discovered there was a clubbing scene in Hull near the university and so I began to go out more here too. I began smoking cigarettes, and this became a habit to the point that I was smoking 20 cigarettes a day, and much more when out at the weekends.

One night I was in the university bar and was due to go out to a club later that night. I was out with one of my housemates, Michael, when I spotted a good-looking guy across the other side of the bar. With my new-found drug-induced confidence I went around and sat next to him and started chatting. His name was Toby and he was a student at the university next door.

Toby was lovely, we found that we had a lot in common and we talked the night away. We laughed a lot. At the end of the evening I asked if he would like to come to a club with me and he agreed. We had such a great night dancing and chatting and then he walked me home.

I fell in love with him that very first evening. He was unlike anyone I had been out with before. We just seemed to click. We were inseparable and I could really envisage a future with him.

Then after a few months, he became very ill. I was looking after him a lot, but his symptoms were getting worse and, in the end, he was diagnosed with glandular fever. He went home to recover for a while. I was glad that he was being looked after and getting the right treatment, but I missed him terribly.

When he came back to university, at first everything was great again. Then slowly he started to make excuses that he couldn't come to see me as he was going out with his mates.

One night I discovered that he had stayed the night at an ex-girlfriend's house. He was adamant that he had stayed on the couch, but I didn't know if I could trust him again. We ended up splitting up over it.

Over the next few months Toby tried really hard to win me back. He wrote letters, he came to see me, he bought me flowers. Because I had been so hurt by other people in my life growing up I just couldn't find a way to trust him again at that point.

I am still so grateful to have known the type of love I felt with him. I thought that I had had my first love at 18 years old but looking back I can see now that Toby was the first man I ever really loved. Over the subsequent years I wondered whether I had made the right decision to split up with him, but then I learned that he went on to marry his next girlfriend and they are really happy and have a family and so I knew that I had made the right decision for both of us.

All this was going on in my final year at University, so it is no surprise that I was really struggling when exam time came around. With the pressure of exams, the heartbreak from Toby, my unresolved trauma and the clubbing, it was a recipe for chaos and it certainly felt that way.

Somehow, I managed to get through the exams but the day after my last exam I collapsed and ended up in the University hospital for a few days. I was utterly exhausted from it all. Amazingly I did pass the exams and I left University with a 2(ii) grade in French and Business Studies. I knew in my heart that I could have got a better grade but was grateful to have been able to complete the degree course at all, the way I had been feeling.

When I moved back to The Wirral in 1992, the UK was in the middle of a financial recession. It was very difficult trying to get a job, especially in the north of England. After applying for several roles and not being successful, after a few months I decided to take a seasonal job over Christmas working at the Top Man clothes store in the centre of Liverpool. This was great as I was surrounded by lovely male co-workers and lots of attractive men were coming in to buy their clothes. It was a fun time. Lots of people working in the store were ravers like me and we would often go out socialising and clubbing together.

I met some guys who lived in Liverpool and we all used to go out to parties and clubs. One of them, Marc, became my best mate. I had never really had a guy as a friend before and we had such a laugh. It was like we were brother and sister. I knew that I could rely on him to look after me and we would often end up talking all night and cracking up laughing. I felt safe with him and sometimes it was as though we were in our own bubble.

There was a whole social scene built up around raving, both in Liverpool and in the rest of the UK. Every week there would be different events/venues/locations with well-known DJs and very often I would see the same people at these events and would therefore get to know a lot of people. It was great to be able to walk into a club and to see a lot of familiar faces that I could say hello to and chat with. I would sometimes walk into the club on my own as I knew that my feelings of anxiety would disappear once drugs were taken. I felt like I really belonged here in the rave community. I felt like I had significance here. And it was a lot of fun.

I absolutely loved my clubbing lifestyle. It was fun, it was exciting and I felt like I belonged. The only problem was that as the drugs wore off, so did the feelings of connection. Without the influence of the drugs in my system I went back to my feelings of pain, fear and insecurity. In fact, they felt a lot worse. Having felt so high on the drugs at the weekend, I came crashing back down to reality every Monday and my 'real' life seemed to get harder and harder and harder to deal with as time went on.

I was so nervous about the idea of giving up taking drugs (as they were my only release from the pain and fear I felt inside), that I lived this clubbing/raving life for the next 10 years. As time went on, the thought of giving them up became more difficult, because not only would I have to give up the whole lifestyle and community that I had built up, but I also knew that I would have to face all those feelings that I had been suppressing since childhood. This was not an option for me at that time. It felt much safer to keep suppressing my feelings and pretend that I was ok, whilst numbing myself with drugs every weekend than to admit the truth of what I was doing – to myself or anyone else.

I felt a lot of shame living this double life. Although my sister Sarah knew some of what I was doing, I hid the true extent of it from her and hid everything from everyone else in my family. Although I was having a lot of fun on one level, I knew that taking the amount of drugs that I was progressively taking was not something I was proud of, and I was terrified of being found out.

With no idea of who I really was I put on different 'masks' to try to fit in wherever I was. I would wear the corporate mask to work during the week and the clubber's mask at the weekend to go out raving. And the family mask came on at family events.

'I am ashamed of who I am.'

I was such a different person in my corporate role than in my clubbing at the weekends. I used to think that if either the people at work could see me clubbing, or the people I went clubbing with could see me at work, they would both be shocked. It really was as though I was two separate people. And neither of these people felt like the 'real' me inside, they both felt like I was putting on an act in order to function in the world.

I worked in the corporate world throughout most of this 10-year period. After working on some graduate apprentice programmes but failing to get a permanent job in Liverpool during the recession, I met a lady (when I was away on a business trip with Dad) who worked for a business publishing company in Surrey, just outside London. She offered me a telesales position selling advertising to hairdressers and so I made the move down to live near where the work would be.

It took a little while for me to settle in. The people in this area were not as friendly as northerners. At home (on The Wirral), strangers would say hello in the street or supermarket, but down in the south they seemed very distant and wary of people they did not know.

I therefore didn't get to socialise with people from work outside of work, but Marc and my friends from Liverpool would come down to London and we would all go clubbing together. I also started to meet other clubbers that I could then meet up with in London on a regular basis.

I would go out raving/clubbing nearly every weekend and start taking drugs on a Friday night after work and, very often, I would not get any sleep until the Sunday night, having been to nightclubs and parties most of the weekend and taking increasing amounts of drugs. Then I would arrive at work on the Monday morning, often feeling disoriented and unable to really focus or concentrate until the Wednesday or Thursday and then Friday I would start taking drugs again.

I tried to hide it from work, but this was increasingly difficult to do. I would often have a Monday off sick or be full of cold, but somehow, I managed to keep putting on the masks and getting away with this double life. I hated the fact that I was lying to people at work and felt shame around this. In one job my boss's leadership style was very like my step-dad. Sometimes she would tell me to do something in a harsh tone and I would end up in tears, when really, I was feeling angry and exhausted – just as I had done as a child. I wished that I could stand up for myself in these moments, but this felt too risky for me as I feared rejection and anger in return. Crying was the safer, if not more frustrating, emotion to choose.

Although I felt like I was having a great time taking drugs, it was all superficially created, and the great feelings only lasted as long as the drugs lasted. Really, I was hurting myself living this lifestyle. I was reckless and took a lot of risks to my health and personal safety. I really didn't care.

Although on the surface I was having a lot of fun, my internal beliefs were playing out in a destructive way. I was acting like a rebellious teenager – only after my teenage years were passed as it had not been safe for me to rebel in my teens when I was living at home.

But over the following years I needed to take increasing amounts of drugs to achieve the same feelings of being high I had felt before. My behaviour was becoming more erratic and my life felt as though it was spiralling out of control. My weekends began to start on a Thursday, I was having more days off sick from work and I was struggling to keep up the pretense. Something would have to give at some point.

I met a great clubbing friend during this time, Siobhan (a different one from the friend from school). We met through our boyfriends who were friends. I remember one night when we had taken Ecstasy I said, 'I feel like making some mischief'. I often felt like this when taking the drug, but everyone else was usually feeling too spaced out to want to join me in my mischief making. 'What kind of mischief?', Siobhan replied, with a twinkle in her eye. We were firm friends from that point on! We ditched the boyfriends and kept our friendship and we created a lot of mischief each and every weekend. We had a great friendship, went to a lot of parties and had a lot of fun during this time.

During these 10 years, I went abroad several times to the islands of Majorca and Ibiza and really loved being away from the UK and the feeling of freedom that accompanied the trips. I never wanted to return home and would feel quite depressed about returning to my 'real' life. It was always as though somehow, I could be more 'me' when I was travelling and returning to England meant I had to fit back into the prison I had built in my mind where I felt disconnected and separate from the world.

Sarah took me on a trip to Barbados when I was 25. She was bridesmaid at a school friend's wedding and she paid for me to go with her. My sister was always so generous and so supportive (we even lived together in a house for 8 years near London). Barbados was a different world from the other places in Spain and Europe I had visited. Exploring this beautiful island with its white sandy beaches, laid back lifestyle and welcoming people had a very calming effect on me. This way of living was so alien to the crazy, busy, partygoing lifestyle that I had been living in London. It was such a contrast to that world, and I loved this new, relaxed way of being.

One day Sarah and I were sitting on the shuttle bus that took holidaymakers to the beaches and back. As usual in Barbados there was no hurry from the driver to get going so we were just sitting there listening to the local radio that the driver had put on whilst we waited.

At one point the DJ on the radio said, 'I've got a really important bit of information I need to tell you', then we heard the rustling of lots of pieces of paper being shuffled about and silence from the DJ. 'Now where's that bit of information gone?' we heard him ask in his strong slow Bajan accent. He sounded so perplexed and Sarah and I just burst out laughing. We wondered what that important information could have been (a hurricane? A weather warning?) and what the consequences might be as the DJ had misplaced it somewhere in his pile of papers.

That summed up Barbados for me, laid back to the point of being horizontal!

When I first arrived on the island we were waiting for a taxi from the hotel to take us out for the evening. I had come from London where the pace of life was so hectic and stressful, and everyone demanded everything be done instantly. And so, when we ordered the taxi the hotel doorman said it would be here in a minute.

We thanked him and sat down to wait. 10 minutes later we were getting cross. 'Is the taxi still coming?' we asked the doorman 'It's coming' he replied gently. Another 10 minutes went by and we asked the same question and got the same response 'It's coming'. Now, Barbados is only 21 miles long and 14 miles wide so when after 50 minutes of waiting we were told 'It's coming' we had to wonder just exactly where it was coming from!

The doorman was bemused by our frustration. In Barbados time is a different concept to the way we rush around crazily in London. To them, things happen when they happen (in their own time) and are not to be rushed.

Spending a couple of weeks in this relaxed space I felt my whole system start to relax.

It was therefore with a heavy heart that I eventually packed my bags to return home at the end of the trip. I clearly remember feeling emotional on the plane on the way back to the UK as I felt like I had to leave this way of being behind and almost put my suit of armour back on, ready for London life and the partying, clubbing, drug taking merry-go-round I was living.

Part of me longed to be the person I felt I could be when travelling, whilst back in the UK but I didn't know how to create that with the chaotic and self-destructive lifestyle I was living.

During this time I started a career in sales and after a couple of years I moved into working in the hotel industry. I loved this job. My first manager was called David and he was one of the best managers I have ever had. He taught me a lot about professionalism, professional relationships and how to create structure and this grounding has stayed with me throughout my whole career to date. More than this though, he really believed in me and this was incredibly powerful for me. In amongst all the chaos of my life there was someone who saw something else in me, who saw my potential and I really thrived on that (even if I couldn't sustain it).

During this time my dad and I were getting on much better. Through his work he was often away at conferences and could take a person to accompany him whenever he went.

By now my two half-sisters Emma and Lucy were growing up and my step-mum Lisa did not want to take lots of time away from them. As Sarah and I were both now adults, Dad would sometimes take one or both of us away with him. I loved these trips and getting to spend time with Dad. The other people on the trips had so much respect for him and I felt proud he was my Dad. I had not seen this work side of Dad before. It also felt strange as these people seemed to know Dad so much better than I did and I really wished that I knew him better.

These trips away with Dad helped to add to my love of travel and each time I returned I would feel sad that I couldn't stay away longer. I began to wonder if it may be possible for me to have an extended trip away at some point, although this seemed impossible at the time as I had amassed debts and could not see how I could clear these and save enough for a bigger trip. I used to dream about travelling though and longed for the possibility that it could happen one day. It was a persistent dream that was always in the back of my mind and I would often tell friends that one day I would go travelling.

If I was ever asked 'What is the one thing in life that if you don't do it, you will really regret it' my response would always be 'travelling'.

CHAPTER 5
The Lightbulb Moment

"May your choices reflect your hopes, not your fears."

Nelson Mandela[9]

Living a double life was putting increasing strain on me internally. I was running out of excuses with family and work for days off and always being ill.

Finally, at the age of 28, the cracks were growing bigger and bigger and my work performance was getting worse and worse. My line manager referred me to speak to someone in the occupational health team. She was a nice lady and I was honest with her about how I was feeling. She referred me to have three free counselling sessions to be paid for by the company. I was grateful for the support and went for the sessions.

Unfortunately, these sessions didn't work well for me. The therapist was slightly odd in his behaviour and therapy style. He would get me to open up about what had happened and then say 'OK, see you next time' – without giving me any advice on how I would then cope, having lifted the lid on all the trauma that I was now reliving.

In the end, I think these sessions did me more harm than good and I ended up taking two months off work to try and recover (and to put the lid back onto my emotions). I had a return to work interview after two months and it was politely worded that it was probably best if I left the company as this job was obviously not working out for me. I felt so ashamed that I went along with what they said. I felt like such a failure.

'I am a failure. I am ashamed of who I am.'

Looking back now, this process had a great impact on my future career and my ability to share at work if I was struggling with my mental health. And so for the next few years I tried hard to ignore the feelings by escaping again through drugs and putting on masks to try to live a normal life.

Eventually, I experienced a mental and emotional breakdown. I sought help from a lovely local GP. He smoked cigars and drank whisky toddies when he had a cold, so I felt that I could trust him not to judge me!

He recommended that I go to the Wimbledon Guild centre for therapy. This was a place where new therapists offered low-cost therapy sessions and I could donate whatever I could afford towards them. When I arrived at the therapy centre for an assessment session, I was initially told by the head of centre that there was a very long waiting list to see the counsellors there and that I might have to hang on for six months or more. I was disappointed as I was feeling so bad at this point, but I couldn't afford to pay for counselling sessions privately, so I resigned to having to wait.

Once in the assessment session, I completely broke down. I told the head of the centre all about what I had experienced so far in my life and how I felt like I was on the verge of giving up altogether. He was shocked to hear my story and that I had received no professional support so far (apart from the few counselling sessions that hadn't worked well for me). He was incredibly supportive and told me that as my story was exceptional, he would find me a counsellor to talk to within the next few days.

The counsellor assigned to me was called Marie.

I felt like Marie really listened to me. She was so non-judgemental and supportive, and she even cried when I told her some of the things that I had been through. A petite woman with a gentle nature she showed such empathy and compassion that I immediately felt comfortable enough to talk to her and to open up some of my innermost held feelings.

With her help I was able to look at The Accident from an adult's perspective. I was able to obtain a copy of the report from the inquest (15 years after it had happened) and read through the witness statements from my classmates. Their statements were virtually the same as mine and backed up how I had remembered what happened on the day of The Accident. This was so liberating for me, as up to that point I had only been able to rely on my own memory. To hear how my friends had seen things the same way was a big relief. And to read how the report held the school to be responsible was enlightening.

I realised that the 'Death by misadventure' verdict was directed at the school and not at me. For the first time, I felt some anger towards the school – how could they have put Sammy and me in such a dangerous and ultimately tragic position? It had all been so avoidable and unnecessary.

Talking everything through with Marie had a healing effect on me, but at the same time I was unable to really let go of the very difficult emotions I was feeling. I was so ashamed of my drug-taking that I didn't even mention it to Marie. I had a lot of rage surfacing in me that I didn't know how to handle, and I was afraid of expressing it. I realise now that I was projecting that rage onto Marie and I got very angry with her for not being able to help me break through it.

I therefore only got so far with my sessions with her before I left and continued my partying lifestyle.

Living with mental and emotional trauma and fear while at the same time living what others consider to be a 'normal' life (going to work, paying bills and being a responsible adult) was a very difficult thing to do.

Although still afraid to believe that there was a God (through fear of being punished) sometimes I would nevertheless pray that if there were someone/something there, would they please come and help me to find a way out of all this pain?

Would they come and help me find another way to live my life that would mean I would become happy?

I was still torn between wanting to believe in a God who could support me and being terrified that if God was real I may be punished and damned to hell. Some of the key questions I asked myself during this time were:

'What is the meaning of life?

Why did The Accident have to happen?

Was I born just to cause misery and pain to others?

Was I just born to live in pain and suffering?

What is the purpose of all this?'

What I didn't realise was that the act of asking these questions set in motion a process to find the answers that would play out over the following years.

I just couldn't believe that the sole purpose of my life had been to create so much misery; both for myself and for other people, although that is how it had appeared to be up until this point in my life.

I remember one day when I was about 10 years old, I was thinking ahead to the future. I worked out that by the year 2000 I would be 30 years old and happily married with children.

As is often the case when you are young, the age of 30 seemed impossibly old and very far away. By the time I reached the age of 30 my life couldn't have been more different from the one that I had envisaged.

I had reached rock bottom. The years of punishing myself through my drug-taking had taken their toll.

I was in a mentally, emotionally and physically abusive relationship with someone who was very controlling and manipulative. His own background was tragic, and he had been thrown out of the house on Christmas Eve by his mum when he was just 11 years old. I had so much compassion for him and wanted him to understand that life could be different for him as he was also taking a lot of drugs and living a reckless party lifestyle.

Looking back, I think I was trying to save myself by saving him, but of course that could never work. The more I gave the more he took, and I felt I was losing myself completely into his rage and control.

Sometimes he would lock me in a room, or he would throw objects at me. He twisted things that I said and had me questioning my own sanity. He was jealous and possessive, and he suspected that any man I spoke to I was having an affair with (and some women he suspected too).

He treated me so badly that I often wondered if I would get out of the relationship alive. When I tried to split up with him he would harass me (once he left me 33 voicemail messages in the space of a couple of hours). In the end I had to get a police injunction out against him to stop him from being in any sort of contact with me and I had to change my telephone number and move to a new house to avoid him knowing where I was.

I had created a life where punishing myself was the driving force:

'I am worthless. I am powerless. I am alone. I am evil. I deserve to be punished. I am unlovable. I am ashamed. I am guilty. The world is unsafe. I am unsafe. I must not be successful as people will reject me. There is something fundamentally wrong with me. I am a victim. I am accepted by pretending to be someone I'm not. I am a failure.'

This destructive way of living could not be sustained any longer. Something had to give. I was heading for a crash...and that is exactly what happened.

One night I was out in London with some friends. As usual, I was the designated driver, as I did not drink alcohol back then (which I did not really mind as it gave me the freedom to do what I wanted to do throughout the evening. I liked knowing that my car was outside and that I could escape from somewhere if needed, it made me feel safe).

I was driving along a main road when I entered a road box junction (with traffic lights). As I entered the junction, the traffic lights I was going through had been on green, and so I was startled to see a black taxi pulling out of the junction in front of me and from my left-hand side.

I panicked and looked back to check that the traffic light I was driving through was still on green thereby giving me right of way, and it was. For some unknown reason, instead of stopping or reversing, the black taxi accelerated in front of my car. I didn't have enough time to brake before hitting the taxi and so I turned the steering wheel sharply to the right to try and avoid a head-on collision with it. It was too late, and I smashed the front passenger side of my car into the driver front side of the taxi in front of me.

I went into shock. Just like with the Accident, I couldn't quite believe what was happening. It was as if everything went into slow motion. I stumbled out of the car and asked the taxi driver what he was doing. The driver refused to say anything, but he handed me a card with his insurance details on it.

Then a witness came forward and told me that he had seen the whole thing happen and that the taxi had driven in the wrong direction out of a one-way street. Then I looked and noticed the one-way arrow pointing in the opposite direction to the one that the taxi had emerged from and I realised that what the witness was saying was true.

Incredulous, and in shock, I suddenly became aware of an acute pain starting shooting across my shoulders. Fortunately, we were within a couple of minutes of the nearest hospital. By the time my friends and I got to hospital I felt like I was in agony. My shoulders and my back were in a lot of pain, so much so that I had to lie down on the floor of the waiting room as I was unable to sit on a chair as it was too painful. I had to wait six hours to see a doctor.

It was diagnosed that I had acute whiplash to my neck and shoulders and my right shoulder was raised slightly. The doctor told me that it would take a few months to heal. A few months! I was so upset.

It wasn't just the car that crashed that day, it was as if my whole world came crashing down.

It was as if life wanted to give me a wake-up call.

And it did just that…

Because I was unable to walk or move very well, I initially went to stay with my dad and his third wife. Over the years she and I have had a difficult relationship, resulting in us now no longer being in contact with each other. But for the purposes of this book I want to acknowledge the things that she has given to me and that I am grateful to her for and for her to know that, despite the challenges, I wish her well.

Although they had been very generous in offering for me to stay with them, it quickly became apparent that things were not working between us and so I left and went to stay with my mum for a few weeks. This gave me the break from the world I had been living in that I desperately needed. It was as though I had got so caught up in running on the same hamster wheel for so long that I had forgotten that all I really needed to do was to step off to take a break and to see things from a different perspective.

Away from the controlling boyfriend and the whole clubbing scene I was able to take stock of what my life had become.

It took a lot of courage to admit that my life was a mess and that I really wanted to change.

I knew that I couldn't carry on with the lifestyle I was living and that if I did I was heading on a one-way trip to killing myself, one way or another.

Some part of me didn't want that to happen. Some part of me that had kept me going all these years through all the dark times and the self-punishment wanted something more for me now.

'A part of me wanted to live and be happy.'

I knew that I would be unable to continue living in London and keep on the road to recovery, so I applied for and got a Sales Manager's position in a well-respected hotel and I moved my life to Leeds. It felt like a fresh start.

I loved the feeling of working again and of wanting to be successful. My self-esteem was still very low, however, and so once again I found myself struggling to be the person that I longed to be. My desire to be who I wanted to be was strong, but the negative beliefs I held about myself weighed heavy around my neck and would not allow me to thrive as I longed to. I believed that to have 'made it', I had to have a good job, be earning lots of money and have a nice home and a steady relationship. I was struggling to hold down the good job and had none of the others as even distant possibilities at this stage.

'**Could I be successful?**' The question lingered in my mind.

And then one day my manager sent me on a sales training course. I had been on several prestigious training courses over the years during my corporate sales career and so I was expecting that this one would be very similar.

This, however, was a Dale Carnegie[10] sales training course. Dale Carnegie was an American writer and lecturer who died in 1955. He developed many famous courses in self-improvement, salesmanship, corporate training, public speaking and interpersonal skills and he also wrote several best-selling books.

Our training was held one evening a week over the course of 4 weeks. It was an external training course and so I attended the training alongside 20 other sales people from different organisations. As part of the course we were told to read two of Dale Carnegie's best-known books, How to Win Friends and Influence People and How to Love Your Life and Your Job. Each week the course attendees had to read several chapters of the books and then we were questioned on them during the course the following week.

As usual, when given homework to do on a course related to work, some people had not bothered to read the books. I, on the other hand, was completely the opposite. As soon as I started to read the books, a strange thing began to happen to me.

It was as if the part of me that had wanted my life to change began to really wake up. Amongst many other concepts in the books, Dale Carnegie talked about how if we think and act positively then we will become positive people.

'If I think and act positively I will become positive.'

This felt like a revelation to me! It was a lightbulb moment. Just the idea that I had a choice as to how I felt was news to me!

'I have choice.'

These words resonated through me... I HAVE CHOICE! I HAVE CHOICE! I HAVE CHOICE!

Up until that moment I had felt trapped in the prison of my own mind. The beliefs I had created about myself (and which had become the foundations of how I lived my life) could all be changed. I could change them.

'I have the power to change'

I could choose to think in a different way and in following that process I could become a more positive person. I could take responsibility for my own happiness and not just be at the whim of life and whatever I thought it threw at me, as I had been living life before. I could consciously create life how I wanted it to be and not just be constantly reacting to it.

With choice came hope. Hope that I too could be happy.

'I have HOPE. Happiness is possible for me.'

New and empowering seeds were being planted in my mind.

I remember one night when I arrived home from the Dale Carnegie training course my housemate, Lisa, was already home. As I came through the front door, she asked me how I was feeling. I started to reply with my usual response about how difficult it was at work and how bad I felt. But then I heard myself and what I was saying, and I stopped, told her to wait just a second and I went out of the house and came back in through the front door.

I asked her to ask me again how I was. She laughed and looked curious but asked me again, 'How are you, Lis?' I took a deep breath and said, 'I'm good, thank you, Lisa. I had a few difficulties at work today but have just been on the most amazing course and have learned some great things. How are you?'

I felt a shift starting to happen.

Right there and then, for the first time in my life, *I had made a conscious choice as to how I felt.* I had decided that I was going to be in control and I had chosen a more positive reply than the usual negativity that was, by now, my automatic default response setting to life.

This knowledge would grow within me over the years to come as I put it to the test repeatedly. Sometimes I would remember in the moment I was feeling bad to choose a different thought to help myself to feel better.

Over time and with repeated commitment to saying it to myself I felt myself becoming more empowered in the knowledge that I could choose how I felt.

At the end of the course we had a sales competition and I came runner-up out of the 21 competitors. The sales trainer was so impressed that he had bought me a card saying how much he loved my zest for life and that I should keep up the great work. This meant the world to me. I felt that I was getting recognition for something positive for a change. I loved it. I had never thought I had a zest for life before, but I realised that that is what must have got me through my earlier years. I was surprised at how different his opinion of me was from how I felt about myself.

At the same time as working as a sales manager, I was also going through the process of a compensation claim for the injuries I had sustained from the car crash. It took me a long time to recover from the mental, emotional and physical injuries sustained.

Having been through a second traumatic incident, my inner fears of being unsafe in the world were heightened.

'I must live life on full alert to be ready to stop anything like this from happening again.'

I saw potential danger everywhere. In my mind I would create exit strategies and protective plans to try to keep me safe. This was exhausting and never went away, although I kept it hidden from others. I now realise that my nervous system was already struggling under the weight of unresolved trauma from the first Accident, and this second one was sending it into overdrive.

One day in November 2002, I was called in to see my manager at work. I could sense something wasn't quite right about the way she called me in, but I dismissed it and put it down to her having a bad day.

When I arrived at our agreed meeting place, my manager was sitting with the personnel manager and the alarm bells started ringing in my head. She said it was with great regret that they were going to have to make me redundant, that the company was restructuring the sales force and that my sales area was being broken up and distributed into the other sales areas.

Initially I was devastated to hear this. It felt like rejection. I had done so well in the sales competition, but in my heart, I knew that my sales performance in the role was not where it needed to be. There just hadn't been time for me to show my newly found determination to alter my mindset from the deeply held negative beliefs that had been holding me back.

Once the shock of hearing the news had passed, I realised that now was the perfect opportunity for me to go travelling! The money from the crash was about to be settled and a great-uncle I loved dearly had died, leaving me a small amount of money. With the redundancy payment included, I now had enough money to enable me to take a year off from work and go off travelling around the world.

Even though I had experienced some sad and traumatic events in the lead-up to the trip, they had all ultimately led to me being able to take a year out and to live my dream. *It was as though some unseen force had come into effect that had enabled me to be in a position to go.* I was incredulous at how all these so-called negative things had happened but had resulted in such a positive outcome for me. I had no idea what was in store for me next, but I was full of hope and excitement and I couldn't wait to get going.

Finally, it seemed that I had taken control of my life again and what had once seemed an impossible longing, my dream of an extended period of travelling abroad, was becoming a reality.

CHAPTER 6
The Awakening

"The wound is the place where the Light enters you."

Rumi[11]

On December 6th, 2002, I arrived at Heathrow airport to begin my yearlong adventure overseas.

Originally, I was going on the trip alone and was intending to begin my trip in Thailand but a good friend of mine, Fordy, suggested I make my first stop in India as he was going to be there DJ'ing at some parties. Although my clear intention was to have time away from drugs during my trip, I thought that a quick stop for a couple of weeks in India sounded like fun.

I had crammed a lot into my backpack for the trip, but that seemed small in comparison to Fordy when I met him at Heathrow as he had a massive suitcase and two big record cases full of records, pre-internet streaming days!

I had met Fordy a few years earlier at an after-club party. Fordy is someone who does not take life too seriously. If ever anything sad happened, he would say 'never mind, hey?' and then make me laugh so I would forget all about whatever had been troubling me. He was great fun to be around and just what I needed to stop myself becoming too depressed. Being a DJ, he would often put me on the guest list to clubs so that I could get in for free and not have to queue, and I would be his driver for the night. We would quite often get to 3 or 4 clubs and parties in one night. So when he suggested I make a stop in India as he was planning to go there himself, it seemed like a great way to start the trip.

Together we boarded a flight to Delhi, India. Fordy was going first to India and then heading to Australia but I had a 12-month, round the world ticket to take me to India, Thailand, Australia, New Zealand, USA and back to the UK.

On the flight to Delhi it finally began to sink in... I had done it at last!

I couldn't quite believe it. After so many years dreaming of this day, I had now somehow managed to be going travelling for a whole year.

For me, this trip was about having a break from the chaos that my life had become. It was about giving my mind and my body a rest from all the negative habits and patterns that had become my life's story. It was about breaking my cycle of going clubbing and taking drugs. It was about taking a rest and recuperating from the pain that I felt I had been carrying like a lead weight for so much of my life.

It was also the biggest challenge I had set myself so far. Going travelling and breaking free from taking drugs meant that I would be facing people as Lis, without anything to hide behind. Was I ready? What if they saw who I was and didn't like me? Unconsciously I was afraid of them discovering that I really was evil. What would I do then?

Overriding all of this, however, was a growing feeling of excitement. This feeling was rather like the feeling of being a child on Christmas Eve, believing that something joyful is about to happen and with a heart full of wonder.

Excited for what? I wondered. I didn't know exactly but I was open and ready to find out.

On the plane one of the air stewardesses started talking to me and Fordy. She said that she loved Delhi, but that it could be quite a shock initially, especially all of the cows. 'The cows?' I asked in bewilderment. 'Oh yes, cows are holy and are allowed to roam everywhere freely in India' she replied.

I had not done any homework at all about India as I was only intending to be there for a couple of weeks and so this came as quite a shock to me. But nothing could have prepared me for the shock of arriving in India! If you have never been to India before it is quite difficult to describe in words the impression that it makes on you.

Right from the moment I landed at Delhi airport I felt as though I had entered a completely different universe from the one I had left only hours earlier. The sights, the smells, the noise, the colours and the heat were overwhelming.

There were just so many people in Delhi along with cars, rickshaws, bikes, monkeys, cows, lorries, buses which created a lot of noise and busyness on the streets. Just observing how all these elements were weaving in and around each other on the roads was quite a spectacle. I couldn't quite believe that there were not more accidents with animals and vehicles bumping into each other, but they skilfully weaved around each other like professional dancers spinning and turning.

As always seemed to happen when I went to a foreign country, almost immediately my old life in England seemed a world away (and not just in distance, I also felt lighter somehow). I had 12 whole months to explore different cultures and countries; 12 whole months before I had to return to face the mess of my life back home (or that is how I viewed it at the time). I didn't want to think about that now. I intended to make the most of every second of my time away and would face having to go back when the time came to do so. Part of me was secretly hoping that I would find a way to stay away from the UK and from my life there forever.

Fordy and I were met off the plane by his Indian friend, Ravi, whom he had met in England through another friend of his in the UK, Chris. Ravi had come to meet us in his chauffeur-driven car. We were then taken initially to Ravi's apartment in Gurgaon, where his butler carried our cases (including all of Fordy's heavy record cases) up to the 11th floor apartment Fordy and I were staying in. Once we had showered, we were cooked a delicious meal by his cook, nicknamed 'Master' by Ravi.

Fordy and I could not believe our luck. This was far more than we had expected on our arrival. Fordy had arranged for us to stay for one night with Ravi and then fly down to Goa the next day. I was so glad to be with Fordy and to have started this journey together. I began to feel a sense of liberation.

Having stayed at Ravi's for a couple of days, the initial thrill of having other people to do everything for me was wearing off. If I wanted a glass of water or a cup of tea, I had to ask someone else to do it for me. I wasn't used to this level of service and I felt quite uncomfortable. Ravi explained that there were so many people in India and many of them were poor. If he, and other wealthier people, didn't give lots of poor people jobs then they might starve. I could understand this, but the whole system felt wrong to me somehow.

From Delhi, Fordy, B (a Danish guy who was also staying with Ravi and who had decided to now come with us) and I headed to Goa, where some more of Fordy's friends were managing some huts on a beach in the south of Goa called Patnem. By this time Fordy and B were talking together in a mixture of English and Danish which they renamed 'Danglish'. It was funny to hear them talk like this, and how they would mix different words together.

Fordy's friend Chris (who had introduced him to Ravi) met us at the airport, as he was staying in Patnem, and we had a beautiful drive back to Patnem beach. I noticed that the earth was a red colour and there were lots of green trees. Along the way there were random stalls in the middle of nowhere selling things and from time to time we would see people working at the side of the road, but it wasn't obvious exactly what they were doing.

We arrived at Patnem when it was dark, so we couldn't really see where we were staying. As all the huts were full, that first night the three of us slept on the roof of the restaurant. We awoke at sunrise and saw our surroundings for the first time. We were staying in the middle of the most beautiful beach I had ever seen. It was about a mile long, curved at both ends and consisted of fine, pure white sand. Along the stretch of beach, around 10 different sets of huts were scattered. Some had their own restaurant attached, as ours did. Looking around my heart felt like it had come home. It was so beautiful and so peaceful there.

Have you ever really looked forward to something so much that often it turns out to be a great disappointment when it happens in reality?

Well, this experience turned out to be almost completely the opposite! This was something that I had dreamed about so much over the years and, when I finally arrived, it was even more beautiful than I could ever have imagined. I loved it so much here that my two-week stay in India turned into five months.

Just having the time to spend here over the next new few months hanging out on this beach and with the community of people who were gathered there, I began to feel a sense of peace enveloping me that I had never experienced before. The sea was great to swim in, sunrises and sunsets were spectacular, the sand was pure white, and I could get a 90-minute full-body massage for just £7.

In addition to that, we had four Nepalese chefs on-site led by a lovely man called Gobin and these men were also staying next to our huts. They had come down to Goa from Nepal for the tourist season in the hopes of making some money that they could take back home to their families at the end. They cooked the most delicious and fresh meals for the cost of around 70 UK pence per meal. I felt like I had found heaven on earth and was in no rush to move on.

As I sat on this beach in South India watching the waves rolling onto the shore day after day after day, I had no idea that an inner transformation was starting to happen…

I found myself again, in many ways, living in a world that was alien to me. However, in contrast to the hectic western lifestyle and stressed people that I was used to meeting in my life in London, people over here seemed so relaxed, so happy, so FREE.

Having lived my life with such a high level of control up to this point, I revelled in loosening up. We each had a key to our huts which we would lock when we were out. I often lost my key or would forget where I put it. I would never had done something like this in England (I think control had been a way for me to stay feeling safe) and it felt fantastic! I felt freer. I went to a local flea market one day where they had a huge variety of clothes on display, along with materials and crystals and wooden carvings. In Indian markets (and some local shops), it is customary to haggle over prices. I hated this initially. It is such an un-British thing to do. We are far too polite in general to haggle well. And I felt terrible trying to haggle over a pair of trousers that was only priced at around £3 to begin with! But the strength of the English pound against the Indian rupee was very strong at that point. And I was expected to haggle over prices. This was the Indian way.

After a while, I got into the spirit of it, and would love to come away with a real bargain. This day at the flea market I was having great fun looking at the different coloured materials, spices and ornaments. At one point I was looking at a stall, when I felt something shove me hard from behind. Indian people have a reputation for pushing and shoving and don't tend to form orderly queues like the English, but the force of this push was so hard that I turned around angrily ready to give someone a stern word and I saw a cow charging off into the distance. I burst out laughing. 'Only in India,' I thought bemused.

The biggest choice that I had to make was 'what shall I eat today?', or 'where shall I travel to next?' And this simplicity of choice was obviously having a positive effect on my levels of happiness. Just sitting on this gorgeous beach, surrounded by relaxed and happy people, I felt something starting to stir inside of me.

'Simplicity of choice = positive effect on my happiness'

A part of me was waking up again… the part of me that had been asleep for a long time; the part of me that had stirred during the Dale Carnegie sales training a few years earlier and the other times I had travelled abroad.

One day I was sunbathing on the beach and, as it was a very hot day, I decided to go into the sea to cool off. Two other girls whom I hadn't known previously were also in the sea near to where I was standing. Suddenly just to my right-hand side a dolphin jumped right out of the water and leapt in front of me several times before swimming back out to sea again.

I just stood there speechless for a second or two, taking in what had happened.

The two other girls were also standing in the water, speechless, and then we all looked at each other smiling and I said, 'Wow, that was amazing!' I felt so privileged to be so close to a dolphin in the wild. It felt very special.

Fordy used to tease me as he never saw dolphins in the water and he thought I was making it all up. 'I don't believe you as I never see them' he joked. 'If you believe it, *then* you will see it!' I replied laughing. And the very next day – he saw some dolphins!

There was a French lady called Dorian staying in one of our huts on the beach with her daughter, Naamah, who was two years old. Naamah was one of the most beautiful children I had ever seen, with huge brown eyes, the cutest smile and long dark hair. Her Dad was Israeli, so she spoke Hebrew and French and some broken English that she had picked up whilst travelling with her mum, which they had been doing for about six months together.

One day when we were playing together she ran up and threw her arms around my neck and said, 'Me love you!'. My heart was beginning to melt around this gorgeous child. She was so free in spirit and so playful and full of fun. I loved to hang out with her and so did Fordy. As he commented, it was good for her to have some other children like us to play with!

We were all walking along the beach one day when we spotted a rather large sandcastle in the corner of the beach with a man working on it. We walked over to see what he was building, and it was the most beautiful, large and intricate sandcastle I had ever seen. It turned out that the sandcastle builder was actually a master sandcastle maker. I had no idea there even was such a thing. It's not something that the careers service at school suggest you launch into when you leave school.

He lived in Goa for eight months of the year and the rest of the time 'worked' in Australia, Canada and Belgium, building structures out of sand. Curious as to how someone had ended up in this profession, I asked him what he used to do before. Apparently, he used to be a door-to-door salesman in the UK then he got cancer and was undergoing chemotherapy when he went down to the beach one day and began to make sandcastles. Realising he had a talent for it he gave up his job, bought a campervan and started to live near the beach and continued to grow his talent.

Now he earns a great living for four months of the year doing something that he loves and the rest of the year he spends in Goa. He had certainly created a great life for himself. He was building this sandcastle on the beach to help to raise donations to buy books for the local village school, as his way of giving back to the local community.

I was so inspired by him, and it got me wondering how many other talents we all have that are yet to be discovered. And what other lifestyles we can create that don't fit into the 'norm' that society expects of us.

As there was not much else to do most days on the beach, books were an important traveller's beach commodity. We would often swap books with each other. I loved reading and had just read *The Lord of the Rings*[12] trilogy in a week (quite an achievement and I didn't have time for much else!)

Zainey was a female British Asian woman who was running the huts that we were staying in. She was also a friend of Chris and Fordy. I noticed that she was sometimes lending a book of hers out, but only to certain people. She wasn't putting this book into the swap pile but would always take it back into her possession again once it had been read by another person.

I became very curious about this book. One day I asked her what was so special about this book of hers and why was she not just putting it into the swapping pile with all the other books?

She told me that it was her favourite book and that she didn't lend it to everyone as she didn't want to lose it. She said that if I promised to look after it and not give it to anyone else, then I could borrow it.

I agreed and couldn't wait to find out what was inside the book.

The book was called Old Souls: The Scientific Evidence for Past Lives:

Scientific Search for Proof of Past Lives[13] by Thomas Shroder. For nearly seven decades psychiatrist Dr Ian Stevenson travelled the world, tracking reports of children who claim to have lived before. Spontaneously they would recall vivid details about complete strangers who died before they were born, people they say they once were.

And when the memories had been checked against the facts of real lives, they matched to an astonishing degree. It took journalist Tom Shroder years to persuade Dr Stevenson to allow him to accompany him on his field research, the first ever to have that privilege. From the hills of Beirut in Lebanon to the slums of northern India, Shroder followed Stevenson as he struggled to understand the mysterious phenomenon of old souls reborn into new bodies.

As I read the book, I felt new possibilities waking inside me. I started to get curious and to ask myself questions, like:

'What if I had lived before in another life? What difference would that make to how I feel in this life?"

"What exactly is it that I have learned, or could learn, through all of my experiences?"

Rather than just a jumble of painful past experiences, what if there was a bigger picture to life? What if I could learn from my past experiences and somehow use them for a greater good?

Hungry to learn more about the possibility of past lives, I bought a book from a local Indian bookstore entitled Many Lives, Many Masters[14] by Brian Weiss, an eminent US psychologist. The book tells of how he had a client called Catherine who came to see him one day to cure some problems she was having in her life.

She had already tried many forms of therapy to help her, but conventional therapy just wasn't working, and she still had many of the original presenting problems that would not go away. Brian began to treat her and, during one session where his intention was to relax her, he accidentally ended up enabling her to regress and she appeared to have entered a past life in which she had lived.

What he discovered was that in remembering her past lives, Catherine would find the root cause of symptoms of problems that she was experiencing in this current lifetime. In finding the root cause and the lesson that she needed to learn from this event, she was able to come back to this lifetime and be free from all the symptoms. She was appearing to have a miraculous recovery after each regression.

At first, Brian struggled with his new findings. He came from a clinical background where things such as past lives were not an accepted topic of conversation. He carried on with his research and he used his regression technique with other clients. Eventually, when the evidence was compelling, he found the courage to share his research with the world and has since written several books on his results.

This notion of living more than one lifetime was so alien to me and sounded like the stuff of fairy tales. Surely, we just lived one lifetime and then we died, didn't we? And yet the idea of living potentially more than one lifetime and learning lessons during each lifetime had a strange ring of truth about it.

This concept seemed to make more sense to me, that we all live many lifetimes and as a result we get to live a full range of experiences rather than just having pot luck in the one lifetime you get to live as to whether you draw the short straw or not. Just as I had felt whilst attending the Dale Carnegie sales training course two years previously, I now had the profound learning that I could not only choose to think more positively but that maybe I had other choices too.

'I could choose what I believed to be true about life and about truth itself'

Building on this, I reasoned that just because I had believed things to be true about myself up to this point, didn't mean that they were in fact true. So, what could be true, I wondered. And what is 'the truth?' or was there even such a thing as one truth for all?

Whilst these new and exciting concepts and ideas were swirling around in my mind, other things started to happen to shift my perception of what I believed to be true also.

One day, a friendly Dutch girl, Adinda, who Fordy had met on the beach that day, asked if she could give me a reiki session. 'What's reiki?' I replied. She explained that it had originally come from a Dr Usui[15] in Japan and that it was an ancient form of energy healing where she would be channelling universal energy.

Energy healing? Universal energy? I had no idea what she was talking about. It all sounded a bit crazy to me!

Adinda said that it was OK and that I didn't need to understand how it worked right now. All I needed to do was to lie down, fully clothed, and that she would give me the reiki session and that I would feel relaxed, which sounded good to me. She did explain that she would be placing her hands above my body and that she would move around my body during the healing.

All I needed to do was lie there and relax – really? Well, that bit sounded OK! I decided I had nothing to lose and agreed to the session.

I was naturally a little nervous and sceptical beforehand, but almost immediately after the session started I began to feel extremely relaxed. Then I started to feel something more. As Adinda moved around different parts of my body I could feel varying sensations occurring; sometimes I felt a tingling sensation, sometimes heat, and sometimes cold. However, by the end of the session I felt as though I was literally floating.

For absolutely the first time in my whole life I felt completely and utterly naturally blissful.

It was one of the most incredibly powerful experiences I have ever had. Some people would describe it as a spiritual awakening, after which my perception of reality changed.

My mind struggled to make sense of it all. What was this reiki? How did it work? What was universal energy, anyway? It had all just sounded like some new age hippy thing to me. And yet, without her even having touched me, I had experienced something so profound – and without relying on drugs for a high – that I could not even put it into words.

Everything that I had believed before seemed to be being challenged. These new insights and new experiences were changing the way that I viewed the world and my place within it.

In my opinion, all this talk about past lives, energy healing and spirituality was for crazy people, wasn't it? That had certainly been my view on the matter before I left the UK. I would have actively ridiculed someone if they had told me they believed all the things that I was now opening up to the possibility of believing, through my own experience of them. And that made me afraid. For so long I had been desperate to fit in and I couldn't see how I could fit back into the life I knew in the UK with these new ideas.

And having been a part of the drugs and clubbing scenes for so long now, I didn't know how to fit into this new, alien world either. And yet everyone in this new world appeared to be so much happier, more peaceful and more relaxed than anyone I had ever met through my drug-taking.

A part of me felt like it had finally come home.

'Was I going crazy?' I wondered. It seemed like the world that I had known before was shifting before my very eyes. I had no reference for these new beliefs, these new ideas and these new experiences. I didn't know anyone in the UK who believed in any of this or who had been through similar experiences to the ones that I was now having.

And so, I decided to keep quiet about what was happening to me until I knew more about this new world that was emerging.

Alongside these new feelings and beliefs, that very negative, critical voice inside my head was still there, full of rage, judgement and fear. It was constantly telling me I was no good and that people would never really like me. It was the voice that I had grown up with inside my head and the voice I had tried to silence these past 11 years with drugs. Without taking drugs I got to hear the voice loud and clear. It sounded like it was booming inside my head yet again, just like Robert's voice had boomed when I was a child. Had I somehow internalised his voice?

I also began to notice that somewhere, deep inside of me, another voice was beginning to emerge.

This voice was much softer and gentler than the other. This voice knew that I had to give up the drugs and the lifestyle that came along with taking them. This voice knew that even if I spent the rest of my life alone, and sober, that it had to be better than the nightmare that I had created in my mind through the life (and lifestyle) I was living before. And although

I could hear its whispers gently emerging, they were often drowned out by the booming inner critic.

'My inner voices control my experience of life.'

Despite the booming inner critic that wouldn't entirely leave me, I also felt like I was reconnecting with that feeling of hope that I had discovered a few years earlier at the Dale Carnegie training. And what a transformation it was having on who I was being and what I was feeling.

Sometimes Fordy, myself and maybe B or other members of our beach community would take trips away for a few days to explore other parts of Southern India and then we would return to the beach we had begun to call home.

My favourite trip was to Kerala when myself, Fordy and two Israeli guys we met hired a bamboo houseboat for a few days and floated along the backwaters, passing paddy fields and local children running alongside the boat and calling to us. It was the most peaceful few days of my life.

Siobhan, my clubbing friend from England came out to stay. Originally, she had been supposed to be coming on the whole trip with me and we had been planning it for a couple of years. One day she announced that she had changed her mind and that she wasn't going to come now. I felt really sad but respected her decision. When I eventually told her that Fordy and I had booked our flights she said, 'Well I didn't think that you were actually going to do it!'. 'Why not?' I replied. 'Because you have been talking about it for so long I didn't think that you would actually go and do it!' was her response. 'Then you don't know me very well' I laughed. I had been talking about going travelling for so long as it was something that I really wanted to do. I knew that if I kept talking about it to other people that I would have to do it, which is why I had spoken about it so often.

Once Fordy and I were in India, Siobhan had persuaded her Dad to take her on a holiday to Goa and at the end of her trip they had come down to south Goa to stay near us for a few days. Siobhan ended up loving it so much that she didn't take her flight back and she stayed with us for about a month before she eventually returned to the UK.

Now we were all back at Patnem beach our time there had to come to an end. Fordy's Indian visa had run out and he had to leave for Australia. I decided to leave too and to continue the onward journey alone and Siobhan returned to the UK.

Travelling alone was one of the biggest challenges that I had set myself to date, but I also knew it was something I had to do for my own personal growth and to prove to myself that I could do it.

I had had some amazing, inexplicable experiences in India that had started to shift my whole perspective on the meaning and purpose of life.

Inside it felt like there was the 'old' me with her very destructive beliefs about herself and the 'new' me wanting to believe more in a meaningful and purposeful world of which she was an integral part. It was becoming a fight internally between these two versions of me. They mirrored the 'me' that had been in the corporate world and the 'me' who had gone clubbing back at home. It was as if there was a 'good' Lis and a 'bad' Lis and I was in constant fear that bad Lis would be found out.

I became extremely aware of the cripplingly low self-esteem that I had been trying to hide from the world. My inability and fear around connecting with other people (without being on drugs) led to me feeling incredibly lonely at times, but I somehow knew that this was all a part of my own journey. I had to learn that who I was without drugs was OK and to do that, I had to spend a lot of time alone with myself. But doing this was also my greatest fear. I was terrified as to what I might discover if I looked too closely inside.

Who was the real me, anyway? Was I really good Lis or bad Lis? Were all these new experiences and feelings the 'real' me? I was too tightly bound to the deeply held core beliefs at this time to just be able to drop them. They still formed the bedrock upon which my life and identity were built.

Internally, however, it did feel as though my core foundational beliefs were being shaken and stirred.

Although it is an incredibly beautiful country, I find that travelling in India can be utterly exhausting. After a while the heat, the dirt, the noise and the smells and constantly being stared at and talked about by the local people everywhere you go can really take its toll on your energy levels. I decided that, after 5 incredible months, it was now time to take my next flight to Bangkok in Thailand and to continue my travels there.

On the plane from Delhi to Bangkok, I felt excited and also slightly nervous. Whatever happened from now on, whatever successes or failures lay ahead, were all down to me. There was no-one else to rely on and no-one else to blame. This was the challenge that I had been waiting for (and feared the most).

And so, with no real plans and just an address in a foreign country given to me by a stranger in Delhi, I headed over to Thailand for the next part of my travelling adventure.

CHAPTER 7
The Test

"Beyond a wholesome discipline, be gentle with yourself. You are a child of the universe no less than the trees and the stars; you have a right to be here. And whether or not it is clear to you, no doubt theuniverse is unfolding as it should"

Desiderata[16]

On arrival in Bangkok in April 2003, I checked into the Mansion House hotel. It felt so luxurious compared to the backpacking venues I had stayed in in India. I had a massive double bed, air conditioning in the bedroom plus a TV, mini bar and a bath. I hadn't stayed anywhere with a bath during my whole time in India (there had only been basic showers available) and so this was such a treat to sink into the hot water and let the dirt it felt that I had accumulated in India wash out of me and down the plughole. I ate a salad for the first time since I had been travelling without having to worry about getting food poisoning as a result. I felt very grateful for all these 'luxuries' as I now saw them, that I had taken for granted in everyday life living in England.

A great learning from my travels was developing gratitude for things my life in England had provided to me every day and that I had just taken for granted. Being brought up in a western 'first world' country there were so many things that I used every day; hot running water, fridge/ freezer, flushing toilets, clean water to drink from the tap, etc. I had not appreciated just how fortunate I was in so many respects before I went travelling, and particularly starting out in India.

I had been so stuck in a very negative way of thinking before that I had not been able to feel gratitude for a long time. I noticed how much better I felt when I focused my attention on being appreciative of what I had, instead of being angry for what I felt I didn't have.

I was now so tired after taking three flights to get to Bangkok the day before (Delhi-Bombay-Singapore) that I slept non-stop for pretty much the whole of the first 24 hours. Although I missed Fordy and the rest of the community we had built at Patnem, it felt great not to have to worry about travelling with someone else, and to just feel responsible for myself and what I wanted to do. I decided to stay in Bangkok for a few days and to get my energy levels back up again before I headed down towards beach life in the south.

Almost as soon as I arrived in Bangkok, my lower back started to ache and so I decided to treat myself to a massage. They are really cheap in Thailand as opposed to in the west where they are a real luxury (and often expensive) to have. As the masseuse massaged my lower back, I cried out in pain. She said that she thought that there might be a problem with my back and that I should see a doctor.

Thinking that my back was probably hurting from having carried my backpack all this way, and that somehow it would get better on its own, after resting for a few days I followed my original plans to get to the backpacker's resort of The Sanctuary[17] on the island of Koh Phangan, which had been recommended by the Israeli guy I had met by chance in Delhi.

All I had was directions from a guy (whom I had met briefly when I stayed in Delhi with Dorian and Naamah) and a Lonely Planet[18] (the traveller's bible) of Thailand to help me to get there.

I felt free and that somehow without knowing what might happen, anything seemed possible. In the West I had always been so caught up with plans. I had to plan where I was going, how I would get there, how long I would stay, where I would go after that.

But now, I just had the address, the Lonely Planet and me. My intention was to travel to Koh Phangan, in the Gulf of Thailand, to see what the Sanctuary was like and if I didn't like it, then I would follow my intuition to find somewhere else. I realised that, although nervous and well aware of the dangers of travelling as a lone female, there were also the beginnings of a sense of trust within me.

I was intrigued to know just what WOULD happen when I lived my life in this way. What would happen if I didn't always need to be in control, if I didn't have to plan everything to the nth degree, if I allowed myself to 'go with the flow' and see where life took me? I saw it as a kind of experiment; 'OK, let's see how this goes and, if it doesn't work, then I can always go back the stressful way of doing things!'

My curiosity had been awakened and I knew that I had to try out this new way of being to see if it would work. The old way of being had been so exhausting and stressful that anything new was worth a try. Up to that point I had been under the misconception that happiness was something that could be gained from things that were external to me. When I had the good job, partner, money then I would be happy. Happiness was always a few steps away from me and something I could never catch up with. With meditation there was the hope that happiness could be something I created internally and was within my control. I was curious to see how this would work in practice.

I had begun to practise meditation in India and had bought a book which I had brought to Thailand and was now trying to practise every day. 'Try' being the operative word! I was really struggling to find any sort of peace when I closed my eyes to meditate. All I found was that I was becoming very aware of all the negative chatter inside my mind. I thought I was 'doing it wrong' and so was very critical of myself.

I found the whole thing quite frustrating and wondered how I was supposed to know if I was doing it correctly or not. I would sit with my eyes closed thinking 'now what? What is supposed to happen now? Should I feel more peaceful, because I don't. Why won't my mind be quiet? I feel so angry now that my mind is so loud'. And so it went on like this every time I tried to close my eyes and meditate. I wondered if anyone else felt like that or whether it was just me? People who I had met who had meditated always seemed so calm and so serene. I felt like an imposter but was determined to persist as I had been told that it can take time before you really understand what it is to meditate. Impatience had been my default up to this point and so it was not an easy thing for me to be patient instead.

I was looking forward to trying to meditate on the beach, where I hoped there would be fewer distractions which would make it easier to do. The meditation book I had bought told me that when you start to listen to your inner voice amazing things can start to happen and fall into place in your life. It all sounded quite weird, and I wasn't sure how that would work but I was prepared to give it a go.

And I had a little evidence that this might be true as I had already started to meet amazing people who had helped and supported me since I had started to try meditation, so I was cautiously optimistic and intrigued at the same time.

Leaving Bangkok, I took an overnight bus down to Surit Thani and then a ferry out to Koh Phangan. I remember standing on the ferry on a beautiful, hot day with blue skies overhead and the warm wind blowing through my hair and feeling a sense of expansiveness and joy.

Arriving on the island, I followed the handwritten instructions I had jotted down earlier; took a taxi to Had Rin (where the Full Moon parties are held), and then took a long tail (fisherman's) boat to Had Tien beach, which is where The Sanctuary is located.

Koh Phangan is a beautiful island with pure white sandy beaches all around its coastline. When I arrived at The Sanctuary, I knew that I had come to exactly the right place for me. The buildings were set back into the Thai jungle and rocks and there was a slope which led down to a rocky beach. The menu was strictly vegetarian (and delicious) and there were daily yoga classes and some workshops and meditation classes due in the next couple of weeks that I could attend if I wished. Just as when I had arrived at Patnem beach months earlier, there was a sense of 'coming home' to this community. I had only eaten meat once whilst in India and had found that a vegetarian diet suited me well. This led me to becoming what I like to call a 'vegequarian' (eating mostly vegetarian with some fish) when I returned to the UK.

I was so grateful to the stranger in Delhi for having led me here. It was odd because when I met this guy in Delhi he had told me that he loved The Sanctuary, that he went there every year, and that he would be there himself in a few days, but he never arrived.

This was my first experience of being in a backpackers' resort and having to initiate conversation, without having Fordy or my other traveller friends around. I sat in the restaurant at The Sanctuary on the first day and everyone around me seemed to know each other. They were all chatting away and then there was me sitting there alone at a table, pretending to read my book (*Many Lives, Many Masters*, by Brian Weiss that I had bought back in India).

I desperately wanted to talk to someone, but I was so nervous. They all seemed so confident and I felt anything but that. What was I afraid of? That they would ignore me? Not want to talk back? Of all the situations in the world, talking to someone who was also travelling was probably one of the least risky things that I could have done. It is not like in the West (and particularly in London) where people are becoming very cautious of one another and who avoid eye contact with each other on buses, trains, and even walking in the street.

So my fear was almost completely unfounded; and yet at the same time it was very real for me. Just the thought of going over and starting up a conversation with someone I would feel panic rising within me and there was nothing that I could do to stop it.

A female traveller sitting nearby to me in the restaurant then leant over, looked at my book and said to me 'Oh I love that book, what do you think of it?'. We started chatting and within a very short space of time I was chatting to lots of other people too. I felt a huge sense of relief.

Rachel was the name of the first person who spoke to me. A softly spoken American lady with long brown wavy hair, she talked to me about Many Lives, Many Masters and some of the ideas and concepts that it talks about, including past lives. Instead of alienating me from other people, my newly forming beliefs seemed to be creating a greater sense of connection. It felt great to be talking to other people who seemed intelligent and 'normal' who were talking about reiki and the concept of past lives as if they were a natural topic of conversation.

Before long, Rachel introduced me to Tina, Sarah, Philip, Rhiannon and Enrico. It was great to meet so many like-minded travellers from all over the world. Rachel and I became firm friends after that (and are still in touch to this day). At the end of our conversation she invited me to meet her the next day for a coffee.

I was to meet her at the huts she was staying in, just at the top of the hill between my beach and Had Yuan which was the next beach along from us.

As I was searching for her hut, I saw an Israeli guy that I thought I recognised from my travels in India. I asked if he had been there and he said yes and that he recognised me too from some of the dance parties we had been to in North Goa. His name was Lior. I loved the way that travellers could bump into each other as our paths crossed over from time to time, in different places and countries, just as Fordy and I had continually kept bumping into Roy when we were in India.

My back, however, remained painful and one day I was lying on the floor in a café that was perched on some rocks on the water's edge near to Had Yuan beach, with my hands on my stomach trying to relieve the pain that I was feeling in my back. A man entered the café and came straight over to ask me whether I was giving myself some reiki. I explained that I wasn't but that I had been looking for someone who might give me a reiki session after it had been such an incredible experience for me when I was in India and I hoped that it might help to alleviate my back pain.

This man (who was a German guy called Upchar) then announced that he was a reiki master and he asked me would I like him to give me some reiki now to help to relieve the pain I was in. Of course, I agreed! Once more I felt a blissful feeling during the reiki session and my back pain also lessened considerably.

'How strange,' I thought, 'that I had been wishing I could find someone to give me reiki and then someone had actually walked right up to me and asked me if I wanted some, without me having uttered a word.' I was noticing that this was happening more frequently. In India I would be thinking about someone and then they would appear. Or I would be thinking about something and then someone else would start talking about it. I had never experienced this back in the UK and I found it really curious, and rather odd at the same time.

Could there be some sort of connection between my thoughts and the reality I was experiencing?

Upchar said that if I was interested then he could teach me the first level of reiki and I would then be able to give myself reiki to help with my own pain relief. I was delighted, and Rachel said that she would like to learn it too.

The next day we both went to learn the technique of reiki I with Upchar.

It is called a reiki initiation where the reiki master (in this case Upchar) attunes the crown, heart, and palm chakras (explanation below) and creates a special link between the student and the reiki source.

The reiki attunement can start a cleansing process that affects the physical body as well as the mind and emotions. Toxins that have been stored in the body may be released along with feelings and thought patterns that are no longer useful. Therefore, a process of purification prior to the attunement is recommended to improve the benefit one receives. Unfortunately I had not had time to go through a purification process and so the attunement then led me into having quite a strong physical reaction. I was sick, and my hands felt like they were buzzing with electricity.

I had heard about chakras in India. There are seven chakras which originated in India within the religion of Hinduism. In the ancient Hindu language of Sanskrit, chakra means 'wheel.' This is because the seven chakras are seen as the spiritual organs in the body, and they are shaped like funnels and spin like wheels. These spiritual organs dominate the physical organs and corresponding areas in the body. These funnels pull energy into the body, and push energy out of the body.

In many Hindu and Buddhist practices the chakras are given great importance, especially while meditating. To understand why you might have a specific illness (whether that illness is physical, emotional, mental, or spiritual), they say that you can look to the chakras to discover the underlying metaphysical cause.

All this information was so new to me, and so alien to anything I had known before. I was still very much in a 'well I'm travelling so I'll try it as a new experience and see what happens', rather than believing it all to be true. My thinking was that *if I tried things and they didn't work then I would leave them, but if they proved of value and/or were a positive experience then I would explore them some more.* This seemed to be proving to be a great strategy as I was learning some weird and wonderful things and meeting some interesting people along the way.

I remember Upchar talking about energy and chakras and spirituality and he believed it all completely. I contemplated how comforting it would be to feel so sure about something that could not actually be proven but which felt right to you. I realised that that could be the definition of faith, to believe in something that you could not prove to be true, except by your own experience.

None of us will ever know for sure what will happen to us when we die, except when the time comes. So *'why not believe whatever gives you the most comfort, especially if you feel empowered by it and it doesn't hurt anyone else'*, I asked myself.

After the reiki initiation, I had a period of 21 days where I had to give myself reiki every day and to try and detox my system as much as possible by avoiding caffeine, alcohol, sugar, etc.

I had a Thai massage one day. After the session the therapist told me he could feel that I had slipped a disc in my back but that he was unable to put it back into place. He suggested that I needed to seek professional medical help. I was shocked. I hadn't thought that my back problem would turn out to be so serious, even though it was very painful.

Now, at this point I was on an island off the Thai mainland, travelling alone with a heavy backpack. It seemed like an awfully long way between where I was now and my next stop which would be Melbourne in Australia which was where I would prefer to seek medical help if there was something seriously wrong with my back.

And yet still I held out hope that if I learned reiki and carried on getting healing from Upchar that the disc just may somehow go back into its place naturally. And so I kept a very positive frame of mind about my back being able to heal itself.

'Think and act positively and you will become positive.'

The Sanctuary was a great place to stay and there were a variety of courses on offer. All around me people were drinking alcohol and taking drugs, but I was choosing not to do so, as part of my 21-day detox but also as I was feeling so much better about myself. I was still smoking cigarettes however, but the desire to quit was getting stronger all the time.

I noticed that I still had a strong desire to be accepted and to fit in. I looked around to see how the 'spiritual girls' dressed and presented themselves. I then tried to copy them hoping that I would be accepted. It seemed to work. Just like when I had started to go raving and I had created my identity to fit in with those around me, now I was doing the same thing here with this spiritual community. It was another role for me to play, another mask for me to wear. My old beliefs were rearing their heads.

'I am accepted by pretending to be someone I'm not.'

It was different this time though. Even though I felt as though I was wearing a mask to fit in, I also felt more like 'me' than ever before. There was something so open and freeing here in this community. There was great food, great people to talk to, amazing scenery and interesting courses to choose from. It felt like a little piece of heaven. The community aspect was strengthened by the fact that many people weren't just passing through on their way somewhere else – it's one of those places where people come for a week and stay for months or, in some cases, years. In the end I stayed for around 6 weeks.

Each day I would head to a café and sit and chill whilst reading a book or meeting up with friends. Just like the community at Patnem, this became another close-knit group where friendships were formed easily and lots of fun was had. There was regular meditation and yoga sessions at The Sanctuary, as well as regular longer courses that I could choose to attend if I wished.

Each week on a Friday evening there was an all-night party next to The Sanctuary in Guy's bar. It was always good fun to go and dance with friends, even without being under the influence of drugs.

Despite keeping a positive outlook on the situation, and despite learning the technique of reiki and having various massage and healing treatments, my back pain was unfortunately getting progressively more acute.

I decided that, as much as I was loving my time here in Thailand, the time had come to seek professional medical help for my back and that would mean moving onto the next leg of my journey and flying to Melbourne in Australia.

Amazingly (with the help of several friends that I had met at The Sanctuary), I managed to get to the airport in Koh Samui without me having to carry my backpack and fly to Australia to seek medical treatment.

Upon arrival in Melbourne I went straight to the nearest hospital where I had an MRI scan that confirmed that I had indeed slipped a disc in my back. I was shocked at first. What would this mean for my trip? Would I need an operation? Would I still be able to carry my backpack and finish my travels? I had waited so long for this trip to become a reality and I was heart-broken at the thought of maybe having to fly back to England only half-way through the trip.

'Bad things always happen to me.'

I could feel the old beliefs wanting to rear their ugly heads, but I was determined to stay positive and focused on getting myself better. I had been having way too much of a good time to allow these thoughts to dominate my experience now. I realised that when I focused on the positive, many doubts and fears would rise to the surface. My life experience had demonstrated that 'bad' things happen, that things didn't work out for me and so I had found it a stretch too far previously to believe that this time would be different. But it was those very doubts and fears that prevented me from getting what I wanted! And it became a vicious circle. Now I was determined to keep staying focused on the positive, no matter what was happening.

In order to try and get the disc back into place, I then had an enforced period of bed-rest for six weeks in a bed and breakfast guesthouse in Melbourne whilst I consulted with doctors and physiotherapists to see if they could help me to avoid an operation. The people in the bed and breakfast were really lovely. They initially gave me a bedroom downstairs in the guest house to make it easier for me and after a few weeks they let me go and stay in a house that they owned around the corner and that also had a bedroom downstairs where I could have more facilities to cook for myself and have more space.

This period of enforced bedrest gave me lots of time to put into practice what I had just learned in India and in Thailand. I gave reiki to myself, I gave time to my meditation practice and I was able to read a lot of books around spirituality and personal development that were available in a bookstore just doors away from the bed and breakfast guesthouse.

'I can choose my experience. I have choice. I have hope.'

I decided to experiment in the bookstore by seeing where my intuition would take me and what books I would be drawn to read. I would run my hand over the books in the shelf (without reading the titles) and see where my hand felt like stopping and I would pull that book off the shelf. This led me to reading some weird and wonderful books in the areas of mind, body and spirit and gaining some powerful insights that I might not have had otherwise.

Halfway through the trip of a lifetime and to suddenly find myself all alone, thousands of miles away from home and confined to bed could easily have tipped me back into my 'life is terrible. Bad things happen to me. Things never work out for me. I am evil. I deserve to be punished'.

But instead, *I chose to have hope, I committed myself to finding my own inner peace and I chose to accept and not fight what was happening to me.*

Unbeknownst to me on a conscious level, I was beginning to gather evidence for the new beliefs that I was trying out. Although I was still smoking cigarettes, I woke up one day and asked myself why did I want to continue poisoning myself like this? If I was ready to embody the new beliefs and to live my life in accordance with who I really wanted to be and not who I had thought myself to be up to this point, then why continue to harm myself any longer?

And so, I quit smoking that same day.

'I am in control of my experience. I am kinder to myself.'

It felt so empowering to be taking care of myself and wanting the best for myself too.

I decided I needed to build on my earlier attempts to meditate so I could try and connect with this other, more expansive, part of myself that I believed now existed. I wanted to see if this turned out to be the loving internal voice I could hear whispering to me.

Trying to meditate now, however, was just as hard as it had been before. My inner critic was still loud and in full force!

I started to write a journal. From deep within me the sleeping writer had begun to emerge. I remembered how much I had loved to write when I was a child and how easily I was able to put my thoughts down onto a page now. I didn't censor or re-read what I wrote; I just allowed the thoughts to flow.

I realised that because of the pain I had felt as a teenager, I had shut down this creative part of myself. I had always found it so easy to write as a child that I assumed that everybody else did too. It was quite a revelation to discover that other people found writing quite a difficult thing to do. I hadn't realised that my ease in writing might be one of my greatest strengths and I had kept it locked away in some hidden place within myself.

Re-opening this creative channel and allowing myself to write again after all these years felt like coming home on another level.

Although I had several physiotherapy sessions and was giving myself reiki treatments every day, after six weeks had passed my back worsened. I was so touched by the generosity of spirit of virtual strangers during my time in Melbourne. The physiotherapist that I went to see offering for me to go and stay with her and her family, Shelley and Steve running the Bed and Breakfast letting me stay in the house they owned around the corner, the local café giving me a free meal when they heard I was having an operation.

I had a relative who lived in Melbourne, Emma, whom I had never met before. Emma is the daughter of my dad's cousin Alan, whom I had planned to visit later in my trip. Emma was such a great emotional support to me during this time. She regularly came to visit me and helped me to get the support I needed. It was a real highlight during this time of getting to know her.

There was so much for me to be grateful for and I was choosing to focus on these elements as I waited to hear about my operation.

The UK had an agreement with the Australia government that British citizens were entitled to free hospital treatment if they had a medical emergency. And so there began a battle between my insurance company and Australian Medicare. My insurance company said my back operation was an emergency and Medicare said it wasn't. This argument went back and forwards over six weeks.

Things got very dramatic in the end. I was awoken one Saturday morning by the telephone ringing in the house where I was staying. Mum was on the other end of the phone to let me know that two nurses had been sent out from the UK and were in Melbourne on their way to pick me up and take me back to the UK on a stretcher on a plane that day.

I was confused. My surgeon hadn't given authorisation for me to fly, and in fact my back pain had become a lot worse in the days leading up to this to the point that my surgeon was planning to operate in the next few days. I started to panic thinking that I would suddenly have to go back to the UK. Mum was away on holiday and so she would not be able to meet me when I got back and at this point walking was increasingly difficult for me due to the intense pain and sciatica.

Mum called Shelley who owned the house I was staying in who managed to get hold of my surgeon. He was absolutely outraged. He said it was dangerous for me to travel and that I could potentially be paralysed by the journey. In my confusion I then tripped over, and my pain became even more acute. My surgeon told Shelley to bring me into the hospital and he would operate on me that day as it was now an emergency and there was no way that I was fit for travel.

So when the nurses arrived on the doorstep of the Bed and Breakfast to take me to the UK they were told that I had gone to the hospital for my operation. They came to the hospital to talk to me, but I refused to see them.

I had my operation and the surgeon said that part of my disc had split off and was pressing on the nerve and that he had been right, it would have been very dangerous for me to travel. The insurance company must have forged the surgeon's signature on a permission document for me to fly, which I found very difficult to believe, considering how dangerous it would have been for me to fly.

The operation was a complete success. I spent 3 days in hospital and then was moved to a rehabilitation centre around the corner.

Because this all happened so quickly mum was not able to fly out in time to be with me for the operation, but she arrived as soon as she could later that week and stayed with me for about five days. It had taken her over 24 hours to get to Australia and her journey hadn't been a smooth one. I was so relieved to see her and so grateful to my dad and his wife for their generosity in paying for my mum to fly out to see me – especially as the day of my operation was the day of their wedding! I had been putting all my positive mindset and affirmations to good use, but it was still a real joy to get a hug from my mum!

When I was a child I had received a lot of love and positive attention from having a physical ailment like glandular fever and tonsillitis. But this time, with my slipped disc, was different. This time I had given myself a lot of the love and attention that I needed (through giving myself reiki and learning how to meditate and reading books that were helping me to develop a positive mindset).

I was determined to stay as positive as I could, but I was being tested to the limit as the physical pain following the operation was intense. It took a few months before I was able to sit up properly and to walk without being in pain.

I wondered how it was that I had managed to have so many sicknesses and accidents as a child that had enabled me to get the attention that I had craved.

'Is there some sort of a mind–body connection?' I wondered. This theory was backed up in some of the great books I was reading (such as the bestseller *You Can Heal your Life*[19] by Louise L. Hay). Louise L. Hay was an internationally known leader in the self-help field. Her key message is: "If we are willing to do the mental work, almost anything can be healed." She has a great deal of experience and first-hand information to share about healing, including how she claims she cured herself after being diagnosed with cancer.

One of my favourite quotes I loved when reading *You Can Heal Your Life* was:

'Remember, you have been criticising yourself for years and it hasn't worked. Try approving of yourself and see what happens.'

This book, and others, were affirming what I had heard anecdotally on my travels. I began to say these positive statements to myself as affirmations. I had heard that this was a great way to retrain your mind into accepting new beliefs. Even if you don't believe what you are saying in the beginning, eventually – and with repetition – the affirmations can help the new beliefs to take hold. I would say things like 'even though I am in pain, I deeply love and accept myself', 'even though I feel this rage, I love and accept myself'. I would repeat these phrases over and over and I did get great comfort from saying them. It stopped me from getting caught up in the pain, the rage or any other negative emotion I might be feeling.

To help me try to make sense of what was happening, and to gain some clarity for myself, I began to write several pages every morning as I woke up, as outlined in Julia Cameron's fantastic book, The Artist's Way[20]. The idea behind writing the morning pages is to allow the thoughts from your left side logical brain to be cleared out so that the right side, more creative brain, can then start channelling your more natural thoughts to come through.

What I personally discovered was that as I began to write, the tone of the writing was usually very negative or painful, but as the writing progressed, a softer, more positive tone would emerge.

Sometimes the softer tone would offer a commentary on the negative writing and help to give it all a different perspective. I began to feel much better for writing out my thoughts and feelings and being able to shift into a different state by the end of my writing the three pages.

Writing helps me to clarify my thoughts and change my emotional state.

I was able to see in my writing for the first time the two internal 'voices' happening inside of my head: the negative inner critical voice that would express itself first; and the second much more loving, supportive and compassionate voice that would emerge during the writing.

'How could I learn to make the loving voice the strongest voice that I could hear inside my head?', I wondered. Could meditation be the key?

This loving voice began to give me a lot of support. On days when my negative voice would berate me and tell me how terrible I was and how nothing would ever work out for me, the loving voice would tell me not to give up and that everything would be OK. And the positive affirmations I was saying were helping too.

I wondered whether I was going mad? Hearing voices could be a sign of schizophrenia, I seemed to recall.

'Am I going mad?'

These weren't external voices that I could hear speaking to me, however. They seemed to be voices of 'me' talking to 'me'. For most of my life these voices had been the narrators of my life from inside my head, and I had had no idea! I had never stopped before to think about the voice(s) that gave a running commentary on my experience. I had never been taught about this at school, or anywhere else. It was a revelation to discover that a whole internal world had been going on that I had known nothing about up until this trip.

Although nothing really seemed to make sense in my life in the way that it used to, I was experiencing feelings of peace, love and happiness that I had never experienced before, and so whatever label someone else may want to put onto the experiences would be OK by me.

The next period of around 3–4 months were very much a testing ground. I wondered, once I had become aware that there was a negative voice running inside my head, and once I had realised just what negative beliefs were driving this voice inside my mind, whether the very fact that I was aware of them would mean they would disappear (more about this later in the chapter).

Sadly, that was not to be the case!

What *did* happen was that I became more and more acutely aware of what was happening inside of me, and this was a painful process, especially as I was also trying to recover from the back operation at the same time. It seemed that the more aware I became, the louder the negative inner critical voice became, and it felt as though I was powerless to do anything about it. Sometimes I wished I had never become aware of any of these voices and wanted to go back to being unaware again. But this was not possible!

Something inside me kept pushing me forward, just as I realised it had always done. It had got me through those tough times and was doing so again. This something had got me out of bed each day and given me the strength to get through each challenge I had encountered up until now.

'There is a powerful strength inside me that I can draw on.'

Looking back I could see just how strong I had been. I had survived The Accident with no professional support, I had left home and passed my A levels whilst living in the council flat, I had found a way to stop taking drugs without help from anyone else and I had utilised the car crash to eventually springboard me into coming on this extended travelling trip.

The loving voice became like a best friend living inside of me who would come to support me when I needed a kind word. It never criticised or judged me, in fact it was completely the opposite. Knowing me like no-one else could, having knowledge of everything that I had lived through, the voice was able to tell me how proud it was of me and how well that I was doing.

Having had a brief glimpse of the possibility of how different life could be for me whilst I was travelling in India and Thailand, and then having all the suppressed negative feelings and emotions coming up so powerfully whilst in Australia, I became afraid and I felt stuck again. I was afraid of

141

moving forward and afraid of going backwards. At times I hankered after the familiarity of living my old life going clubbing and taking drugs which, although ultimately destructive, had also been a lot of fun and had given me a sense of connection and belonging.

Yet even in my darkest moments now, the loving voice was still there. It would not go away (no matter how loud and strong the judgmental voice became) and as time went on I could hear it more and more frequently, gently coaxing me to keep going.

'I am supported.'

The teachings of Dale Carnegie came back strongly into my awareness. I knew that this was a good time to put those teachings into practice. I hadn't chosen to slip the disc in my back, but I could choose how I responded to what was happening. I could choose to believe that 'bad things always happen to me' OR I could choose to believe that things just happen – it is how we respond to what happens that matters the most, just as Louise L. Hay was advocating.

I realised just how naïve I had been to think that I could just be positive and that in doing so all my negative beliefs would simply vanish!

On a very basic level Dale Carnegie was correct I now knew, but there was also something missing for me in his teachings. If you have core negative beliefs about yourself (as I had had, such as I am worthless, I am evil, etc), then those beliefs are what you will continually live from and no matter how much positive thinking you do, unless you get to the core beliefs and change them you will never be able to sustain your positivity and you will keep yo-yoing backwards and forwards between the two, which is exactly what I had been experiencing.

I learned about how beliefs are created and how they impact our lives and also about how our minds are created into three parts; the conscious, unconscious and superconscious minds. These parts overlap but also have individual functions:

Conscious mind

As the name suggests, the conscious mind is everything that we are consciously aware of. The conscious mind thinks rationally and helps us to set directions/goals.

This part of our mind is what makes decisions and it has free will to decide what it chooses. Where the conscious mind makes the decisions, the unconscious mind helps to make them a reality, or becomes the block to us creating what we want.

When you decide to make a cup of tea, go shopping, go to work, etc, the decision is coming from your conscious mind.

Unconscious mind

If the conscious mind is everything that you are aware of, then the unconscious mind is everything else. According to the Neuro-Linguistic Programming (NLP) communication model[21], there are over two million bits of information per second streaming into our unconscious minds from the external world and we can only process 126 bits per second.

So how do we know which bits to process and which not to? We all have our own individual filters that act as barriers or gate openers to all this information. The filters of the NLP Communication Model are Meta Programs, Belief Systems, Values, Decisions, and Memories. I won't go into too much more detail about this model here but there is a lot of readily available information available online if you wish to know more.

The unconscious mind has more power over our decisions than the conscious mind. It is why some people feel that they are permanently yo-yo dieting. The conscious part of their mind really wants to lose weight and be slimmer. But in their unconscious mind if they don't believe they deserve to be loved, or if they feel that men are dangerous then those deeper beliefs will ultimately sabotage any conscious attempt to lose weight, leading to frustration. This pattern I know very well having been on many diets myself over the years. The deeper beliefs act as a protection, trying to keep us safe. If we feel that men are dangerous, for example, then our unconscious mind will not want us to lose weight and become more attractive to men, as this could lead to danger.

What I found important for my own learning was the discovery that there was a whole world happening in my unconscious mind based on the beliefs that I had created, the experiences I had had, the decisions that I had made, and so on. And even though my conscious mind had been set on being happy, what was happening in my unconscious mind wouldn't allow this to happen.

The exciting thing was knowing that all learning, behaviour and change happen in the unconscious mind and that if I could delve inside my unconscious mind, discover what was in there and what was holding me back, then it was possible to create change in my life.

Once more I felt empowered and that my own peace of mind and happiness were in my control. This was great news!

'I have control over how I feel.'

The unconscious mind is where:

•   Memories are stored

- Memories are organised (in relation to time, etc.)

- Memories with unresolved negative emotion are stored

- Repressed memories may be presented for resolution or repressed for protection

- Associations are made and learned quickly

- The body is run and preserved

- The emotions are stored

- Perceptions are controlled and maintained

- Energy is generated, stored and distributed

- Habits are generated, and instincts are maintained

Superconscious mind

The superconscious mind has also been called the Collective Unconscious, Higher Self, Universal Mind, Higher Intelligence, Higher Mind, Inner Mind, Universal Intelligence, etc. The scientific community sometimes refers to it as "The Unified Field" or the "Infinite Field of Potentiality."

Whatever you prefer to call it, the superconscious mind apparently has no limitations or boundaries (unlike the conscious and unconscious minds). The superconscious mind is said to be the realm of intuition and inspiration and a field of pure potential. When we connect with the superconscious mind we can feel 'in the flow', 'on purpose', 'intuitively guided'.

When our conscious and unconscious minds are in rapport, it is thought that we can access the superconscious mind much more easily. We can help to build that rapport by clearing out any negative emotions/limiting beliefs from our unconscious minds so that communication between all three becomes much clearer.

With these realisations, I understood I was on a journey and that working through my negative beliefs would take time and patience (still not my strongest point at that time but the meditation was helping to make it better). The most powerful part was that I could choose to change, and that I have control over how I respond to life.

'I can choose to change. I have control over my response.'

I liked this idea of a superconscious mind being an 'Infinite Field of Potentiality'. I wondered if it was a connection to this that I had experienced initially in my reiki session in India and then at various times since. This felt right to me. We definitely have a conscious mind and an unconscious mind, so why not a superconscious mind too? And believing that I was connected to a field of infinite intelligence and potential from which everything is created (from ideas and inspiration to worlds and even us) felt more empowering to me than religions had up to this point.

'Believing in something greater than me, and of which I am an integral part, brings me comfort and joy'

It took me five months to recover from my back operation in Melbourne. All my original plans of buying a second-hand car and go travelling up the east coast of Australia had to be altered completely. I was literally halted in my tracks.

My surgeon had agreed that I could continue to travel once I had recovered sufficiently from the operation, but he told me that I would not be able to lift my backpack; either now or in the future. I was shocked initially to hear this news: it had never crossed my mind that I'd end up in this state physically. What would I do? How could I travel if I couldn't lift my backpack? What would I do with all my belongings? All these questions whirled around in my mind.

'You have two options,' he continued. 'The first is to buy a bag on wheels and the second is to find an Australian man to carry your bag for you.'

'I think I'll go with the first option,' I replied, laughing. 'It might be easier'.

The next leg of my trip I had planned to meet my sister, Sarah, and to travel around New Zealand together in a campervan. She had flown out with a friend to Sydney where she had tickets to see England play in the Rugby World Cup, which England won. She therefore arrived feeling on a high to Auckland airport where we met to begin out travels together. She had also lost her voice through all the shouting and celebrating during and after the rugby final.

We had talked about travelling around New Zealand for many years and I was really looking forward to seeing her again after nearly a year of being away. I wondered if I shared some of my new experiences and learnings with Sarah, what would she think of them?

I decided to wait and see what happened during our trip as to how much I would share with her about my experiences so far. I didn't have to wait too long for the first opportunity to arise.

We had hired a campervan in which to travel around New Zealand. Unfortunately, as we had had to wait for my visa to be approved for New Zealand before we booked it, we had to take the only campervan that was available, and it wasn't in great shape! Various things were missing inside and the seats that folded into a bed at night did not quite match up which always left me in fits of laughter whilst watching Sarah try in vain to make this an easy process each night. As soon as she pushed one side down, the other side would fly up – much to her dismay and my amusement.

Unfortunately for her, I was unable to help her due to having had my back operation so recently and was therefore not able to apply any pressure (which made it all even funnier for me not being able to help). She was not amused as much as me, however! We named the campervan Bertha and set off with excited anticipation for our trip.

One of the first evening stops that we made was in a campervan site in the North Island. They had a hot tub there, and Sarah and I sat in it for a while to relax after a long day's driving. Upon returning to the campervan, Sarah suddenly realised that she did not have Grandma Ida's wedding ring on (that she had been wearing since Grandma died several years earlier).

Getting into a complete panic she started frantically trying to find the ring but to no avail. We both loved Grandma so much and the thought of losing the ring was devastating. I tried to reason that the ring was just a ring and that it wasn't Grandma herself, but Sarah would not be pacified and I understood how responsible Sarah she felt for the ring's safe-keeping.

We retraced our steps to the hot tub and back again and everywhere inside the Campervan, but we could not find the ring anywhere.

I had read a book whilst waiting for my back operation in Australia called *Healing with the Angels*[22] by Doreen Virtue. Although it was one of the more 'weird and wonderful' books I had read, I had found great comfort in asking angels for help, whenever I was feeling afraid or stuck in an uncomfortable emotion, or when I needed guidance about next steps. I had no idea whether angels were 'real' or not, but I did find that when I asked them for help, help would appear. I wondered whether to share this with Sarah and get her to ask angels to help to find the ring, or whether she would think I had gone slightly crazy?

With Sarah being so upset, I thought I had nothing to lose and so (a little nervously) shared my idea with her. I think that at that point in time she was prepared to do anything to help to find the ring and so she consented to ask the angels if they would help her. And so we did ask them.

Having retraced our steps and also having turned the van upside down, a couple of minutes later the manager of the campervan site appeared out of the blue walking past our van and asked if we needed any help. We explained what had happened and he replied 'Oh, this happens all the time. Have a look down the side of the folding table inside the van and see if it has fallen down there and onto the wheel arch underneath'. We unfolded the table and peered down and right there, resting on the wheel arch was Grandma's ring!

Sarah looked at me in slight disbelief. I could see that she was wondering whether this was just a great coincidence? I just shrugged my shoulders and smiled.

The rest of the trip flowed really smoothly. I can honestly say that I have never laughed so much as we did in those four weeks spent travelling together. We initially went around the North island and then travelled to the South Island. We swam with dolphins, went into Milford Sound on a boat in the rain, flew in a helicopter over the Franz Josef glacier and Sarah did a tandem skydive over Lake Wanaka (my recent back operation gave me the perfect excuse not to have to do it too!). Sarah loved it and it was a definite highlight of the trip for her.

A massive fan already of the British band Coldplay since their first song 'Yellow[23]' had been released, their album 'A rush of blood to the head[24]' became the backdrop to our trip. Sarah and I both loved to sing along to the songs as we drove around the islands. Over the years I have loved how my own personal journey has been in synchronicity with the journey of the band. Their songs and music have been such a support and inspiration to me, as well as the great philanthropic work that they have done.

During our travels around New Zealand I read *The Power of Now*[25], by Eckhart Tolle. Just as when I had read the book on past lives whilst staying on Patnem beach, I felt tingles in my body when I was reading this book too.

Eckhart writes that everything that has ever happened, is happening and will happen, is happening now. There is no past or future only the eternal moment of now. 'This book is twisting my noodle!' I exclaimed to Sarah and she laughed. The idea that there is no past and that there will be no future as everything is happening in this moment was too much for my brain to cope with…and yet it made complete sense at the same time.

One of the things that I took from the book was that change happens now in this very moment. No need to wait for some far-off future date to make changes in my life when everything is happening in this moment of now, so may as well make it now now!

I was also delighted to read what Eckhart wrote about voices inside of our heads. He echoed my earlier anxiety and said that if someone went to the doctor and said that they could hear voices, they might be sent for a psychological assessment. And yet Eckhart confirms that virtually everyone hears a voice, or voices inside their head all the time, which he describes as our involuntary thought processes that we just don't realise we have the power to stop.

Yes! This was the evidence that I had been looking for. Relieved to understand that we all have voices that are inside our head, I felt reassured about my own!

Eckhart continues that we may have an experience of seeing someone in the street who is talking to themselves incessantly and who we may have labelled as 'mad'. He says that these people are not so different from us, it's just that our voices speak inside our heads and not out loud.

One passage really resonated with my own experience: 'It is not uncommon for the voice to be a person's own worst enemy. Many people live with a tormentor in their head that continuously attacks and punishes them and drains them of vital energy. It is the cause of untold misery and unhappiness, as well as of disease'.

But there was another ray of hope for me from Eckhart's teachings: '*The good news is that you can free yourself from your mind.* This is the only true liberation.'

'I can free myself from my mind.'

It was such a relief to understand that what I was going through was a normal experience and that other people felt the same way as I did. I didn't have to keep listening to this attacker/tormentor voice inside of me that had created so much suffering in my life, without questioning it's validity.

Eckhart also explained about the pain-body. If we don't deal with pain when something happens to cause pain, then it can accumulate over time and join with other pain we have suppressed, and it becomes like a collective negative energy field, which he calls the emotional pain-body. This pain-body can be dormant in some people and quite active in others. Some people live their lives almost completely in their pain body and others only dip into it and experience it in certain situations (like close relationships or when they have been hurt emotionally or physically). The pain-body can be activated very easily by one word uttered from someone else that acts like a trigger into the suppressed pain we have been trying to avoid feeling.

One moment we may be happily going about our daily lives and then suddenly we feel thrown into the grip of a very difficult and negative emotion (we may feel rage towards another person, for example). This emotion can feel overwhelming and intense and we don't feel able to control it. I would often feel rage if I believed that another person was trying to control me, which happened with some managers in my early career. I was immediately transported back to being a child and all of my suppressed rage about my step-dad would come rushing to the surface, much to my discomfort. I knew that my reactions were then over-exaggerated to what was happening in the moment. I dearly wished that I could find a way to make this stop as I found it quite debilitating and it was also impacting my close relationships.

When you live in the pain-body, as I recognised that I had been doing, Eckhart says that the pain wants more pain. Although on a conscious level someone will be adamant (as I was) that they did not want more pain, on an unconscious level the pain-body is creating thoughts and behaviour to keep the pain going. It is as though the pain body creates a false self that we believe is who we are and our 'real' self is actually living free from the pain, but we can't feel it when we are associating with the pain-body.

The way out of living like this, and into the 'real' self, is to bring conscious awareness to what is happening, and to face the pain we are feeling inside. I had been living in my pain-body, I could sense this to be true. And I had made a start at bringing conscious awareness to this fact and turning to face the pain. I knew that I was on the right track to living in my 'real' self and this was very reassuring. At the end of the month spent travelling together, Sarah and I flew back together to Sydney, Australia and spent New Year there before Sarah headed back to the UK. We spent New Year's Eve on a boat in the harbour watching the spectacular fireworks display which was incredible. I felt very grateful to have spent this amazing trip together.

I was sad to see Sarah leave but I also knew that I would be seeing her again in just a few months' time once the rest of my trip was complete.

After she left I travelled North of Sydney to stay with my dad's cousin Alan and his wife Poss who looked after me really well and it was wonderful to meet their daughters and extended family. After staying with them for about a week it was time to head back home to the UK. I decided to fly back to the UK via Thailand again. My original flight had been back via the US but as my recuperation from my back operation had taken so long, I was now over the 12-month validity of my round the world ticket and therefore had to forego my US flight tickets. As I had loved Thailand so much I decided to go back there again on the way home instead.

By pure 'coincidence', Upchar (who had taught me my first reiki initiation) was also going to be back in Thailand from Germany with his girlfriend at the same time as me and so we met again on Koh Phangan, and he was able to teach me reiki level II.

He asked me how everything had been since the last reiki initiation and I told him that, although things had been very difficult with my back operation, I felt like a light switch had been turned on inside of me during the initiation, and that every day since then the light had been getting brighter and brighter.

'There is a bright light inside me. It keeps getting brighter.'

I also expressed some concern that at the same time as the light was getting brighter, the pain inside of me seemed to be getting stronger and louder. Upchar told me not to worry and that this was all part of the process that I would now be going through. It was as though the light was shining on all the suppressed hurt and pain so that I could see it to heal it.

This gave me comfort although a large part of me had been hoping that if I set a clear enough intention that I would be able to bypass the painful part and go straight to giving and receiving unconditional love!! Unfortunately, this was not to be the case.

In our time together Upchar asked me what it really was that I wanted. I paused for a moment and replied, 'Peace of mind'.

From all the trauma and pain I had experienced my mind had become so loud, and sometimes chaotic and busy. What I really longed for most was to feel calm and peaceful at last. Peace of mind became my sole focus over the years to come. I was on a mission to find it.

Whilst doing the reiki course, I had been staying back at The Sanctuary and once the course was over I noticed that there was a different course coming up, an eight day course to learn about shamanism. My curiosity was now well and truly open to all things new on this trip and, thinking I could just squeeze one more course in before I returned to the UK I signed up for the course, not really knowing what I was signing up for. I was just following my newly found intuition wherever it wanted to go – and this course seemed to be it for now.

The course was run by Vinod; an English guy who had become an Osho Sanyassin[26] and who now lived on Koh Phangan with his (then) girlfriend (another Sanyassin) called Shashi.

Sanyassin is a Sanskrit word that describes someone who has reached the life stage of sannyasa, or "renouncement of material possession." A sannyasin has turned away from all material possessions and emotional ties. Osho himself described the sannyas movement simply as the movement of the seekers of truth.

Vinod and Shashi were both of English origin with English birth names but who now lived and worked in Thailand. They had taken their new names during a ceremony when they had decided to become Sanyassin.

The course was absolutely amazing. Vinod was a lot of fun. He wore a sarong with a huge sun image on it that you could see when looking from behind me. 'I wear this', Vinod smiled, 'to remind myself that the sun really does shine out of my backside'. He was great, very irreverent and quirky. The course would start at odd times like 11.08am and he would get us to question a lot of the 'norms' we were used to.

Most days he would guide us into what are called 'shamanic journeys'. We would lie down on a mat on the floor and with his drum he would guide us with a rhythmic beat into a deep meditation or 'journey', allowing our unconscious minds to give us the symbols, images and words that we needed in order to heal. I had never been on a course before where the majority of the time you lay down and delved deeper into your imagination and unconscious mind. It was great!

We learned about shamanism and what it means. Shamans believe that all things are energy and that all things are alive. Shamanism encompasses the belief that shamans are intermediaries between the spirit world and the human world. Shamans treat illnesses by mending the soul which in turn brings the person's physical body into wholeness again. A shaman may also enter supernatural realms to obtain solutions to problems that they bring back into the present.

Vinod explained how to make medicines by taking the essence of different plants. Shamans very much believe that it is necessary to communicate with nature respectfully and that we have lost touch with this in the western world. They say we have lost our connection with nature and how to commune with it.

So I spent the eight days lying down and going on amazing journeys within my imagination, learning about different medicines and plant essences, learning about energy and how to use it, learning about different healing techniques. I loved every single minute of the course and I felt like I was Harry Potter[27] going through Hogwarts School. I had always loved reading the Harry Potter books by J.K Rowling and now I felt like I was living in my own version of the story. It was quite surreal, great fun and also very powerful.

On one of the days Vinod set us all a task, to go into the Thai jungle and to respectfully ask a tree for a branch to make a wand and then to bring this wand back to the course. He said that the tree would let us know whether it was the right tree or not and whether we had permission to take a branch to make a wand. Inside I was laughing. It really did feel like Hogwarts now! I kept thinking 'if only my friends back home could see me now'. I was highly sceptical of the exercise when I set out into the jungle that morning.

I was slowly walking along and just enjoying the feeling of being immersed in nature when I asked myself the question 'so how on earth will I know whether a tree has given me permission or not to take a branch to make a magic wand?' when out of the corner of my right eye I saw a branch waving slightly. I stopped abruptly and turned towards it. There was no breeze at all as it was a really hot day and so the movement of the branch took me by surprise. I stood in front of the tree and asked if I could take this branch and, to my astonishment, it moved again.

'I'll take that as a yes!' I exclaimed and thanked the tree as I took the branch and almost ran back to the course to share my story with the others. Everyone on the course had their own story to tell and they had all brought a branch back with them. It was amazing to see how much each one fitted with their individual character. There was an American lady who was very petite, and she brought back a tiny branch with a single green leaf on the end, and a loud American man who brought back a branch that was more like a staff that could reach down to the ground whilst he held it in his hand. This was just like a staff I had seen Gandalf wielding in the 'Lord of the Rings' movies. I loved the way the individual wands seemed to be reflecting everyone's individual personalities, and I felt that mine (which was a kind of in-between these other two) was perfect for me too.

I was loving the exploration of different ways of being that this course and the whole trip was giving to me.

During the 8 days of this shamanic course even more of my ideas and beliefs about 'the way that things are' were being turned on their head. I marvelled at all of these new concepts and began to realise just what a curious world we really do live in.

Finishing the course meant that my whole trip away had come to an end. One day I was in the Thai jungle making magic wands and two days later I was in the kitchen at Sarah's house in Kingston, England.

It felt completely surreal to cross from one world to another so abruptly and it actually took me quite a while to readjust to life in the UK once more.

I had absolutely no idea how I could now fit back into UK life again. I was worried about being drawn back into the old clubbing and taking drugs lifestyle that I had lived for the previous 10 years and that I had built my life around.

But I also knew that I was a very different person from the one who had left the UK just 16 months earlier. I had opened up to exploring many different perspectives than I had known before, I had begun to unravel some of the negative beliefs that had been holding me back in life and

I had formed close relationships with other people that weren't based around taking drugs.

And so it was with curiosity and optimism that I came back to the UK in March 2004.

CHAPTER 8

The Fresh Start

"Peace comes from within. Do not seek it without."

Siddhārtha Gautama[28]

My primary question when I returned to the UK in 2004 was 'what would happen next in my life?' Would I be seduced by the temptations of my previous life? Would I be able to resist going back to nightclubs and to taking drugs again? Where would I belong now? What would I do to earn a living?

Upon my return, it initially seemed as though my whole trip abroad had been just a dream and that now that I was back in the UK, I was being woken up to 'reality' again, just as I had felt coming back from my earlier shorter trips abroad and also from living in Paris. I just could not initially see how I could create the peace that I had discovered within me whilst travelling, back here in the busy, noisy and hectic life of London. Was it even a possibility?

'Is peace of mind possible living in a noisy city?'

Everything and everyone appeared to be the same as before; everyone that is, except for me.

I moved back to London and I got a job back in a sales role within the hotel industry – the career I had known before I went away. In practical terms, I really needed some money to live on and so the most obvious thing for me to do was to go back into the industry that I knew from before and which, I believed, would pay me the most money.

Having felt so free whilst travelling, the reality of being back in a 9–5 job was quite sobering. In order to soften the blow of having to work again, I had accepted a job with a hotel chain that only had hotels overseas and none in the UK. I knew that in my sales role that this would mean

I would get to travel abroad and to stay in the hotels, so it seemed like a great transitional role for me whilst I adjusted to life in the UK again.

Everything started really well. With improved confidence in myself I was able to jump straight into the role and to get great results for the company that I was working for. I was able to prove to myself just how much I had changed in the 16 months that I had been away.

Bit by bit, however, uneasiness was building inside me. I kept trying to ignore how I was feeling, but the job and the company were not in alignment with my new beliefs and values and I felt I was playing a role once more, and not one that felt very empowering. To make myself feel 'better', I began smoking the odd cigarette here and there, and soon I was back to smoking 10 a day.

I did, however, manage to stay away from nightclubbing and taking drugs, which, looking back, was a great achievement. I was fully committed to developing my peace of mind and feelings of happiness and so I cut ties with a lot of the people I had known through the clubbing lifestyle I was leading before.

This meant that in a way I was starting my life all over again. Initially I spent many nights sitting at home on my own, which was the hardest part for me. I then moved in to share a house with my sister Sarah and I was grateful for her support and encouragement.

Around eight months into my role at the hotel company, the disc in my back slipped again. I wondered if this was the mind-body connection in action, as Louise L. Hay had talked about? I questioned whether I should really consider changing professional career as I felt that working in sales for hotels was no longer working for me and maybe my back was giving me a strong signal to push me in another direction? It certainly felt that way.

Over the previous 18 months several people, including Sarah, had talked to me about life coaching and I felt intrigued to find out more about what it was exactly. Not being able to work with my slipped disc meant that now I had the opportunity to investigate it more thoroughly. A life coach, I discovered, is someone who empowers other people by helping them make, meet and exceed goals in both their personal and professional lives. This sounded perfect as a potential new career for me. I felt so motivated to help other people to break free from what may be limiting them in their own lives, as I felt I had started to do in my own.

One day, as I was lying down resting my back, a compelling vision came into my mind. This vision was of me standing on a stage in front of hundreds of people, and they had all come to hear me speak. It seemed so real and so surreal at the same time and I knew it was not something I could ignore. It had a clarity unlike other thoughts I'd had. This image was accompanied by a feeling of such absolute certainty that this was a future reality for me. I felt like I had had a glimpse of my future career, but it seemed so far away from the reality of where I was at that time (lying flat on my back and barely able to move) and I was also terrified of speaking in public! I wasn't sure how this vision could possibly become a reality for me, and yet part of me really felt it to be true.

My back eventually improved, and I was soon back at work again. After investigating various life coach training courses, I found a week-long residential training course with an American coach training company and I booked myself onto it. I decided to hand my notice in at work and to jump into my new career.

With growing excitement around becoming a life coach, I worked through my notice period at work. And then my disc slipped again. I could not believe it. I was trusting that I was doing the right thing for me. So why had this happened to me again?

'Bad things happen to me. I am evil. I deserve to be punished.'

Although my old beliefs had been shaken deep inside, they were still there and stirring up feelings of anger and fear. Sometimes I felt like I was on a merry-go-round of the same inner thoughts which were stuck on repeat cycle.

As I had already resigned, I had to leave work at the end of my notice period. At this point I struggled to sit in a chair for longer than 15 minutes at a time. I went to my life coaching training but had to spend most of the course standing up as I was in so much pain.

The course was great. It was even better than I had hoped that it would be. I liked the way that coaching was solution-focused and helped people to learn more about who they are and what they really want. I liked the 'coach approach' which included the idea of 'kind curiosity'. In normal life when someone is talking, we often have thoughts that pop into our minds that relate to our own experience of what the other person is saying. We may then jump into the conversation to give our (unsolicited) advice to the other person 'I know what you should do, you should do this', etc. which can be very disempowering for the other person (especially when they haven't asked for advice). I really liked the idea of having kind curiosity when a person is talking, it enabled me to focus more on the other person and less on me and my interpretation of what they were saying. It was also much more empowering for the other person. I felt that I had gained key skills for life, as well as for my new profession.

I was excited to get the qualification and to start working as a life coach. Unfortunately, after the course had finished, I spent the next six months getting my back into a healthy state again – and during this time I was unable to look for any permanent work to support me whilst I built my business up.

Because of this I started to build up a lot of personal debts. I had paid for my training course on credit and had some debt already accrued. Because I was unable to look for any paid employment I had to use my credit cards to pay for rent and bills, and very quickly my debts escalated.

There was something about money and me that did not seem to be connected. It was as though there was a relationship between my deeply held core negative beliefs about myself and my relationship with money.

'I am worthless.'

And my bank account agreed. 'Could my inner beliefs have created a physical reality through my finances?' I questioned?

By the end of 2005 I was in a severe financial crisis.

My faith, too, was also in crisis.

My newly acquired empowering beliefs were on very shaky ground. What I had expected to happen by taking a 'leap of faith', handing in my resignation at my old company and retraining myself as a life coach was that life would now flow very easily for me and that I would be happy.

The reality I experienced was very different. Yes, I had undergone my new life coaching training, but I had then been unable to work for a long time, had amassed a huge amount of debt and I was feeling completely out of control of my life – again!

I decided that I may have been much better off before I had heard about any of this spiritual and personal development.

Now here I was stuck inside of my house most of the time, with hardly any close friends, no social life and deeply in debt.

'How could you do this to me?' I raged at life (and 'God'). I felt utterly betrayed. It seemed cruel to have allowed me to dare to hope that my life could be different and that I could be happy. Maybe I had misunderstood the whole thing. Maybe my desperate desire to be happy and to have peace of mind had made me blind to 'reality'. Maybe I really was mad, bad and also stupid, after all.

Maybe I was just born to be miserable and there was nothing that I could do about it? Maybe I should just go back to wearing all the masks from before and just making do as best I could? Maybe I should just start taking drugs again; at least then I had friends and a social life and some fun every weekend?

And yet... and YET, something inside of me still had hope. Something inside of me said that ALL of this was a part of the journey along the road to where I wanted to be. This voice was still smaller than the tormentor, but it was definitely there, and it was persistent. I clung to it with everything I had.

Having experienced a life with hope I could not bear to go back to feeling hopeless again. Looking back I can see how courageous I was to trust on such a deep level and to take such a big leap of faith, but also very naïve in the practicalities of supporting myself through the process.

A few months later, Sarah told me about an organisation that she had been to called 'Alternatives[29]' – a not-for-profit organisation that hosts inspirational talks and workshops in London. They are dedicated to raising awareness and offering practical, inspiring and alternative solutions for everyday living.

Many of the leading personal and spiritual development teachers from all over the world come to give talks at Alternatives when they are in London. I was excited as a lot of the authors of the books that I had been reading over the past year were on the speakers or workshop list.

Here, it seemed, was my opportunity to rediscover a connection with like-minded people and to make new friends. 'Maybe I can recreate some of the community I met while travelling but here in London, after all?' I thought. I went along to some talks and workshops and then applied to become a volunteer member of the Alternatives team and was delighted that I was accepted. This meant that every Monday night for the next few years I attended the talks and assisted on some of the workshops at the weekends.

I became a workshop 'junkie'. I went to workshop after workshop after workshop. Some were through Alternatives and others were ones I chose to go to myself. I was like a sponge, soaking up all this new learning. I felt part of a community and I built new friendships that were like the ones I had created when travelling. I met an incredibly lady called Mary Daniels and she went on to become a great friend and mentor, as well as a Director of Alternatives.

Mary has since written a book about her life experience and subsequent learnings published by Hay House which is called 'Wild Awakening: 9 Questions that Saved my Life[30].' I am very grateful for Mary's friendship over the years, which at times has not been easy for either of us (as we have at points been powerful mirrors for each other's pain) but through which we have both grown and our friendship matured. She continues to inspire me hugely and she gives so much love everywhere she goes.

During this time I also went on many training and development seminars to improve my confidence in my coaching ability. I was on a mission to find answers to the questions that were continuing to circle within my mind, *'Who am I? What is my purpose in life? What is the purpose of life? How can I achieve peace of mind?'*

I needed to know the answers and I would not stop until I had them. It almost became like an obsession of mine to discover 'the truth' and the answers to these questions.

'What is 'The Truth' anyway?' the question re-emerged and lingered with me.

Whose truth was 'The Truth'? Was it the Catholics', the Protestants', the Hindus', the Muslims', the Jehovah's Witnesses'? Was it those who followed a shaman's path, was it The Truth of atheists, agnostics, mystics, spiritualists?

Surely there can't just be *one* that is the *right one*, I wondered to myself. That just didn't seem to make any sense to me.

During the next couple of years, I was relentless in my quest to discover answers and I pushed and pushed myself. I was not going to give up my search, no matter what the cost.

As the years went on I had several crises of faith. Sometimes I would feel in my heart that everything was great and happening exactly as it was meant to happen. But next I would be feeling a lot of pain and raging at life and at 'God' as to why I had to go through any of this at all. On these days life just seemed so painful, so unfair and so unjust.

'Why couldn't I just be happy and leave the past behind?' as other well-meaning people said I should do.

I saw my pain as something that I had to annihilate, to get rid of. I equated pain with bad and happiness with good. Having suffered most of my life, I was now trying to disassociate myself from my pain as quickly as I possibly could. Any time that I felt any pain I would book a session with someone to help me to move through it so that I could go back to feeling better once more. It became like another addiction. I tried hypnotherapy, reiki, NLP, acupuncture, Emotional Freedom Technique, meditation, and many, many more!

The healing 'fix' would only work for a short time. I would then become impatient that I wasn't 'cured' and move onto something new instead to see if that had better results. Some seemed to work better than others, but I always seemed to fall back into pain again before too long. I had heard that in meditation I needed to go 'beyond my mind' and so I translated this to mean that I had to somehow get rid of my mind and move into some more enlightened state. Every time I tried to do this, however, my mind fought back…hard! It just would not go away, no matter what I did.

On one course I went on during this time I did a process which is designed to take you through different layers of negative beliefs you hold until you get to the core belief that is driving the others. When I say there are layers of belief, by layers, I mean the degree, intensity or strength of a belief being held in your mind. A core belief is the strongest and most deeply held belief that we have and other beliefs can be attached to it and be driven by it.

During this process I could feel myself dropping through different belief layers until eventually I heard myself saying "I need to suffer to be closer to God!". The words were being uttered from my mouth but I didn't know where they were coming from. It was a strange feeling. The words resonated with me as being true but I had had no conscious realisation at all that this was my belief, deep down inside.

I had been christened a Catholic and had gone to Sunday school as a child but had not had my Confirmation and was not brought up a practising Catholic. Somehow the belief system around needing to suffer to be closer to God had become embedded in me at a very early age and had been unconsciously driving my behaviour as an adult. On some level I believed that suffering was going to bring me closer to God, in other words that it was something I really needed to do. I was astounded. And it made so much sense. I had been suffering for a very long time. I wondered how many other people around the world might have this core belief also? There was so much suffering in the world and I was curious as to whether a belief system like this might be at the root of some of it.

It was incredible to think how deeply belief systems are held within us and how we may have no real conscious idea of what is driving our behaviour and our experiences in life. At this point I was not sure how to really change this belief system, but it was a great first step to have uncovered its existence.

During this intensive period of my life I had a lot of fun learning many new things. As well as the courses I was going on I learned more about the power of the mind; I walked over hot coals, I broke a wooden board in two with my hand and I put a plastic straw clean through a raw potato in only one attempt!!

On one of the courses I was told how powerful our names are. I thought about my name. My first name Elisabeth apparently is Hebrew in origin and means 'consecrated to God' and my last name is Cashin 'money-in' so I had both religion and money in my full name (and this has become a core learning over the years of how to integrate spirituality and money in my work!).

Whilst on this course I realised that I had been spelling the shortened version of my name as Liz (short for Elizabeth). I had spelt Liz previously with a z as I didn't want to cause a fuss by saying 'it's Liz with an s'. Learning the power of names I decided that from that point on I would be called Lis (or Liz with an s!). It was interesting as just in changing that one letter I felt somehow more fully myself.

Around this time I met an incredible lady called Judith (Jude) Davis who was going through a similar process in her own personal development (having lost her son very suddenly when he was 13-years-old). She became such a great friend and it was invaluable to know that I had someone to turn to, someone with whom I could share what I was going through, someone who understood trauma from their own personal experience and someone who listened to me in a non-judgmental and compassionate space.

Judith is one of the most loving and generous women I have ever met. There have been some really tough times when Jude has been there to hold me, encourage me and to tell me that everything was ok. We also laugh a lot and she has a wicked sense of humour! I am truly blessed to call her a friend. She is also an astrologer and breathworker[31] and her healing sessions are incredibly powerful.

'Just because you have always believed something to be true (about yourself) doesn't mean that it is.'

This was a phrase that I had initially heard in India and was repeated to me during a workshop in London one day. I felt it resonate on a deeper level than before. 'Just because I have always believed myself to be bad, doesn't mean that it is true!' I had such an immense feeling of relief at the possibility that I might not be evil after all, but I was far from believing it to be true.

I realised just how much I had been projecting out into the world because of the beliefs I was holding inside, and how I had been blaming other people for how I was feeling. I took 100% responsibility for my own peace of mind.

'I am responsible for my own peace of mind.'

I saw I had pushed a lot of people away from me through my own deep insecurity and fear that they would hurt or reject me (as I had experienced in my childhood). I expected people to cause me pain and guess what? Yes, that became my experience of them. Pushing people away was my protection to ensure that nobody got too close to me ever again. The more that I tried to stop people from hurting me, the more I experienced them doing exactly that.

Once again, I knew that now I had a choice.

'I have choice.'

I knew that whenever I experienced pain because of someone else's actions that I could now choose to look inside *myself* for the cause of my pain.

This was very difficult at first for me to grasp. I wanted so badly to blame someone else for all the pain that I had felt during my life. I so badly wanted to blame my parents, my school, ex-boyfriends, my friends, even 'God' for hurting me. I struggled to let go of this blame and instead wanted to keep myself feeling like a victim who had been wronged by life.

I came to realise that my anger and rage at some of the things I had experienced were all valid for the child who experienced them at the time, but in holding onto these negative emotions I had created pain and suffering for *myself* and would continue to do so, unless I could find some forgiveness and extend it towards those who had hurt me in the past.

Knowing this became like torture for me. I knew that on some level I could choose to stop feeling like a victim and yet I was still feeling so much rage and fear inside. I felt like I was playing an inner game of tug of war with these old and new beliefs – each one trying its best to become the winner of the game. Was the belief system of needing to suffer to be closer to God still playing out in my life? Or was it something deeper still?

As a volunteer with Alternatives I had the chance to attend a personal development course called The Essence Process[32] led by Dr. Menis Yousry. This Foundation course along with their Advanced course I went on to do next gave me some profound insights into myself and I gained some lifelong friends too. One lady, Sanja, it transpired lived just around the corner from me at that time and we became firm friends, along with Jacky who we also met on the same course. Even though I have moved several times since we met we have all remained great friends and I love meeting up with them and putting the world to rights!

My relationships with my mum and my dad strengthened during this time. I was able to start to open up with them about how I had been feeling so much shame and guilt, how I had taken drugs to escape the pain for a long time and how I was trying hard to reclaim my life. I had to be courageous to do this and was shaking at times as I felt shame and like I was risking their rejection, but in fact it began to build bridges between us. I also felt that, having been so honest with them about what I had been doing, the shame I was feeling started to lose its grip. Dr. Brene Brown[33] says about shame ""The less you talk about it, the more you got it. Shame needs three things to grow exponentially in our lives: secrecy, silence, and judgment."

I had been so determined to hold onto blame and rage, particularly towards my parents for not having rescued me as a child, but it was eating away at me. One of the best and most authentic speakers I had the privilege to assist on at Alternatives was Byron Katie[34]. She has created a very simple and yet profound four step process called 'The Work[35]' to

get people to question the validity of the negative emotions that they are holding onto. I highly recommend you visit her website and download the free resources that she has there.

One of my favourite all-time quotes from her is '*If you argue with reality you will lose, but only 100% of the time*'. Most of the time we want things to be different from the way that they are or were for us. We say things like 'S/he shouldn't have done that to me'. What we are doing is trying to argue with reality, as the fact is that the person did do whatever they did and by us saying they shouldn't have done it we are hurting ourselves and it is not changing what happened.

By accepting that what happened did happen (not condoning it but accepting it) we can then be free to choose how we want to move forwards, but as long as we are still living in blame and 'should/not' we are going to keep ourselves stuck. I realised that, in order for me to feel the peace of mind I longed for, I was going to have to fully accept what had happened and to forgive the adults involved, understanding that they were doing the best that they could. This was not an easy process for me but one which has been so instrumental in my own personal growth.

I assisted on a few of Byron Katie's workshops with Alternatives and she was the only speaker in all of the five years that I was a volunteer who came to meet the volunteer team and to allow us to answer any personal questions we had during her lunch break. She then invited us all onto the stage at the end to receive a round of applause from the audience. This is a lady who really walks her talk!

Another gem of a book that I read was *Ask and It Is Given*[36], by Esther Hicks. This book tells us how well-being is our natural state and we either feel well-being, or resistance to well-being. Esther talks about the law of attraction being what we focus our attention on we attract into our lives. If you focus on not having, you will continue to not have. You draw to your experience what you predominantly think about. So if you are constantly worrying about not having money and not being able to pay the bills you will continue to have more of the same.

In this way, worrying is using your imagination to create something that you don't want. The stronger the beliefs and thoughts that you hold about something, the more you will attract them into your experience. For example, if you say that you want to lose weight, but in your unconscious mind you are holding deep beliefs around being unworthy or unattractive then these beliefs will prevent you from losing weight and/or sustaining it in the way that your conscious mind wants to.

Esther says that we all have an inner guidance system which is based on our feelings. Instead of giving your attention to whatever is in front of you, you can guide your thoughts to different thoughts that make you feel better, using the emotional guidance system.

I had heard about the law of attraction before and had watched the film The Secret[37], based on the book by Rhonda Byrne. In this book Rhonda states that whatever we focus on we will attract. I found it very useful but also simplistic. I knew a lot of people were frustrated as they kept focusing hard on what they wanted but were attracting/creating something very different in their lives (myself included).

Esther took things one step further. She informed us that whatever we were predominantly focusing on in our *unconscious* mind is what we were attracting, and not what our conscious mind is focusing on. This helped me to clarify why I had been trying so hard to create happiness for myself, as my conscious mind had wanted it to happen but my internal (unconscious) beliefs were so negative and so destructive that sustained happiness had just not been possible. I had created a deep inner conflict and it certainly felt like that. In fact it seemed like the more I focused on happiness the more conflict that I had created instead.

'Ask and it is given' is created in the following way:

1. Ask for what you want

2. Allow it to come into your experience

What generally happens is that we ask for what we want and when it doesn't appear straight away we start to worry or say things like 'this is rubbish. I knew it wasn't going to work' and then that prevents what we want from showing up, because we are not allowing it to, or believing that it is possible. The 'trick' is to focus only on what you want and not on what you don't and to ensure that you clear away any negative beliefs that might be preventing you from receiving it.

By this point I had had several years of in-depth personal work and training and my mind had become overloaded with so much information and the inner conflict seemed to be getting progressively worse. In my relentless quest to find peace of mind I had (ironically) not given my mind any peace! The pushing and pushing eventually took its toll on me.

Everything finally came to a head in early 2009. Nothing was working out how I wanted it to, no matter how hard I tried or pushed for it to happen. Unable to work consistently and therefore not able to pay my rent I had begun to accrue debts again which was sending me into a state of panic. I was feeling so deeply depressed that I just couldn't function properly. I went to visit the doctor and was signed off work and told that I would need some time without working to recuperate.

I didn't argue. I had tried and tried and tried and pushed myself to the absolute limit. I had done everything that I could possibly think of to break free from my pain and yet I seemed to be feeling more pain than ever before. I was at absolute breaking point. I gave up. I had no energy to fight anymore. I was absolutely exhausted with life.

My life was falling apart, and I needed somewhere to go.

It was at this point that my dad and step-mum offered for me to go and stay with them. As the previous time I had stayed with them had not ended well, I was very nervous about going to stay (as I'm sure they were too) but I was also very grateful to them both for wanting to support me now. I knew that I needed somewhere to stay where I would not have to worry about paying the bills for a while and so I headed to Yorkshire to stay with them.

I rested and recuperated with them for a short time and I took some part-time work to support myself. It wasn't an easy time for any of us living together again but for my 40th birthday present they surprised me by supporting me to fly back out to India, which was what I really longed for at that point and was a generous thing for them to do. Through his charity work, Dad had helped to raise money for the Parmarth Niketan Ashram in Rishikesh (a spiritual haven in the Himalayas) several years previously and, through his friends the Solanki family, my room was booked at The Ashram.

I felt glimmers of happiness flickering through the pain. I felt as though after a very long and very tough six years since I had been in India previously that I was now turning a corner. If I could find peace of mind anywhere in the world, I thought, it would be in India.

And so, another phase of my journey began…

CHAPTER 9
The Heart Opening

"The best and most beautiful things in this world cannot be seen or even heard but must be felt with the heart."

Helen Keller[38]

And so it was on 31st July 2009, that I found myself flying out from Heathrow to Delhi for the second time. Just like the first time when I had left the UK for India seven years previously, I felt like a child on Christmas Eve. I hoped with all my heart that this would be another incredible and life changing experience, but I had no idea how it would turn out to be.

I arrived in Delhi and instead of going south as in my previous trip to India, this time I went north, to Rishikesh where I would be staying in Parmarth Niketan Ashram[39] on the banks of the River Ganges. An ashram is a residence of a religious community and its guru. The guru at the head of the ashram where I was staying is called Swami Chidanand Saraswatiji Maharaj[40] (or Swami-ji as he is referred to). Swami-ji means 'Holy man' and there are many heads of ashrams in India who are referred to in this way. The Swami-ji at this ashram has such a gentle and loving presence and a deep wisdom that he shares with those who come to visit. Quite a small man, with dark greying longer hair and beard, he wears orange robes to signify his status.

He has an American lady devotee Sadhvi Bhagawati Saraswatiji[41], PhD, who lives at the ashram and who works alongside Swami-ji delivering his charity work around the world. Bhagwati, as she is known, grew up in an American family in Hollywood, California, and graduated from Stanford University. She was completing her PhD when she left America in 1996 to go and live permanently at Parmarth Niketan Ashram. She has been living there for the last twenty-two years, engaged in spiritual practice and dedicated service. She was officially initiated into the order of Sanyas herself (monastic renunciation) in the year 2000, by her guru, Swami Chidanand Saraswatiji. A beautiful lady with long dark hair, Bhagwati also now wears orange robes to signify her status.

The River Ganges has particular significance within the Hindu religion in India. The river, personified as a goddess, is worshipped by Hindus, who believe that bathing in the river causes the remission of sins and facilitates liberation from the cycle of life and death. Pilgrims travel long distances to immerse the ashes of their kin into the river, so that their loved ones will pass on to heaven.

It was therefore a very holy place for me to visit and to spend time. I had booked initially to do a yoga course at the ashram.

When I arrived, the ashram was not what I had been expecting. I had longed for it to be a tranquil, quiet and peaceful place on the banks of the holy river. What I discovered instead was that, because it was such a revered and holy place it was very busy and there was a lot of noise due to the steady stream of the Indian people on pilgrimage who came every day to worship and to admire the statues in the grounds.

My mind was longing for a peaceful place to rest and so in the beginning I felt unsettled there. I thought that I had made a mistake in coming here and that I needed to leave and find somewhere quieter as my mind now was feeling in turmoil and chaos. I went into Bhagwati's office to thank her for her kind invitation for me to stay longer in the ashram and to tell her that I thought that I needed to move on and that I was leaving the next day.

She said of course that was OK if it was what I really wanted to do. She asked me to sit me down and then she chatted to me for over an hour. During that hour I felt all the tension that I was holding onto so tightly starting to melt away. I felt that she knew just how I was feeling.

'What is it that you are looking for, Lis?' she asked in her soft American

accent.

'Peace and quiet,' I replied, 'and a place to let go of this pain that I am carrying.'

'Can you not do that here on the beautiful banks of the holy River Ganges?' she questioned. Up until that point, I didn't think that I could. It had all seemed too busy and noisy.

'You will never find what you are looking for while you keep moving,' she continued.

'Here we think that western psychotherapy has everything back to front. It encourages a person to continuously keep going into the pain, into the pain, into the pain and then people have become experts at analysing their pain. What we are not good at is moving into something else *from* the pain'

She repeated something that Swami-ji had told her:

'In the West you sit around in a dark room discussing the details of the darkness. You measure every molecule of darkness. How many protons? How many neutrons? How many electrons make up these atoms? How long has it been dark? Whence did this darkness come? Is it darker than yesterday or is it perhaps getting slightly less dark? You go around and discuss the way the darkness makes you feel. You encourage each other to express your frustration at sitting in a dark room. This goes on endlessly.

In the East, we run our hands along the wall looking for the light switch. We know that once the light switch is found and the light gets turned on, then it no longer matters how dark it has been or what the molecules of darkness are made of, or from where the darkness has come. What matters is that now there is light.'

I was reminded with this metaphor of the statement that I had made to Upchar six years earlier when I had told him that having my reiki initiation felt like a light switch had been turned on inside of me and that it was growing brighter every day. It seemed fascinating to me that we had both used such a similar metaphor and the memory of that time came flooding back to me.

Bhagwati added that one of the greatest gifts that Eastern psychology has to offer to the West is to help people to find a way out of the darkness. She says that it is important to go down into the darkness. It is important to see, to feel, to know the reasons why we are the way we are (our deepest fears and fantasies) but then it is equally important to be able to find our way back to the light. It is equally important to know when to stop discussing the darkness and begin to look for the light switch and to turn it on.

'What we need to do', Bhagawati continued *'Is help Lis to learn to love again.'*

When I went in to see Swami-ji later that night for Darshan (an evening audience where devotees come to give reverence) I waited patiently as a steady stream of people came in to see him and then left. Finally, I had a moment alone to speak with him. He told me to come and sit closer and then I started to cry. I told him that I had been close to leaving that day but that Bhagwati had persuaded me to stay and the words that she had used around learning to love again.

'Loving is giving,' he said.

I had heard these words many times throughout my life and intellectually I understood what they meant. And yet this time, when Swami-ji said these words to me they seemed to penetrate right into the core of my being. 'Loving is giving' – the words had a deeper resonance than before.

These words were exactly what I needed to hear. I knew that I had been circling around and around in my pain for such a long time and had not been able to find a way to break the cycle. I knew every square inch of my pain; why it was there, how it was there, what the lessons that I had learned from it were.

But how would it be possible for me to live in love?

And what did giving mean in the context of loving?

Those were very different questions and I did not know the answer to them. Returning to my earlier conversation I had told Bhagwati that I didn't know where to even start doing what she suggested.

She said that what was needed was a programme around *'helping Lis to learn to love again'* and that to begin this programme she was going to put me in the ashram school for a couple of hours every day.

She continued that she was not employing me as an English teacher but that she was happy for me to go into the school and to just have fun with the children. She said that if I could learn to open my heart and to trust these children then it would be a first step to learning to trust in adults too.

It all sounded great. I had seen the children in the school, as my room in the ashram overlooked the school block. The school was for local children of families with low incomes from the ages of 3-14 years. In the morning, the school had classes for children aged 3-8, and in the afternoon for 8-14-year olds. The school was a very plain building – rectangular in shape and the classrooms were very basic with rows of pews and a blackboard and chalk at the front of the class. The school was located right on the banks of the River Ganges.

I thought that going into the school and hanging out with the younger children could be a great chance to have some fun and to let my inner child come out to play. After a few moments of reflection, I thanked Bhagwati for the opportunity and decided to stay for a while to at least give her school idea a try.

Going into the ashram school on that first day I felt a little apprehensive. I could not speak Hindi (the Indian language spoken there) and the children either did not speak any English or they spoke only a few words.

As Bhagwati had informed the teachers that I was coming in and she had told me that she wasn't expecting me to be a teacher, I had assumed that I would be there to just have fun and to play with the children, as she had suggested.

However, on arrival in the school the head teacher welcomed me, then ushered me into a classroom where she told me that she had put two of the older classes into one and that I would be teaching them both. And then she promptly walked out and left me alone in the room with about 40 young children aged 5-8 years all staring incredulously at me.

I couldn't believe it! I had no idea about being an English teacher to children. I had no books, no lesson plans, no teacher training, no clue about how to lead a class. And I couldn't even speak the same language. I felt fear and panic rising inside me as reality was sinking in and I had a classroom of children all looking to me for learning.

There were a few moments of silence as all the children stared at me, probably wondering who this strange white giant was standing in front of them, and I stared back at them, wondering what the heck I was going to do now. I reckoned that I had around one minute before the shock factor of a tall white woman standing in front of them wore off and all hell could break loose. I started to perspire.

I had to act quickly and think on my feet. Suddenly an idea came bursting into my mind, I smiled at the thought of it and then slowly began to sing. 'The wheels on the bus go 'round and 'round...' a child's rhyme that many UK children learn growing up. This was an inspired thing to do! The song has a very repetitive nature and there are lots of actions that you can do that accompany the words of the song. Before long I had all the children performing the actions along with me and some of them were trying to sing along too.

It was a truly magical experience. I realised that having fun transcended any cultural or language boundaries and enabled a deep sense of connection with the children.

After finishing 'The wheels on the bus' I continued to think of any songs I could remember that are sung to children in England, like 'Heads, shoulders, knees and toes' and before long the children would be up on their feet and copying my actions and trying to sing the words.

I was just making some of the words up as I couldn't fully remember all the verses. But it didn't matter as the children couldn't understand what I was saying anyway, and they had not heard the songs before.

As the hour progressed I felt myself relaxing more and was even starting to enjoy myself. This was great fun!

After an hour the head teacher returned and asked me how I had got on and whether I would return the next day? I said that I would only return if she could promise to be in the classroom with me and to translate the words into Hindi for the children, which she gladly agreed to. I felt that if I was going to be seen as an English teacher then I would do my best to ensure that they actually learnt some English along the way, and for that I would need a translator.

As the days and weeks went by, I felt my heart opening more and more as the love from these gorgeous children poured into it. I would spend the time away from the class looking forward to going into the school and to the time spent together with the children. I was the one who was supposed to be teaching the children, but I learned so much from them, their openness and also from the teacher's generosity of spirit. And I felt I was able to give love to them also, through the play and the fun that we were having together.

Bhagawati had been right. If I could open my heart to these wonderful children and teachers, then there was hope for me in the outside world too.

I was extremely grateful that Mum sent me out many books including a book and CD from England called 'Singing English' to support my lessons and Dad and my step-mum sent out paper and pens and other fun things for the children to do. I was grateful for the loving support of both Mum and Dad at this time.

'I am grateful for what I have.'

I improvised the lessons as best that I could. We played the Singing English CD every day and then the children could draw and have fun. The most amazing thing was that the teachers (who came into my lessons to help me translate) said that they had learned a lot from me! And the children, because they were singing and having fun, learned a lot of English too.

Initially the children were quite worried when I gave them some paper and said that they could draw something they wished. They were so afraid to get it wrong and they kept asking me what they could draw. When I said 'anything' they just looked in a state of confusion. One of them asked me 'Can we draw a flag?' and when I replied 'yes' he turned to the rest of the class and said, 'She says we should draw a flag' and then every child drew a flag! As time wore on they got more confident about being able to express more of their creativity.

Loving, I was discovering, *is giving*. And in giving, I was also receiving so much.

'In giving unconditionally, I receive so much.'

A friend of mine said that when they watched me leaving the school each day I looked like a mother duck with her ducklings following behind, as there would always be a line of children following me saying, 'hello, hello, how are you?' or counting 'one, two, three, four, five...' or other things we would have learned together that day!

In tandem to this, I had also been sick for most of the time that I was in Rishikesh. I had flu, tummy bugs and a foot infection that became so bad it had turned into mild septicaemia. It was the monsoon season and the dirty paths were being constantly flooded with rain which allowed germs to spread easily and it was very difficult to keep wounds clean.

Outside of the Ashram there was a pathway that leads along the river to a bridge that you need to cross if you want to go anywhere else. All along this narrow pathway market stalls and shops have set up selling CDs, clothes, food, etc. I loved to smell the wafts of incense as I walked along this strip. It is quite a busy and noisy walkway every time you leave the Ashram. The first shop you came to was a CD shop and this was run by two brothers in their early twenties called Nicky and Amit. I would often stop and have a chai (tea) and a chat with them and they became like my younger brothers, along with their friend Sandeap.

In India, I was advised to be cautious as people can sometimes be very nice to you and say that they don't want anything in return but then at some point they will tell you of a problem they have that needs money, etc and ask you to help by giving them some money. This happens a lot and so unfortunately it was easy for others to become sceptical of people's motives.

With Nicky and Amit, my experience was the reverse of this. For my birthday they took me out for a pizza, when my foot was really bad they got some plants from the jungle and their mum made them into a paste for me to put on my foot. If I wanted to go anywhere they always offered to take me and pick me up. And they never asked for anything in return, although I tried to buy them cakes and tea, etc as often as they would allow me to.

I was glad that I had gone against advice of forming friendships with these boys as they really looked after me very well. We were always laughing and joking, and I knew that I could rely on them. One night when I was on a trip staying a few miles away I had a nasty experience with some other people and Amit and Sandeap drove through a roadblock on their motorbike and came to fetch me in the middle of the night.

After teaching in the school for several months, I knew that it was time to move on and go somewhere else – but I had no idea of where that would be. I was sad to leave the school and my 'brothers' in the CD shop but also excited at what the next part of my trip would bring.

On my last day in the school I was in my room in the ashram getting ready to go to class and I overheard the children practising all of the songs that we had learned during our months together. I felt a surge of emotion well up inside of me. I felt like a proud mother hearing her children singing. When I arrived at the school building the head teacher told me that the children had been practising for my arrival. I admitted to her that I had overheard them from my room but that I would pretend I was surprised when I walked into the classroom.

Turning the corner into the room the children were lined up in two rows facing each other. As soon as I appeared in the doorway they launched into a rendition of all of our songs, back to back. They had remembered all the words along with all of the actions that we had made up together. It was quite a performance and I loved every minute of it.

In general in India it is not customary for people to show emotion to each other and so I was trying really hard not to shed a tear as the performance was drawing to a close. At the end I thanked them all so much and they rushed forwards to hold my hands. I have a lovely photograph of me with a beaming smile surrounded by around 10 children. It's one of my favourite photographs.

One of the children turned towards the teacher and spoke to them in Hindi so I could not understand what they were saying. What I now know they were asking was 'How do you say this in English?' followed by repeating the translated sentence to me of 'We will miss you!'. At this point I couldn't hold back the tears any longer. I was so genuinely moved by their performance and all of the time that we had spent together. Then the teachers were in tears and we all had a very emotional farewell.

It was a time that I will never forget and that will always have a special place in my heart where I really did start to learn to love again.

Moving on from here I was initially invited to stay with a lovely friend, Sushila, and her husband, Pradeep, who lived in Delhi. I had met Sushila on my yoga course when I first arrived at the ashram and we had had a lot of fun, together with another wonderful lady Vita, and we had kept in touch since. She even returned to the ashram during my stay and I had met Pradeep during that trip.

They were such a lovely couple and very modern in Indian terms. Pradeep had a managerial position on an Indian newspaper and Sushila worked with organisations around humanitarian issues. She was from the South of India and he from the North, and it was still very unusual at that time for couples to marry from different parts of India. I felt like they were trailblazing in their own way.

It was so lovely to arrive at their modern, comfortable apartment block in Gurgaon, Delhi. After having spent months living in very basic conditions it felt so good to be back in western style luxury again. I really appreciated the hot shower, the comfortable bed, the air conditioning, the kitchen, the washing machine – all the things that I had taken for granted back home. And, as with all middle-class Indian families, they had a cook and a chauffeur to support them.

The day after I arrived at Sushila's apartment my neck went into complete spasm. We visited the local doctor who told me that I needed urgent intensive physiotherapy and that I would be unable to travel for at least another week (that actually turned into being two weeks). As I had only been supposed to stay with Sushila and Pradeep for a few days I was worried as to what their reaction would be.

'You mustn't worry at all,' Sushila said immediately. 'You must stay with us until you are feeling well enough to travel again.'

And that was that. I was welcomed into their home and given the time and space that my neck needed to heal. I am so grateful to them both for their love and their support during this time. Once more life had given me support when I needed help.

'Life supports me.'

Being able to rest at their apartment for a couple of weeks gave me a bit of time to work out where I would like to go to next. I decided it was now time for me to do a 10-day Vipassana meditation retreat[42]. Vipassana meditation was brought to the West by S.N Goenka[43] and is a specific meditation technique that is taught in Vipassana meditation centres around the world. Vipassana means 'to see things as they really are.' I had first heard of these retreats when I was in India years before but the thought of spending 10 days in silence with nothing to do except observe my busy, critical, noisy mind had been too much to consider back then.

Seven years later and back in India, the time now felt right for me to go on retreat. I was naturally nervous about the whole thing but also keen to discover whether I would finally get to the root cause of my pain. During the retreats you sit in a room with around 1-200 other people in noble silence for 10 days. Noble silence means that you are not allowed to look at anybody else or make any kind of contact with anybody else in any way. You are not allowed any kind of distraction and so you give in any books, notepads, phones, iPod, etc to the management team there and you only pick them up when you leave.

You have to imagine that there is only you there and to block everything else out of your awareness. This enables what they call a 'deep surgical operation of the unconscious mind' to take place. It is an intense experience and should not be undertaken lightly!

Fordy, when he heard where I was going, couldn't believe that I would not be able to talk for 10 whole days. In our clubbing days he had given me the nickname 'She who talk a lot' as I talked incessantly when I was on drugs. He even used to warn people not to talk to me and he would come back hours later to find me still chatting away to them and he would give them an 'I told you so' look. I wasn't sure myself if I would be able to be in noble silence for 10 whole days, but I was very keen to try. After practising meditation back in the UK, by listening to meditation CDs and reading books and meditating on my own, I felt like I was ready to take my practice to another level.

I researched centres in India and the only one that had a course coming up in the next few weeks was down in Chennai in the South-East of India. I booked a flight to take me there and once my neck was moving more freely I thanked Sushila and Pradeep and set off on my journey to the Chennai Vipassana Centre.

Upon arrival, we had one day to settle in and during this time we were allowed to communicate with our fellow meditators. The women and the men were segregated to ensure that there was as little distraction as possible. I was to share a bedroom with a lovely Slovenian girl called Spela and we had a little bit of time to chat before we were going into silence for the duration of the retreat. Once the retreat began we had to share a room and bathroom but not communicate with each other verbally or through eye contact. It was actually an incredibly moving experience for us both and we felt a closeness by the end of the 10 days and realised how much people communicate, without having to say a word.

There was a very comical moment a few days into the retreat when Spela and I had an ant invasion in our room. We had to somehow get rid of the ants whilst not looking or communicating with each other. At one point we just both burst out laughing. Another day I was feeling in a lot of pain and I was crying in our room and it felt very comforting to know that she was there, and the next day she was crying, and I was holding the space for her.

On the first day at the centre, we were told that this was going to be a very challenging process for everybody to go through and that at least once during the 10 days we would probably want to stop the process and to leave the centre. They got us to recommit to staying for the full 10 days as it can be really dangerous to leave halfway through the process.

And so began an incredibly intense 10 days. Because my conscious mind had no distractions it allowed my unconscious mind to reveal exactly what was inside. I found that, with no external distractions, my mind wanted to create distractions and so I would often notice that my conscious mind had 'wandered' into a daydream or into a worried projection of some future possibility.

I kept bringing my focus time and time again back to the Vipassana process and my mind struggled, fought back and then got really, really angry. By day 3 my head felt as though it was literally going to explode with rage. The tormentor inside was in full force. I found sitting still practically impossible to do. I became really hot and I found that trying to focus my attention on my breath was virtually impossible. The meditation teacher said that this was all a really good sign and that I was to be grateful that I was having such an intense experience as it signalled that I was releasing some very deeply held suppressed emotion. I wanted to punch her! Gratitude was the last thing on my mind at that point.

On an intellectual level it was a great thing to know that the teacher thought that I was releasing some deeply held emotions. In the reality of my experience at the time I just wanted to scream and yell and vent my rage at someone or something. Which, of course, in a silent meditation retreat I was unable to do!

'Just keep focusing on your breath,' the teacher instructed. 'Argh!' the voice inside my head screamed. In the end I could not contain my rage any longer and so I left the meditation hall and walked as far away (within the centre confines) as I could, and I started to have an internal dialogue with myself.

'This has got to stop' I yelled at myself. 'I cannot live with this rage inside me anymore and I am choosing now to release this rage so that I may live a peaceful and a happy life.' For about 15 minutes I raged at myself. I felt like I was asserting my power and letting my unconscious mind know that 'I' was back in charge and that I wasn't going to be controlled by it any more.

The next day I felt that I was still angry, but the heated rage had abated which I was grateful for. It was at this point that I felt like I was losing a grip on my mind. It felt as though I really was now going to go mad. The best way that I can describe it is that it felt like my whole mind was constantly moving and I could not keep focused on any one thing.

It was terrifying. I told myself that if I was 'going mad' then I was in the right place to do it and that I was sure that somebody there would take care of me and make sure that I was safe. I just didn't care anymore, and I surrendered completely to the 'madness'. It was a very difficult day to live through and I was glad when it was over. I understood why the centre had been so strict about getting us to reconfirm that we promised to stay at the centre, no matter what happened as I had been so scared that day that I really was losing my mind.

I believe that, in a way, I was losing my mind. I was losing the old habitual patterns that were stored within the mind that my mind had identified as being 'me'. What I was able to come to realise was that these habitual patterns of thought weren't actually me and that, by observing them, I was able to detach from them even more.

'So who was doing the observing and who was doing the detaching?' I wondered. 'And if I wasn't these habitual thought patterns that I had believed myself to be all of my life, who in fact was I?'

My whole perception of 'reality' was shifting again, just as it had started to do back in India many years previously. And this time, I really knew that I was on the way to finding the happiness that I had been searching for. It wasn't to be found in the workshops or the seminars or in the healing sessions that I had been on. It was always there. It had always been there. It was an essential part of who I really am, it was just that I couldn't access it through all of the pain that I had been feeling before. I had to really sit with the pain; to see it, to hear it and to let it know that it mattered to me.

The rest of the retreat I found was still very powerful but not quite as intense as it had been in the first 5 days, thank goodness. What I discovered was that when my chattering negative unconscious mind was forced to be still, that the clearer, brighter voice that had been hiding for so long emerged. This voice, it appeared, had amazing insights into my pain; where it was from and what were the root causes. I had lots of memories from different times and places coming back into my mind to help me to understand myself on a deeper level.

On the 10th day, all the retreat participants got to speak to each other – if they wanted to. Spela and I hugged each other and thanked each other for our support and we laughed about the ant 'incident'.

Leaving the retreat centre after 10 days (9 days of which had been in complete silence) was an interesting experience. I travelled down to Pondicherry (further in the South East of India) and stayed in a guest house there. After being in silence for so long it seemed as though the guest house was incredibly noisy. I spent the whole night sitting and doing the Vipassana meditation technique. I just allowed the anger to be there, but I did not attach to it. I just let it be. It was a liberating experience as I realised that I did not have to react automatically anymore in the way that I used to.

'I have choice over how I respond to life.'

I spent a few more days in Pondicherry and then I headed to Auroville. Auroville aspires to be a universal town where men and women of all countries are able to live in peace and progressive harmony above all creeds, all politics and all nationalities. The purpose of Auroville is to realise human unity.

It is an 'experimental' township in the Viluppuram district in the state of Tamil Nadu, near Pondicherry and is based on the vision of 'The Mother' and Sri Aurobindo[44] (both of whom are now deceased). Sri Aurobindo was an Indian nationalist and freedom fighter, major Indian English poet, philosopher, and yogi and The Mother was a French devotee who lived within his Ashram in her later life (and who was revered in her own right). I was reminded of Swami-ji and his American devotee Bhagwati. It seemed as though Western women had come to help these holy men to be more connected and prominent in the West. Compared to some of the more rural parts of India I had visited before, Auroville is very modern. There is a bakery with fresh western style bread and lots of restaurants serve salads that are safe to eat (as Auroville ionize their own water systems making them safe to drink). I really enjoyed the idea of this relative luxury and decided to stay for a few weeks to do some writing here.

I met some lovely people in Auroville and we used to spend a lot of time together. Another community was formed, outside of the official Auroville community (that we found to be quite exclusive and we were not invited!) and we named ourselves the Auro-fringe. There were some guys from different nationalities who were all working on an alternative currency model from their computers. It was all super top secret and they said that they had to move regularly so that they would not be caught. By whom I did not dare ask! It felt very furtive and I was really curious to know more, but never did. In recent years I have wondered if it was cryptocurrency that they were working on.

Heather was a great English woman who I met one day through another friend Filippos. From the moment we met we became firm friends. From Leeds, Heather has a no-nonsense approach to life, and a wicked sense of humour along with a big heart and I loved spending time with her.

It was New Year's Eve, 2009, in Auroville. Since returning from my first travelling trip many years previously I had subsequently spent several New Year's Eves alone, reviewing the year just gone and looking forward to the year ahead. I thought about what I had achieved that year past, I celebrated my successes, and I thought about what I wanted to let go of coming into the new year.

I usually carried this out in the form of writing/setting intention/ visualisation/giving thanks/meditating. This new year in Auroville I did what I usually did, but this time with around eight friends. We then headed to the open-air Tibetan Pavilion in Auroville. It was truly beautiful. There were thousands of candles all lit around the pavilion and in an Om sign (universal symbol of peace) just outside the front door. There was a full moon that night, which made everything extra special. There were hundreds of people inside the pavilion, many seated around the centre, and Tibetan chanting was being broadcast.

As I sat down very close to the centre I looked up and saw the full moon shining in a clear, black sky. It was a perfect night and I breathed a contented sigh and said a prayer of gratitude for being in this peaceful place. Then I began meditating and had the most blissful experience. There was something about the energy there that was incredibly peaceful. I began to see all the people that I love come into my consciousness and I was sending them all love and gratitude.

I stayed there for a couple of hours, not wanting to stop this feeling of expansiveness. Eventually I left and drove back to my friend's place on my moped. Now, I just want to add something here. If you have ever been to India, then you will know that the roads are completely crazy. From the moment I had stepped off the plane on my first visit I had been in awe of how it all just seemed to work.

Firstly, as well as cars, buses, bikes and lorries, there are also monkeys, cows, goats, dogs and people that all share the road with you! Not only do they drive on the left-hand side but also on the right, or even in the middle of the road. They also cross the road in front of oncoming traffic, expecting them to slow down and allow them to cross. Basically, they do whatever they like!

Once I asked someone if there were any rules on the road in India. He just laughed, shook his head and replied, 'No, no rules.'

'But do you need to pass a driving test?' I enquired.

'Oh yes, but you can just give the examiner some money and he will pass you,' was his reply. That explained a lot about the chaos on the streets that I had witnessed! Normally I would never drive on Indian roads. Auroville, though, is completely different. It is like a mini world inside of the rest of India. The roads are better, they have tarmac and are generally quieter.

It is also incredibly difficult to get around Auroville if you do not have a moped. Most of the bikes are like the one I had, which was only 65cc engine, so not capable of driving at the same high speeds as the motorbikes.

Everybody I knew there drove mopeds, so I decided to get one as well. After a couple of hours driving I got the hang of it and was driving quite well. I had been driving for a couple of weeks before New Year's Eve came around. So, after the lovely evening that I had already had, I then went back to my friend's place where we lit a bonfire and welcomed in 2010. It was quiet and peaceful and one of my most favourite New Year's Eves ever.

At 12.30am I was tired and left to go home. I said goodbye and, alongside my friend, Heather, we set off to ride our bikes home. At one point I lost Heather as she stopped to wait for another friend to catch up. I was tired and now cold and so decided to drive on ahead. We said goodbye and I set off.

I admit that I was driving a little fast, not breakneck speed but just eager to get home and into bed. I was also completely sober. The roads were very quiet as most people were still partying for the New Year. As I drove home at various points there were groups of Indian men congregated together and drinking alcohol. They would shout 'Happy New Year' as I went past.

After about 15 minutes I was approaching the guesthouse where I was staying. The road I was driving along sloped down and eventually came to join a main Indian road at the bottom of the slope. This road was a main bus route and was always busy at all times of day and night. I would never dream of driving my moped on this main busy Indian road. Fortunately, my guesthouse was on the left-hand side before the junction.

As I neared the guesthouse I went to apply my brakes, and nothing happened. My speed increased as I was driving downhill, and I suddenly felt real fear. I tried the brakes again and nothing happened. Panic took over . What's happening? Where are the brakes? How can I stop the bike? The main road was looming closer and I was gathering speed towards it.

In a split second I knew that I had to stop the bike somehow, without the brakes working. At first, I tried to stop the bike with my foot by putting my foot on the floor to slow it down, but I was going too fast for that to have any real impact.

At the last moment I turned the bike off the road, onto the bumpy grass verge to my left outside my guesthouse and tried to stop with my foot. I almost made it but still crashed into the side of the house where I stayed. My right knee took the brunt of the impact and I crumpled underneath the bike.

There was a group of Indian men standing and drinking just opposite where I stayed and they all came running over. They were drunk and shocked at having just watched the accident happen. Some of them were laughing nervously and others started to pull me up and pull the bike. 'The brakes have snapped in two,' one of them said and some others looked and agreed with him. 'Either someone has cut your brakes, or they have worn and snapped as sometimes happens,' they added.

'Are you OK, are you OK?' they were shouting in my ear and pulling me quite forcibly up. I was in total shock and couldn't quite believe a) what had just happened and, b) that I was still alive. As I tried to stand up a searing pain shot through my right knee and I thought that I had broken it.

Here I was, alone, and surrounded by a group of rowdy and drunk Indian men and unable to walk on my right leg.

I shouted at them that I needed some space and that I didn't know if I was OK or not. I was trying to get my shocked and confused mind to logically think of what I needed to do to ensure my safety and also to see if I was seriously hurt or not.

I sat down on the edge of the road and put my head into my hands. Everything was like a whirlwind inside. 'What had just happened? How can it have happened? What if I have broken my knee? Will I be insured for driving a moped? How will I manage if I cannot walk? I have to go to Sri Lanka to renew my visa in 10 days – how will I manage if I cannot walk? Why has this happened?

Memories of having to have my back operation in Australia during my last travel six years ago came flooding back. HOW HAS THIS HAPPENED?? All this was whirling around and around and around in my mind.

For a brief time, I wanted to shout and scream. *Why does this keep happening to me?* I could feel how much I wanted to allow this voice to dominate. This familiar voice that screamed 'why me?' at the incidents that happened in my life. Anger accompanied this voice and I could feel the intensity of it now, bubbling just below the surface.

And once more I knew that I had a choice.

Did I really believe that I was still a victim of life? Did I still really believe that this had happened to hurt me, to punish me from some punishing God 'out there' somewhere?

Or did I want to trust now? Trust that things just happen sometimes? It's how we respond to what happens and learn from it that really matters.

As it was New Year's Eve and there were no taxis around to take me to hospital, I had to wait at home until the next day to seek treatment. I had to have help to support me to hop back to my accommodation as I could not put pressure on my right leg. As I lay in bed the shock really took hold and I was shaking really badly. I was so cold, and I put layers and layers of clothes and covers on, but I just could not get any warmer (and I was in south India where the temperature was hot).

I decided that the best thing to do would be to focus on my breathing to try and get it to calm down. In my mind I said,

'If I have broken my knee, I accept it. If I need to go back to the UK I accept it.

Whatever happens, I accept it'. I repeated these lines over and over and over again all night long

I did not sleep but just kept trying to bring my focus back to slowing my breathing down and accepting the situation as it was, and not wishing that it was any other way. As it was New Year's Eve I couldn't get hold of any of my friends on the phone to come and support me.

The next day I went to the hospital and was relieved to know that I had not broken any bones, but something had been torn inside my knee which made it incredibly painful to walk on.

I accepted my situation and experienced a feeling of relief . My next challenge was going to be the fact that I had to renew my visa in Sri Lanka and I had a flight booked in a few days to take me from Chennai in India to Colombo in Sri Lanka. And I was walking with the aid of crutches.

What I didn't know at the time was that I also had a bigger challenge to come.

CHAPTER 10
The Acceptance

"Clearly recognising what is happening inside us, and regarding what we see with an open, kind and loving heart, is what I call Radical Acceptance."

Tara Brach[45]

I had originally applied for my year-long multiple entry tourist visa to India whilst still in the UK. Once approved there had been a condition to the visa that I could not be in India for longer than 6 months before I had to go outside of the country and get a re-entry visa stamp to come back in again for the final 6 months of the visa. This was how the visa system worked. Tourists were used to this process and so would generally book a short trip over to Nepal if they were in the North of India or over to Sri Lanka if in the south. As I was in the south I planned a visit to Sri Lanka for a few days as it was the closest neighbouring country and I thought it would be nice to spend a few days there, get my re-entry visa stamp and return to my friends in India.

Unbeknown to me, the Indian visa rules had changed a few weeks before I was due to go and get my re-entry stamp. Apparently, the terrorists who planned the Mumbai terrorist attacks that occurred in November 2008 had used multiple entry tourist visas to plan and carry out their attack and so the Indian government had made a snap decision to change the visa system rules to try to prevent this from happening again.

It was decreed that anyone leaving India on a multiple entry tourist visa had to be out of the country for 60 days before they could return. I had heard a rumour about this in the few days prior to me having to go to Sri Lanka but had also been told that if a person was a genuine tourist and could prove it then they would be allowed back into India in the usual way. I had already pre-booked internal flights in India and had proof that I was going to stay with a cousin who was living in Mumbai as well as confirmation that I had been accepted onto a second Vipassana meditation retreat. I could also show that I had been staying in Rishikesh at the ashram and so I felt confident that I would therefore be allowed back into India as I had my travel itinerary scheduled.

On the Tuesday of my trip I therefore packed my bag for a couple of days, left most of my stuff in Auroville and told Heather and my other friends I would see them in a couple of days on the Thursday that week. On arrival at Chennai airport my passport was stamped 'no return for 60 days'. I tried to reason with the Indian airport staff, but they insisted I needed to go to the consulate in Kandy in Sri Lanka to plead my case.

I went to the consulate in Kandy immediately upon arrival, and the man behind the counter told me that it was OK and that I could return at 5pm and my passport would have the 60-day ruling revoked. I was so relieved! My knee was still hurting from my moped crash, so I just went to sit in a shopping mall in Kandy before I returned at 5pm for my passport. I arrived at the counter to be told by the same man, 'Sorry, I made a mistake. You will have to stay here for 60 days.' No amount of reasoning or pleading would do – he was adamant that there was nothing else that I could do to change what was happening.

Initially I panicked. What would I do in Sri Lanka for 60 days, with very little money and a damaged knee? It was nearing the end of my time away and my money was running out quickly. I had everything planned and budgeted to stay in a very cheap place in India, but I had no idea how I could support myself here in Sri Lanka.

As there didn't seem to be much else I could do, I decided to practise acceptance of what was happening and look to see what might be possible for me to do here in Sri Lanka. I initially thought that I could look for a Vipassana meditation centre as I would not now be able to get to my second Vipassana at a centre in Delhi that I had been booked onto.

'I accept what is happening to me.'

I found that when I told myself that I accepted what was happening, I felt calmer and more in control and was able to think more clearly.

I researched places where I could go on meditation retreats and found a meditation centre called Nilambe[46], situated about an hour's drive south of Kandy. I could also stay at Nilambe for the whole of my 60 days and they had a place available for me to stay, which was a massive relief.

Heather, who I contacted back in Auroville to let her know what was happening, immediately said she would lend me some money and that it was no problem at all. Once more I felt a huge sense of relief and gratitude wash over me.

I felt a strength rising inside me. I knew that, no matter how difficult this situation appeared on the outside, I had accepted it and would find a way to make it work.

With the money situation sorted, out I headed off to Nilambe. When I arrived, I realised that this was the place that I had longed to find in India, but never had. It was situated at the top of a tea plantation in the hills below Kandy, with breath-taking views and stunning sunsets that filled the whole sky. The energy there was so peaceful, and my heart immediately felt a sense of coming home. I knew that I could be in this place for a while. It felt almost as if it had just been there, waiting for me to arrive.

I joined in with the group meditation schedule every day. Although the schedule was very much like it had been at the Vipassana centre (starting early in the morning and finishing late at night) you were allowed to practise whatever meditation you liked, rather than it being fixed and everyone following the same meditation practice. I preferred this more relaxed way. There was a walking meditation slot and a working meditation slot which meant the day was more varied and interesting. People could talk to each other at allocated times throughout the day, unlike in the Vipassana centres.

People came and went from Nilambe, some would be there for a week and others for much longer stays, like me.

There was a variety of people there when I was first arrived. There was a loud Irish man who wheezed and made a lot of noise; even his clothes were noisy! There was an Italian man with a moustache who was always late for the meditation sittings and would come bursting in and briskly walk the whole length of the meditation room to find a space to sit and he would spend ages loudly plumping up his meditation cushions before eventually sitting down and settling into the meditation. Many nationalities were represented there; the German psychic astrologer, the American yoga teacher, the Israeli boy, the lovely (and eccentric) English lady, the Canadian lady who now lived here and several local Sri Lankan people to name but a few.

I had only been at Nilambe for a day when I realised that, as well as the main accommodation blocks for women, there were also two self-retreat houses. Upon enquiry I found out that it was possible, with the teacher's approval, to go into self-retreat whilst at Nilambe. Going into self-retreat meant that you were living separately from the other meditators and that you could choose to go completely into silence, the exception being that you could speak to the teacher or the staff if you had any problems during the retreat.

After a week I arranged a meeting with Upul Nishantha Gamage, the teacher at the centre, and he agreed that a self-retreat would be a good idea for me. Just as Swami-ji, the head of the ashram in Rishikesh had told me that 'Loving is giving' I found Upul to be a great living example of this.

A relatively young man to be leading a meditation centre, Upul started to meditate in 1977, at 13 years of age. At that time, he was instrumental in establishing a Youth Society at a Buddhist Temple near his parents' house in Sri Lanka and got involved in many activities as the secretary of the society. In the late '80s, he had offered to help Godwin (the founder of Nilambe) to run courses at Nilambe. Subsequently, when Godwin passed away Upul became the new teacher at the centre.

Upul would regularly give talks at Nilambe in the evenings. One night he talked about the journey that we are all on as human beings. Most of us use our unconscious minds, he said, like a rubbish bin and dump all sorts of ideas into it. If we let suppressed emotion arise, accept it and let it go then our unconscious mind will become just like a photo album of memories with no emotional charge attached to them. He added that we need to make friends with our ourselves and our emotions. I longed to be able to file some of my childhood memories like a photo album in my unconscious mind, instead of feeling the intensity of emotion that would explode whenever they arose.

Before I had spoken to Upul about doing a silent retreat, I had envisaged maybe going into silence for a week or 10 days (like Vipassana) and then assess how things were going. When we spoke Upul immediately said that he thought it would be good for me to be in silence for three weeks. Three weeks! My goodness, I have to admit that I was a little afraid of going into silence for that length of time. When I had done the 10-day Vipassana meditation retreat I had found that I was really just starting to make progress towards the end, and so thought that a longer period of silence may be even better for me at this stage. And so I agreed to do the three weeks.

One of the first things that Upul said to me was, *'You have to stop being so hard on yourself.'* I heard the words, but in my head, I was thinking, 'I'm not hard on myself, that is how I used to be. No, now I am loving and kind to myself', and on hearing these words in my head, I remembered a friend in Auroville asking, *'Why do you keep hurting yourself?'* after my moped crash had occurred. I had a sudden realisation that they were both right.

Under the pretext of being on a personal journey I had told myself how loving I was being to myself. Isn't it the most loving thing to be on a path to inner peace and happiness? The answer is yes, of course.

But how are you walking that path? How are you communicating with yourself internally – in a loving or critical way?

'You need to develop a friendliness towards yourself,' Upul continued. *'Find a way to accept yourself. Developing Loving Kindness towards yourself is the Key.'*

And so, as an extension to finding acceptance in the events that happened to me, I was now being encouraged to develop acceptance of myself. This was a whole new ball game!

'Developing loving kindness towards yourself is key.'

Before I could give love unconditionally to someone else in a relationship I had to learn how to give it to myself. At first, I did not understand how I could do this. How could I develop Loving Kindness towards myself? Isn't that what I had been trying to do these past few years, with obvious limited success? I didn't know where I had been going wrong and felt that I had tried really hard to make it happen.

'Awareness is the first step,' he said.

I was so exhausted with trying and trying and trying various things over the last few years, all of which appeared to have had some success, but none of which had given me the lasting peace of mind or the happiness that I so longed for. *How many times did I have to feel as though I was going around in circles?*.

And then the day came, Feb 2nd, 2010, and I put on my 'In Silence' badge and I started my segregated retreat.

One thing Upul warned me about before I went into the retreat was not to spend all day in my room alone meditating. He said that the danger would be that I could withdraw so far into myself that it would be extremely difficult at the end of the retreat to come back out again into the world. These words stayed with me throughout the whole retreat and I always tried to go to at least two group meditations a day and I would sit with the others at mealtimes even though I did not speak to them.

In the silence I was feeling a lot of anger rising up again.

I just allowed this anger to be. Instead of reacting to it and coming up with a mind story to justify how I was feeling and how other people had 'done me wrong', I just allowed the emotions to come. And come they did! All of the suppressed anger that I was holding onto about the accident, my family, friends and boyfriends all came to the surface. Anger turned into rage.

But I was determined to really accept it now and not to fight it any longer. I knew that there was no sense in hanging onto it. I knew that this was causing me a great deal of harm. It was so hard for me. I still wanted to hang onto the anger; to make me the injured party, the victim, the 'poor me' in the story. Of course, events had happened that had given me much ammunition to warrant holding onto this anger. I did not have to look far to come up with many justifications. But that is what they were, justifications.

Yes, I did have the right to be protected as a child; both by the key adults in my life and by the grammar school that I attended. But holding on to this rage was not hurting them, it was just hurting me. It was eating away at me and robbing me of my happiness. I needed to find a way to release it for my own sake.

One afternoon, as I looked out onto the surrounding hills, I could see one side of a hill that had been burned in a recent forest fire. The hillside looked like a shadow of its former glory and it seemed to me to reflect what holding onto this rage had done to me, having burnt away all the light and goodness and left me feeling desolate and burned.

To the right of me, I could hear the birds singing and the warm air was blowing against my cheeks and hair. I could hear music coming from a village far down in the valley below. It sounded very soothing against the backdrop of this rage of mine. Cockerels were crowing in the distance although dawn had been and gone many hours previously.

During the retreat itself, I would swing from feeling really intense negative emotions to feeling calm and blissful. I seemed to drop through many internal emotional layers and images and events from the past would flash through my mind to accompany whatever emotion I was feeling at that time.

I would find that whatever emotional state I was feeling that day in my silent retreat would be projected onto how I experienced the others in the group when I joined them in the meditation sittings. If I was feeling angry then I would be really annoyed by the sounds they would make that disturbed my peace. If I was feeling peaceful then others would seem peaceful too. I realised the impact that my inner state had on my experience of life and how much we can all project how we feel onto other people and then blame them for us feeling that way! It was fascinating to realise this.

'We project how we feel onto other people and blame them for us feeling that way.'

Throughout the retreat, the loving inner voice that I had connected with back in my earlier travels in Australia and during the Vipassana retreat was becoming clearer again and had more certainty now when it spoke to me. It would talk to me and tell me what was happening inside my mind to help me to make sense of the process I was going through. It seemed to have a wisdom and a deeper insight that went way beyond anything my conscious mind could understand.

'Where is this voice coming from?', I wondered. Was it possible that this voice was from the superconscious mind that I had read about previously? Did it have access to more intelligence than I had accessed before?

One day, I had the realisation that in my life experience, control + anger = love. This is what I had experienced 'love' to be. 'If I make you angry and if you can control me then I know that you love me'. This is not the love that I wanted in my future relationships. I committed to finding a different way to define love moving forwards.

This understanding made sense of why I had attracted some men in my romantic relationships where anger and control were the predominant factors. Somewhere in my unconscious mind I had made the decision that anger and control = love, based on my experience with my step-dad growing up. And so when I was looking for love, I had attracted anger and control instead (believing on a deep level that that is what love was). No wonder I had felt so bad in these relationships!

I had experienced love as taking, and not as giving as I had heard Swami-ji tell me in the ashram years earlier. I committed to staying single until I could redefine what love is for myself and learn to attract more healthy and unconditional loving relationships into my life. I didn't realise at the time, however, just how long that process might take!

As the retreat progressed, and as I dropped through layer after layer of repressed emotion and uncovered some of the more destructive beliefs that I was holding about myself, I realised that beneath everything was something else underpinning it all; I really hated myself.

'I hate myself.'

In light of this revelation, I felt how much pain this was causing me, on my mental, emotional, spiritual and physical levels.

This was the black cloud that had been hanging over me since childhood. And I could feel at every level just what a devastating effect self-hatred had on me. In believing that I was not good enough and that there was something fundamentally wrong with me I had rejected myself on a core level.

And this was not something that someone else was doing to me, this was entirely self-inflicted. *This was me turning in on myself. This was ME punishing myself.* I didn't need life, God or anyone else to punish me, I was doing a really good job of it all my own.

'I am evil. I deserve to be punished.'

I felt the pain that this and other beliefs I had created over the years had caused me and that they were all self-created. I had created them, and I had believed them to be true.

I had hated myself for not being 'better' in some way. 'If I were better, then Sammy would not have died. If I were better, then my family would have loved me more. If I were better, then my step-parents would not have hated me so much. If I were better, I would not have been bullied at school. If I were better, I would have been able to live a 'normal' life like everyone else seemed to', and so on and so on went the hating voice inside my head.

'If I were better, my life would have been different.'

'I don't deserve to be happy. I should suffer. No-one will ever love me,' the critical voice continued. I just let the voice speak, without judgment. I knew that this voice and the beliefs supporting it were what were really running my life; the beliefs that if somehow, I had been fundamentally 'better' in some way, then my life would have been completely different.

All those years and years of blaming other people and I realised, in that moment, that *I am the one who keeps* hurting myself. It was a revelation. And it was the hardest thing to face; really feeling the full force of how much I had hurt MYSELF.

It felt like a huge relief to finally admit this to myself. It felt like on a very deep level, I had been living a lie. I had been so terrified of uncovering the 'real' me in case I would discover something really horrific to be true.

And in fact, *what I had discovered when I looked closely inside myself was a hurt and lonely child who was desperate and in need of love* – from me. With this realisation, the floodgates of my heart opened.

I cried for a while. I hadn't acknowledged to myself before how much I had wanted to be 'normal', to have a normal life (children, a husband, a house, friends and so on). I just wanted to have some stability and some normality after the craziness of living my life. I grieved for the life that I had not been able to live.

I remembered just how awful it had been for me living my life as a child. Memories came flooding back of feeling alone and scared and trapped. All of those painful memories seemed to come and hit me all at once. I felt an intense heavy pressure on my chest and it became difficult for me to breathe properly. I was hot and raging inside and I just allowed all of the emotion to surface and to just be.

There was no judgment in this space.

The pain grew stronger and stronger and stronger until I struggled to contain it. The pressure was bearing down on my chest and I found myself screaming:

'I have suffered enough! I ask for forgiveness from those I have hurt, and I forgive myself. I forgive those who have hurt me. I have punished myself enough.'

'I have suffered enough.'

I felt this statement resonate through every single cell of my body. I had had enough of suffering. I did not want this belief system of needing to suffer to be closer to God to be playing out in my life any more.

By allowing myself to fully surrender to the process, by giving myself absolute space without distraction to be able to fully listen and to hear what I was suppressing inside myself, by allowing the suppressed emotion to surface without trying to stop it or to judge it, by allowing all of these things to happen whilst embracing myself with loving kindness I knew that I had had the breakthrough I'd been praying for all of these years.

'Surrendering to the process, deep listening without judgment and loving kindness are key to self-acceptance.'

In that moment I began to develop something that I had not felt before, and that was compassion for myself. In the painful realisation of feeling how much pain that I had caused to myself I felt a shift happening internally and I moved from a space of hating myself to one of having compassion for myself.

'In the realisation of the suffering I had created for myself, my self-compassion was born.'

I was reclaiming my personal power. I vowed that I would no longer give my power away; that I would stand up for myself and not allow anyone else to bully me. I vowed to protect and support myself from this moment onwards. I vowed to stop suppressing my own power.

'I am powerful.'

Throughout the 21 days of being on self-retreat, I systematically worked my way through the feelings of anger, sadness, fear, shame and guilt along with happiness, peace of mind and bliss. I felt like I was on an emotional rollercoaster. I did not know from one minute to the next what would happen. I just completely surrendered to whatever arose in each moment and did not attach to it being good or bad, just that it was all ok. I accepted it all.

I had some moments of really feeling like I was fully in the present moment which brought a feeling of expansion within me. I felt an integral part of everything in the world, just as I had in my first reiki session on the beach in India. I realised that this was similar to how I had felt years previously when taking ecstasy and was probably what I was searching for all that time through taking drugs. My internal negative mind chatter stopped in these present moments and I also felt blissful at times.

Years previously I had taken LSD and had a very bad experience where my thoughts had become very negative and I had felt afraid. A friend at the time had told me that (when taking drugs) if a negative thought comes into your mind and you catch the thought, to just let it go and think of something else more positive, and to do this as quickly as you could. He said that you could tell yourself that if the negative thought was really important you could come back to it later. It really worked, and I held onto this insight and found it worked well whether I was taking drugs or not! If I could catch a negative thought and replace it with a positive one as soon as possible then I was always able to change the way I was feeling. The 'knack' was catching the negative thought in time before it had a chance to really take hold and for negative feelings to develop.

I realised that, if I am able to detach from my thoughts and to witness them, that I am not my thoughts.

Being in the present moment fully was about letting go of thought, any thought. And the space in-between felt like the expansiveness I had felt previously when I had taken ecstasy.

I wondered what might happen if everyone who takes drugs knew that they could reach a state of bliss naturally? (like I had done through reiki and also through meditation). Would they want to know more about how to create that for themselves? Was everybody taking drugs really looking for expansiveness and connection to something greater than themselves?

For so long I had labelled myself and my negative emotions as being bad. Having allowed them to surface and holding them in a space of loving kindness I could finally see them for what they really were; *parts of me that I had rejected and that were feeling the pain of separation*. By holding them in a space of love and in allowing them to just be and giving them a voice, I realised that I was able to really see, hear and validate myself in a way that I had always wanted other people to do. I was giving myself the love and attention that I had craved all my life from external sources. I realised that all of this time I had been blaming other people for not being able to give me what I had been unable to give to myself.

I committed that from this moment on I would try to love myself more and more each day. I would really try to stop judging myself or blaming myself and that I would deliberately focus on developing acceptance and compassion for both myself and for others too. Moving forwards, I would deepen my practice of accepting whatever happened.

No longer would I automatically default to judging somebody else by the actions that they took. I knew that every hurtful action comes from a place of pain inside and so having compassion for the other is the key to change for them. People who are suffering need to learn how to love and accept themselves, just as I was beginning to do in my own journey.

By the end of the 21-day retreat I felt absolutely, totally and utterly exhausted from being on such an emotional rollercoaster. But at the same time my heart was opening more and more as feelings of love and compassion were developing within me.

In feeling my heart opening I knew that life would feel different. I had connected with what I had been searching for. The glimpse of happiness and peace of mind that I had first touched upon in India years earlier, and that had eluded me again up until this point, was getting clearer. What had been learned could not be unlearned. From this day on I committed to develop my love and compassion towards myself and to help other people to find a way to love and accept themselves too.

Loving is giving, the words reverberated in my mind once more.

CHAPTER 11
The Choice

"The most beautiful people we have known are those who have known defeat, known suffering, known struggle, known loss, and have found their way out of the depths. These persons have an appreciation, a sensitivity and an understanding of life that fills them with compassions, gentleness, and a deep loving concern. Beautiful people do not just happen."

Elisabeth Kubler-Ross[47]

Although I only officially had to be out of India for two months (in accordance with) my '60 day do not return to India' visa stamp, I was officially allowed to stay in Sri Lanka for three months and in the end stayed at Nilambe for two and a half months as I was benefitting so much from my stay.

I had connected strongly with the compassionate 'real' me and I was really enjoying the connection. It was great to finally begin to feel some compassion and not just hatred towards myself. It was early days, but the connection had been made and once again I felt a surge of hope.

'I have hope. I have choice. Happiness *is* possible.'

After completing the three weeks of silent retreat, I continued onto the standard daily meditation schedule with the rest of the people staying there. I loved the routine and the daily practice of meditation, and the times I could talk with my fellow meditators. I distinctly remember coming out of the silent retreat and speaking to people for the first time. It felt so odd! After speaking only a few sentences my throat felt sore. My mind had become so calm and peaceful during my retreat that now it hurt to think and speak. I could see why some people devoted their life to be in silence as the feeling of peace you feel is so wonderful.

One dark evening, I remember sitting outside the meditation hall on a bench waiting for the other meditators to come outside. Suddenly something moving on the floor caught my eye. I thought it was maybe a frog as we had a lot of frogs appear at Nilambe that week. I shone my torch in its direction and to my horror saw a very fast-moving green snake next to my foot. I jerked my foot up onto the bench and continued to shine the torch on the snake as the others were now filing out of the meditation hall and coming towards me – and the snake.

Trying to get someone's attention to help me when everyone was in silent contemplation was, on one level, quite amusing, but in a split second the panic of having a snake that was heading in their direction forced me to get their attention and quickly. The cook from the centre came over, saw the snake and ran in the opposite direction, shouting 'danger, danger!'

Not much use to me. The manager came next and ushered the other meditators away from the snake and I continued to shine my torch on it until we saw it safely slither off into the bushes. 'Don't worry, if it had bitten you it wouldn't have killed you,' the manager told me, 'but you probably would have lost your leg! That's why we tell all the participants to carry torches at all times,' he continued. What a close call.

This and other incidents that occurred over my final few weeks' stay seemed as though the things that I feared the most were presenting themselves to me, so that I could observe my reactions to them and start to make a change in learning to respond, and not just react to my fears.

I had a fear of snakes, and a snake appeared. I had had a recurring fear of men breaking in and attacking me at night for many years, and one night a local man tried to break into some of the other women's sleeping spaces. I had woken up to hear their screams and had gone to see if I could help, with one of the other ladies who was staying on retreat.

'I can choose to respond, not just react.'

My habitual reaction to either of these incidents would have been to panic and to find more evidence for my fears. I would have added fuel to my pain-body, as Eckhart Tolle describes it. What I realised was that the practice of meditation when done regularly can give a moment of space when events occur, that opens your mind and you can then choose how you want to respond. You get to reflect on your initial reaction (anger, judgment, etc) and then choose to respond in a different way (with empathy, compassion, etc).

I realised that learning how to respond and not just to react was going to be essential if I were to change the way I lived my life. Living from my old beliefs had become a habitual way to live in fear and I had been *reacting* to life through these beliefs.

'I am evil. I deserve to be punished. The world is unsafe. I am unsafe. I am unlovable. There is something wrong with me. I am worthless. I am powerless. I am alone. I am a victim. I am not good enough.'

Reacting to life through these beliefs, it was no surprise that my life was not turning out the way I would have liked or that I was feeling so depressed much of the time.

I could see this so clearly now.

'Between stimulus and response there is a space. In that space is our power to choose our response. In our response lies our growth and our freedom.' —Viktor Frankl[48], *Man's Search for Meaning.*

I love this quote from Viktor Frankl. He had been sent to Auschwitz and other Nazi concentration camps during the Second World War. Despite living and working in inhumane conditions and witnessing the atrocities of war, Viktor realised that if a person cannot change a situation he is in that causes deep pain, he can still choose his attitude towards it and himself.

He describes in chilling detail how his captors took from him virtually everything of personal value and basic human dignity. The only thing that they were unable to take away was his choice as to how to *respond* to the deprivation, degradation, and trauma to which he was subjected. He made a conscious decision to focus his energies on 'owning' that small but all-important space between the stimulus (whatever was said or done to him) and his response to it.

I realised that events had happened in my life over which I had had no control. And through reacting to these events with limited awareness I had created beliefs and built a very negative picture of myself which had become my identity that I had wrongly assumed was 'who I was'.

Now with this new awareness I could start to question the validity of these beliefs and to develop new and more empowering beliefs in their place. I could learn to respond to events in a very different way from before.

'I have a core inner strength I can draw from. I have choice. I have hope. I am powerful. I am lovable. I am worthy. I am enough.'

So now building on the awareness I had discovered on the Dale Carnegie training - that I had choice - I now realised that daily meditation and mindfulness practice could really support me to be aware of my thoughts moment to moment which would enable the choice to become easier, over time.

I could choose to change my thoughts, leading to the development of new beliefs.

It all sounded so easy. What I would come to realise over time is that it is actually very *simple*, but not necessarily easy in practice! And it can take time to change deeply held core belief systems that may also need more professional support to uncover and process. I also realised how damaging it had been for me to keep pushing myself to 'be fixed', when in reality there was nothing to fix. In reality I was just someone who had experienced trauma and rejection and had learned to suppress deep feelings of pain in order to function in the world.

What I had learned during my time at Nilambe was that there were different parts of me that were in a lot of pain. However, rather than discovering some monster lurking deep inside me as I had envisaged before, I had instead uncovered 'trapped' parts of me that had been created when I had experienced pain and trauma as my younger self. Not having had the support I needed at the time to process what was happening, I had tried to push these parts carrying pain away – leading to me feeling split, separate and confused.

What I had feared the most was feeling this suppressed pain. I was afraid that it would be too overwhelming for me to feel. And so I had created all sorts of distractions and addictive behaviours to try and do anything except to feel the pain inside.

'Pain is inevitable. Suffering is optional.' – His Holiness, The Dalai Lama XIV

Pain is something we can all expect in our lives and – unfortunately is unavoidable. *Suffering*, however, is lasting pain that gets created in our minds and which prolongs the feelings we hold about our experience. With awareness and understanding, we can choose to let go of the suffering, which is what I now committed to do for myself.

Knowing now that happiness and peace of mind was a choice that I was making, I prepared to leave Nilambe and fly back to North India on the final leg of my journey before I had to return to the UK.

After flying to Delhi, I spent another night with the very welcoming Sushila and Pradeep before making my way up to the mountains in the north of India. My destination was Mcleod Ganj where the Dalai Lama lives in a monastery when he is in India. Initially it felt very strange to be out of the meditation community I had been staying with at Nilambe and I took a while to adjust to being in the busyness of India again.

Having spent a lot of time in meditation I realised how much I speak and say things which are unnecessary. I think I felt uncomfortable with any sort of silences when I was with other people and so would always attempt to fill in these gaps with anything I could think of. This then led to chatting about the most irrelevant things. It also meant that my mind was constantly busy with thoughts, with hardly any space at all.

'It is in the space where we can create choice.'

We are constantly reacting with and to each other from our individual belief systems, leading to potential misunderstandings, frustrations and falling out with each other – almost as if we are on automatic pilot. Not understanding the process around this we can then project our unhappiness onto those around us and potentially blame them for how we feel.

I was reminded of my earlier learning that *'I am responsible for my own peace of mind.'*

The day I was heading to Mcleod Ganj I had to get to New Delhi train station for 4.30am. I arrived at the station to be informed that I had come to the wrong station and that I needed to be at Old Delhi station. 'But it says New Delhi on my ticket?' I asked, confused. 'Oh, that is just where it was printed,' was the reply. Nowhere on the ticket did it say Old Delhi train station. I love India but sometimes, like this time, it infuriates me.

Not knowing if what I was being told was true (having been given wrong instructions before at train stations to the point of being on wrong trains several times), I asked a few more people and got a mixture of replies – some thought New Delhi, others Old Delhi. Finally, I found some policemen and they agreed it was Old Delhi so in haste I had to get a rickshaw and head across Delhi to catch my train.

Fortunately, at that time in the morning the traffic was lighter than usual, and my rickshaw driver drove as fast as he could.

Arriving at Old Delhi station I was now very late for my train and just had around 10 minutes to board before it departed. I grabbed my bags from the rickshaw driver and ran inside the station. Having had my back operation in Australia during the last extended trip away, I now had a bag on wheels as my main bag, a small rucksack on my back and a small across the body bag with my passport, purse and a notebook inside.

With no time to lose, I summoned all my strength to carry my bags up the staircase leading across a bridge to the platform where my train was waiting to leave. I got to the top of the first staircase, very out of breath but determined to push on through until I made it to the train, and I hurried across the bridge.

To my right-hand side, a young Indian guy aged around 14-15 years pushed me. This is not unusual in India. I had been pushed and shoved many times as Indian people crossed my path or jumped in front of me in queues.

This time, however, felt different. The boy who had pushed me so hard then didn't cross my path but instead remained to my right-hand side.

Suddenly, out of the blue I heard a very loud voice coming from inside my own head that shouted, 'You are being robbed'. Shocked, I looked to my right and left and saw a gang of young Indian guys all around me – and also behind.

Feeling afraid but also determined to get away I shouted, 'NOOOOO!' really loudly (and another expletive I cannot repeat here!!) and pushed the guy to my right out of the way as I came to the staircase leading to my train platform and hurried down it to my awaiting train.

Flustered and afraid that something valuable had been taken, I took a moment to stop and catch my breath and assess my belongings. I was shocked to discover that the bag on wheels had knife marks in it where someone had tried to rip it open, my small rucksack had been unzipped so that it was wide open (the lock having broken the day before) with the contents now openly on display (but when I checked my laptop and camera and everything else was remarkably still in there) and the small over the body handbag still had my passport and purse inside – just the notebook was missing.

I couldn't believe how lucky I was. And where had that loud voice in my head come from? There had been so many of the boys having surrounded me on the bridge and yet I had somehow managed to escape with only my notebook missing. I was a little sad about this as I had some email addresses of people I had met whilst on my travels in the notebook, but I was definitely counting my blessings. I began to jog along the platform to find my carriage as the train was about to depart in a couple of minutes time.

Just as I was about to board the train, I had a tap on my shoulder. Afraid that maybe some of the boys had followed me I turned around nervously only to see a strange-looking Indian male beggar standing behind me with his hand outstretched. His hair was wild, and his eyes were blue which is very unusual in India. And even more astonishing, in his hand was my notebook.

I stood there in bewilderment. I had travelled quite a distance along the length of the train to find my carriage. He must have run all the way behind me. 'Dhanyavaad,' I said (thank you in Hindi). 'Thank you,' he replied in English, then turned and walked away.

I was confused. He hadn't even asked me for any money! And even though I had spoken to him in Hindi he had replied to me in English. This was without doubt one of the strangest experiences of my entire life.

A blue eyed, long-haired Indian beggar who spoke English had somehow appeared out of thin air, with no expectation of reward to give me my missing book. I felt as though I was in a dream.

Incredulous, I boarded the train. Seeing my shocked and slightly dishevelled appearance a lovely Indian lady sitting next to me on the train asked me if I was alright. I explained to her about the boys and the beggar and we also chatted about my experience of narrowly avoiding a poisonous green snake in Nilambe.

'All these events are showing you how protected you are,' she smiled. 'And the snake represents Lord Shiva. This is a very auspicious sign for you.'

Well, that is one way of looking at it, I laughed to myself! But not the way I would have looked at it, I realised. This lovely lady had automatically interpreted the events that had happened to me as something really positive to be glad about. Lord Shiva is the third god in the Hindu triumvirate. The triumvirate consists of three gods who are responsible for the creation, upkeep and destruction of the world. The other two gods are Brahma and Vishnu. Brahma is the creator of the universe while Vishnu is the preserver of it. Shiva's role is to destroy the universe in order to re-create it.

I could have processed being nearly bitten by a snake, then getting to the wrong train station and then being surrounded by a gang of Indian thieves through the lens of my old beliefs 'bad things always happen to me'.

OR… I could choose to interpret them through a different lens now.

And it didn't matter whether I believed in Lord Shiva or not. The fact was that I could choose the lens of how I interpreted the events that had happened. I took a deep breath and decided to choose my response.

'I am safe. I am protected.'

I settled with a sense of comfort into the rest of my journey.

McLeod Ganj is a beautiful village set in the mountains of the *Himachal Pradesh district of India.* Many travellers come to stay here, and I found myself feeling part of another traveller's community for a few weeks.

I found a lovely and cheap room to stay in. It was positioned on the side of a hill looking across to the other parts of McLeod Ganj and also out across to Dharamsala spread on the land miles beneath us. Dharamsala is the second winter capital of the state of Himachal Pradesh.

My room was part of a traveller's guesthouse and, as mine was the corner room, I had dual aspect views and a lot of light coming into the room. There was a peace and tranquillity here that created a welcome landing place for me to transition before heading back to the UK.

I was able to do a lot of writing about my experiences of the trip and I met some really lovely people here too.

After five wonderful weeks, I packed my belongings for the final time this trip and made my way back to the UK.

CHAPTER 12
The Integration

"Whatever you can do or dream you can, begin it.
Boldness has genius, power and magic in it. Begin it now."

Goethe[49]

Finally, after an incredible and enlightening year away, I made my way back to the UK. Arriving back this time was easier than it had been the first time I had been travelling. This time around I had mentally prepared myself more fully for the transition, I knew what it would be like and I was able to ease back into UK life more gently than before.

On one level I felt again as though I had lived in another dream while I was away. Just as I had experienced in my first trip to India, so many strange and wonderful experiences had happened again (like the blue-eyed beggar in Old Delhi train station!) and I had learned so much more about myself too. I knew I had made a connection to a more loving and compassionate part of me and that now that this connection had been made I just could not go back to the punishing way I had lived my life before.

I was excited to see how this translated into my 'real' life now.

I sometimes felt on a rollercoaster of emotions, but this was much less than before and there was increasingly more stability in my life. I tried to develop a daily practice of meditation. Some days/weeks/months were more successful than others. Sometimes I would feel as if I had made no progress at all and then other days I would feel more alive and fulfilled than before. I noticed a big difference in my life and in my ability to respond (and not just react) on those days when I had taken the time to meditate before I started my day.

After my experience of teaching the children in Rishikesh, I now developed a strong desire to work with teenagers. I felt that having begun to develop compassion for the traumatised teenager inside of me, I would like now to support teenagers who may be struggling in life to develop skills and mindset tools they could draw on when needed (the things that had helped me and that I wished I had had when younger)

I loved this work. I loved the energy, passion and enthusiasm of teenagers and found working with them very rewarding.

Initially working one to one and delivering coaching and training sessions with various different youth organisations I found myself very quickly moving up into senior management roles (setting up and running youth programmes). I was making a positive difference through the work that I was doing, which was incredibly fulfilling.

Transferring all the life coaching and personal development tools and experience I had previously developed with adults I was able to quickly adapt to working with teenagers.

I didn't want anyone else to suffer as I had.

'Loving is giving.' Swami-ji's words echoed once more. I had felt the truth of those words when I had given the English lessons to the wonderful children in the Ashram school and now I felt it again in working to support teenagers to overcome challenges and to build emotional resilience and live fulfilling lives.

I realised the joy that comes when you give to others; when you can bring together your own gifts, strengths, skills and life experience to the benefit of someone else.

I also realised the joy of being self-employed. Being located in an office for five days a week had never felt good to me, which is why my previous sales roles had worked well as I would spend most of the week out on appointments with clients. Now I set myself up as a self-employed coach, trainer and programme development consultant and, although being self-employed brought about its own challenges, I loved the sense of personal freedom it also brought.

Just as I felt my inner child had come out to play in the classroom with the beautiful children in India (with the songs and dances we had developed together), now I felt that the teenager inside of me was having fun, especially on some of the residential camps that I was working on, alongside some amazing and very talented young people. I was also a mentor to some young people who had difficult home lives and I felt very empowered seeing how they were turning their own lives around.

In my management roles, some of my responsibilities included becoming the safeguarding and health and safety lead during the programmes. This meant that I had overall responsibility for the safety and wellbeing of thousands of young people. Although I loved the fact that I had a big role to play in developing these programmes, and therefore improving the outcomes for the young people taking part, it also put me into a high level of anxiety feeling that I was responsible for their safety and wellbeing.

'What if something bad happened and I was found to be at fault?'

Looking back (and following the notes in the coroner's inquest report), I knew that my school had not put everything in place that they needed to in order to protect Sammy and myself on the day of The Accident. Inside I was absolutely terrified that something might happen to one of the young people on the programmes I was running – and that I would be held responsible. Having felt so happy and fulfilled working with young people I was now feeling re-traumatised at times. I didn't know how I could cope if I was the one found to be negligent and someone else died as a result of something I had overlooked. I developed some empathy for the teachers back in my own school as I felt the weight of responsibility when you are accountable for the lives of young people in your care. I was determined not to leave any stone unturned when I was the one in charge.

I tried to reason that everything was different now and that I was very thorough in my role and that it was highly unlikely that anything really bad would happen, but I was feeling more and more panicked at the thought it might.

I performed my role with absolute diligence. I could spot potential dangers everywhere and was able to mitigate a lot of these risks in a way that other people could not. I would not rest until I felt that all the highest safety measures possible were in place. I was therefore really acknowledged for my work in this key area by the organisations that I was working with, but on a personal level it was taking its toll on my mental health and wellbeing.

One summer I was in a role of Camp Director for an amazing youth charity. Their mission is to improve the emotional wellbeing of young people – giving them the skills and inspiration to overcome the challenges they face, to navigate the divisions in society, and to lead confident, healthy and purposeful lives. I loved the programmes that they delivered and had been in the role of Head of Programme Development supporting the organisation to grow for the previous year.

This particular 8-day residential camp was one of the annual core programmes for around 50 young people and 25 staff. The camp was held down in Devon, UK. As Camp Director I was responsible for the safety and wellbeing of the young people and the staff during the camp. I had developed some training modules which I delivered to staff before the start of camp. This was to make all staff aware of their roles and responsibilities around safeguarding and health and safety. The training was designed to either prevent incidents from occurring in the first place or to know just what to do if, despite best efforts, something happened whilst they were working on camp. The training went well, and I felt confident all the staff team would know what to do if an incident took place during camp.

One afternoon, about halfway through the week of camp both the young people and the staff team were all standing together in a circle in a field receiving instructions for the next activity. A 15-year-old girl began to cough and I saw a staff member running over to her and moving on with her into the next field.

Then another member of staff ran across. Shortly afterwards a member of the team dashed over to me and said that the girl was not breathing properly. I ran over and saw that she was struggling to breathe. We knew that she was asthmatic and thought she was having an asthma attack. Her inhaler did not seem to work and so we very quickly put our emergency plan into action.

Being on a field in remote countryside in the UK, we were very worried as this girl's condition was deteriorating rapidly until she was barely breathing at all. All the staff involved at the site and also on the camp team were incredible in supporting her as much as they could, especially a lady called Katie who was holding the girl and supporting her to breathe. After what seemed like an eternity the ambulance arrived, the paramedics injected an adrenalin shot into her leg and immediately called for the air ambulance that came and airlifted her straight to hospital. The girl's condition was by this time critical and as the air ambulance took off, we had no idea what the outcome would be for her survival.

Standing on the field that day and watching as this girl struggled to breathe was agonising. Flashbacks to standing on the school field following The Accident (when I was not much younger than this girl) came flooding back.

'Bad things always happen to me.'

'Please don't let this girl die. Please don't let this girl die' I repeated inside my head. I could feel the panic rising, but I kept trying to reassure myself that now was completely different from back then. I knew that I had done everything I could to ensure that this girl was supported and that we got the appropriate help as quickly as possible.

Once the air ambulance had taken off, I got in my car and followed it to the nearest hospital around 10 miles away. Driving along that day I did not know on arrival what news I would be told. I just prayed that this girl would survive.

Filled with absolute fear and dread at hearing similar words as when I went to the hospital to see Sammy with mum all those years ago (that Sammy was going to die), I entered the hospital building.

'She's going to be OK,' the nurse said. 'She's going to be OK!' Oh, my goodness, I cannot tell you the relief I felt. I was so grateful to all the team who had collectively supported this result. I broke down in tears. The doctor informed me that everything we had done at the camp and everything the ambulance men did had saved this girl's life. (It transpired that she had an allergic reaction to something in the field and had gone into anaphylactic shock.)

'Bad things DON'T always happen to me.'

The cycle felt as though it was broken. I had new evidence to draw on.

It was as though I had reached a full circle in my life.

Sammy had died, this girl had lived – and I had played an integral part in both incidents.

My next work contract role involved me initially researching the setting up of a community for young people to overcome addictive behaviours. I was working alongside three guys, Ray, Gordon and Dave. As a part of my research I was curious to see how other communities around the world were structured and how they worked. Someone told me about The Esalen Institute[50] in America and I decided that I wanted to go and stay with them to experience the community there first hand. Esalen has a community of people who live and work there year-round, along with a varied programme of workshops and courses from teachers who come to stay for differing lengths of time. I applied and was accepted for a scholarship place on one of their work-study programmes.

In May 2014, I travelled to The Esalen Institute to spend a month there studying Tai Chi and volunteering in the kitchen. Esalen is a non-profit American retreat centre and intentional community in Big Sur, California, which focuses on humanistic alternative education. The Institute played a key role in the Human Potential Movement beginning in the 1960s. According to their website, 'Esalen is more than a retreat centre or an educational institute. Anchored by the inspiring beauty of Big Sur and an unparalleled intellectual history, Esalen is a world-wide network of seekers who look beyond dogma to explore deeper spiritual possibilities; forge new understandings of self and society; and pioneer new paths for change.' This community is based on the cliff edge at Bir Sur and has an incredible view out to the Pacific Ocean with spectacular sunrises and sunsets. I was really looking forward to immersing myself in their culture.

As a work-study student I spent five hours working in the kitchen each day and then I got to learn Tai Chi with Kenn Chase[51] in my other time. We had some scheduled free time also, as well as group and team check-ins each day/week where the community could come together in big or small groups to talk about how they were feeling. The facilitator of the group would use the gestalt method to facilitate and hold the space for participants. When I arrived at Esalen on my first day I was informed that

I would be staying in a wooden cabin about a mile-long walk away from the main Esalen site. The walk was along the Pacific Highway and I had a fantastic view of the ocean walking along this road to work. Not a bad commute, I laughed to myself thinking of all the people back in London who would be travelling to work being squashed into tube trains, like sardines in a can, as I had done in the past.

I loved staying in Esalen. It was such a beautiful place. In addition to my Tai Chi classes there were regular dance events, meditation sessions and the site has natural hot springs that are cut into the side of the rock. One of the best features of Esalen is being able to sit in the hot tubs looking out to the ocean. Apparently Esalen's cliff-side hot springs have been in ritual and healing use by the Esselen Indians and others for more than 6,000 years. I met some fabulous women who were taking part in the same month-long programme as me. Mary-Lys I met on the minibus on the way to Esalen from Monterey and we bonded straight away. Hailing from outside Dublin in Ireland Mary-Lys has a great sense of humour and we laughed our way through most of the month. We have remained good friends and she has been to visit me in the UK. My 'roomies' in my wooden cabin were Elizabeth, Milly and Susa and I loved sharing with these funny. Intelligent and caring women.

Kenn Chase and his lovely wife Vicki were great teachers. I loved finishing my work shift in the kitchen knowing that I could go and really relax into the Tai Chi and Feldenkrais sessions with Kenn and Vicki.

Feldenkrais[52] is an educational method focusing on learning and movement, which can bring about improved movement and enhanced functioning. It is named after its originator, Moshe *Feldenkrais* (1904-1984), an engineer and physicist as well as a Judo teacher.

Tai Chi[53] essential principles include mind integrated with the body. The ultimate purpose of *tai chi* is to cultivate the qi or life energy within us to flow smoothly and powerfully throughout the body.

We also had a lot of fun together in our group. Our practise sessions with Kenn would sometimes take place on the wooden deck next to the swimming pool. One day we were in the middle of practising our sequence of movements when a whale and her calf swam past us in the ocean. It was a truly magical moment for me.

On the last day of our Tai Chi training programme our group travelled to a local monastery to meditate there together. It was a beautiful experience. Then we headed to Sand Dollar beach to go through our Tai Chi movements on the beach. It was the perfect ending to our time together.

Whilst at Esalen, I heard about an amazing guy called Jules who did one-to-one sessions in something called Cortical Field Re-education[54]. Some of my fellow work-study participants had been for sessions with Jules and they always came back looking as if they were floating on air. I booked a session, curious to see what Jules delivered. The session was great. I had an initial chat with Jules about how I was feeling and then I lay down on a massage couch and he very gently stretched my arms and legs or rocked my pelvis or other parts of my body. Sometimes I felt an emotional release after a making a particular body movement. Sometimes when Jules was lifting my arm, it felt like it was being stretched and stretched. At one point I thought I would look like Mr Tickle (from the Mr Men children's book series) by the end of the session. I had to open my eyes to check and was relieved to see a normal-sized arm still attached to my body.

After the session I was sitting up on the side of the couch, getting my bearings before I stood up. I wasn't consciously aware of it, but my feet were on tip toes and not flat on the floor. Jules came around to the side of the couch and knelt down next to my feet. I was about to ask what he was doing when he very gently took my feet in his hands and placed them flat on the floor. As he was doing so he said, 'It is safe for you to be here now'.

I wasn't prepared for the intensity of emotions that poured out. With this very simple gesture he had got to the heart of the matter, around how unsafe I was feeling in the world. Jules said that part of me was always on alert and ready to run away, that's why I had been on tip toes and not with my feet flat on the floor. I realised that I often sat with my feet on tip toes, not feeling safe enough to just 'be here now', always ready to run if feeling under threat.

When the month at Esalen came to an end, I travelled across America to Florida. It was my dad's 70th birthday and as a treat he had hired a villa and wanted all his daughters (and their partners and children) to stay with him and his wife and to go to Disneyworld together. When I had been a small child, Dad had promised to take me to Disneyworld and I had been heartbroken when it had not happened at the time. It was very special and thoughtful of him and his wife to have organised this trip.

A few years before, we had all been to the Isle of Man (an island in-between Liverpool, UK and Ireland) for a Cashin family reunion. My surname Cashin originates from the island and a relative had organised a reunion there for Cashin family members, who had gathered from all over the world. On this trip, my dad and his wife had hired a house and myself and my sisters had all stayed together for the first time, along with my step-sister from Dad's third marriage. As my half-sisters Emma and Lucy had not really known me or my full sister Sarah growing up, it was a great chance for us to spend some time together.

Sarah had by this time met John, and Emma was married to Tom (they had two lovely boys, James and Jack). This trip was the first time I had really met my nephews and I fell in love with them from the beginning. I loved my newly extended sister family. The sisters all got on well together and bonded very quickly.

Following on from the Isle of Man trip, I spent more time with Emma and Lucy and so going to Florida on this trip with them all was really lovely. We had a wonderful time in Florida and made lots of happy memories for life. My step-mum Yvonne was instrumental in organising both the Florida and Isle of Man trips and in therefore helping to bring the sisters closer together and I am incredibly grateful to her for that.

Coming back, my relationship with my half-sisters has gone from strength to strength and I can't now imagine my life without them. My sister went on to marry John and they are very happy in their life together.

Having felt so rejected in my early life, one of the greatest gifts I have received is my new extended family. It feels like they have all filled a gap that I didn't realise was there until they filled it.

On my return from America, I began to have reiki sessions with a lovely guy called Sean. A friend of mine Nichola had known Sean for a number of years and she recommended I go to see him for some reiki sessions. Reiki had been such an incredible experience for me whilst in India and so I relished the opportunity to keep myself in balance by going for regular reiki sessions.

Sean had received his training with Master Yu Tian Jian[55]. Master Yu Tian Jian, also known as Master Yu and Dechan Jueren, was a Chinese Buddhist monk. He was the 49th lineage holder of Chinese Esoteric School of Buddhism, also known as Hanmi Esoteric School or Hanmi Mystery School.

Master Yu Tian Jian is the latest in this line of living Buddhas. The Hanmi school believe 'in a universal loving spirit… an Indestructible, Absolute and All-Aware Presence[56]', that all life is one, that there is one intelligence and creative power that expresses itself as the universe. This was very much in alignment with my own views that I had developed since travelling in India in 2003.

Sean had been to China several years earlier to experience an in-depth training with Master Yu. Bringing back these teachings to the UK, Sean was teaching in the local Buddhist temple and also giving reiki sessions from a dedicated room at the Atlantis Spa and gym[57] that he runs with his wife in Tiptree, Essex.

Every time I lay down on the massage couch for a reiki session, I would feel enveloped with love and compassion. I would feel so relaxed by the end that I never wanted to get up. And each time I would notice a palpable shift in my life in the weeks following the sessions. It was as though having the session with Sean would help to balance whatever I was feeling at the time into a more positive state.

Around this time, I became aware that I was not giving my physical body as much attention as I had been giving to my mental, emotional and spiritual aspects. My poor body, which had carried me through all of my life and had done such a great job, was being neglected. I would have times when I would be determined to lose weight and so I would focus on my health for those time periods but invariably I would 'fall off the wagon' and start to eat unhealthily again at some point (this yo-yo dieting stemming from the unconscious beliefs I was holding, as explained in a previous chapter).

I was now managing to eat a much more balanced diet on a regular basis. My comfort food when upset was still to default to eating sweets, as I had done in secret as a child but overall, I managed to eat really healthily.

I also went for regular walks in the countryside and I felt recharged and more relaxed when I did. I had an assessment with an ayurvedic[58] practitioner, Annie, and she told me that my physical system was running on empty. She prescribed me taking a concoction of different herbs into a powder with hot water 3 times daily. They really boosted my energy levels and became a great source of support to my emotional healing process. I became physically stronger (with regular visits to the gym) and my overall mental health and wellbeing improved.

In order for me to heal fully, I realised that all the physical, mental, emotional and physical aspects of myself were inextricably linked and they all needed to be healed; i.e. the whole of me.

CHAPTER 13
The One I Have Been Waiting For

"It's not your job to like me – it's mine"

Byron Katie[59]

Lots of great things were now starting to happen in my life.

One day I was having a reiki session with Sean and he said that he thought that I needed to have some more fun in my life. I agreed. When I went home that night I was contemplating what I could do that would be fun. The Graham Norton show was on the television and I found myself laughing out loud. I wonder if I could get tickets to go and watch his show? I thought.

I went online and found a website where you could book tickets to see TV shows and the tickets were free. When I tried to get tickets, all The Graham Norton shows were fully booked, but I could apply to go and see The Jonathan Ross show instead. I also found Jonathan Ross to be very funny and so I applied for tickets. I was online on the Saturday. On the following Monday morning I got an email to say that I had got tickets for filming the show on Wednesday that week… and that Coldplay were playing live. I was ecstatic! Over the years of my personal development journey I had been a massive fan of Coldplay and Sarah and I had travelled around New Zealand with Coldplay as our backing track in the campervan adventures. I immediately called Sarah to see if she wanted to come with me. She was as delighted as I was.

On the day of the TV show recording, we arrived at the studio and realised that, even though we had arrived much earlier than we needed to, the queue in front of us was very long. I was sad as I thought that this would mean that we would be seated towards the last section of the audience and we would therefore not be near the band. As predicted, when we went inside the studio the first two sections were full and we were seated in the 3rd section nearest to the exit, about 10 rows from the front.

Slowly, however, it dawned on me that the first section of the audience was seated in front of the seating area where Jonathan Ross would be interviewing his guests, the middle section had nothing in front of it, and the 3rd section (where we were sitting) had the band set up. We were sitting right in front of where the band would play. Amazing!

The show began and eventually, after all the interviews had taken place Coldplay came out to play their latest single 'Adventure of a lifetime'. Chris Martin, the band's lead singer, said that he was going to come into the audience at one point during the song and asked the audience if that would be OK. He pointed in the direction of where Sarah and I were sitting, and we were very excited. Then Chris came running up into our section and stood two people away from me at the end of our row and sang part of the song there. The best part was that after the song was finished they had to do it all again as Chris was told by his manager that he had to change his shirt. We were delighted.

On leaving the show recording that day, I reflected how this experience had all happened so quickly. Sean had given me the suggestion, then I had taken immediate action and, as a result, had had such a fun and uplifting experience.

'I can create fun in my life. Good things happen to me.'

This filming happened in November, although it was the Christmas show that would be shown on television in December. I was staying at Sarah's house for Christmas and my mum was there too. We all watched the show together. When Chris Martin came onto the show initially it was to be interviewed by Jonathan Ross. I turned to mum and said 'This is Chris Martin. He's my hero. Sarah and I love Coldplay' and I told Mum the story of travelling around New Zealand listening to their songs and also about the concerts we had attended. Chris did his interview and then walked across the studio to where the rest of Coldplay were waiting to play. Mum looked perplexed as she had done for a few minutes and she asked me 'Why do you call him Mahimo?'. Now it was my turn to be puzzled 'I don't,' I replied. 'No, mum, MY HE-RO' Sarah repeated loudly and slowly. We all burst out laughing. To this day Chris Martin is known to us as Mahimo.

Something that I had wanted to do for many years was to learn to play the drums on a drumkit. I absolutely love the sound of a drum beat and my feet automatically begin to tap if I hear it in a song. I had developed the mindset that I was too old to learn, but as a part of my wanting to create more fun in my life I decided I would take the plunge and have some lessons.

It was great fun. My lovely drum teacher Ian was very patient with me and passionate about playing the drums himself, which was infectious. I voiced my initial concern about my age and he said that his oldest student was in his 80's. 'How fantastic' I thought, to still be going for your dreams in the later stages of life. I bought an electronic drum kit and continued with lessons for around eight months, before I had to move to a new house and the lessons had to stop.

For the next few years I found that I was able to integrate what insights I had learned over the previous 10 years and my daily practices were supporting me hugely.

As I had tried to do on previous occasions, most days I would do around 10 minutes of meditation. I would either listen to a meditation with someone else talking me through the process, or I would sit in silence and focus on my breathing and let my mind settle before the day began. Again, I definitely noticed a difference in my state of mind on the days when I managed to do this and the days when I didn't.

Since coming back from Nilambe years previously and having had so many incredible insights and realisations about why I had suffered as much as I had, my personal journey had since been one of knitting together new beliefs and new neural pathways in my brain. This wasn't a seamless process and instead was one of feeling as though I was taking two steps forwards and one step backwards. My pain-body was so strong, and I would sometimes find myself sucked back into it, but with awareness and continued commitment to my happiness and peace of mind I had the tools and the support network to re-balance myself once more. I was going to see Sean regularly to have reiki sessions as a part of this process.

When I went to visit Sean, he would talk to me with such kindness and compassion and he helped me to gain a deeper level of acceptance for the process I was going through. 'Not many people have the courage to look into themselves so deeply,' he said. Rather than feeling that I had somehow got it all wrong and had completely gone off-track at times, he would help me to see that everything I was experiencing was a part of the process for me to heal. Because I had had such intense pain and trauma in my childhood, it was natural that it would take some time for me to come to terms with it all and to feel safe enough to face those deeper aspects of myself. Although the visit to Sean was often a 3-4 hour round trip, I felt that these sessions were a lifeline for me and helped me to keep functioning.

Around this time the opportunity arose for me to go and live with a wonderful lady called Mary. Mary was 88 years young when I moved in with her as part of a national scheme called Homeshare.[60]

Homeshare matches a person who needs some help to live independently in their own home (householder) with a homesharer. Householders will have some support needs or may have become isolated or anxious about living alone. The idea is that with reassurance and companionship householders will continue to live full, happy and healthy lives. Householders will also be able to pass on their skills and experience to enrich the lives of those that share with them

My own relationship with my grandma had been such an important part of my life and for a long time I had wanted to do something that would enable me to connect with older people and to give back in some way. Initially nervous about the possibility of giving up some of my own personal freedom living in another older person's space, my nerves quickly abated when I met Mary. She has a real zest for life and a twinkle in her eye. At 6pm on the dot she would appear in the kitchen to pour a drink. 'It's gin o' clock,' I would often tease her. She lives a busy life playing bridge, attending the Women's Institute group, going to jazz nights locally and being a part of her local church group. In addition to this she has many friends and a loving and close family calling and coming to visit. I loved living with her, giving her practical support and learning more about her interesting life.

I also started to do some part-time nannying for two lovely girls, Elsa and Amelie. A couple of times a week I would pick them up from school, take them home and we would have fun creating things, dancing and laughing until their parents came home.

With these two roles (in addition to my self-employed work), I found that in giving to other people I was supporting myself to feel better. I also reconnected with an old friend from school, Sally. I had lost touch with everyone from school up to this point and I was really nervous about meeting Sally as I was still holding onto some painful memories and unsure what seeing her would bring up. But when we both realised that we lived near each other in London, we agreed to meet.

From the first moment of seeing her again I felt an overwhelming sense of relief. I was so happy to hear how successful her own life had become, and we became good friends. She has since supported me in many ways (including being one of the first people to read this book!) and it has been very healing for me to have her in my life.

Sean's sessions were really helping me to keep feeling more balanced overall, but I frustratingly still had episodes of feeling panic and fear.

I had learned so much about beliefs and values, how the mind works, the different levels of the mind, about coaching, mindfulness and meditation and all sorts of other modalities that had all really supported me in some way. I felt now that I wanted to speak to someone with more specific qualifications to help me to process the deeper levels of the trauma that I had experienced.

I was recommended to go and see a lovely integrative psychotherapist called Merry who I started to visit on a weekly basis. Right from the start I felt comfortable talking to Merry. She very much believed in looking at the person as a whole being and she had spiritual beliefs which were similar to my own. I was able to share with her just how bad I had been feeling and it felt a relief to be able to share in a non-judgmental space and to really feel heard. I went to sessions with her for around a year.

Around this time, a friend of mine recommended a yearlong mindfulness training with Youth Mindfulness[61]. Situated on a stunning 550-acre estate on the River Dart in South Devon, UK Sharpam House would be the setting for the training.

On this year-long training there would be 4 x 5-day retreats and at the end of the year I would also be qualified to deliver an 8-week mindfulness training programme. Believing that this would support me on both a personal and a professional level, I signed up to the training. It was one of the best decisions I have ever made.

On arrival at the first retreat, I felt very nervous. Who would these people be that I would spend the next year of my life with? Had I made the right decision coming on the course? I imagined that there would be a small group of around 15 people on the training but on arrival quickly gauged that there were many more of us, 37 in fact!

From the very first moment the training began, I knew I had absolutely done the best thing possible for myself. The course trainers, Lindsay, Michael and Will, along with their supporting team of Jasmine and Kareem, held the course and the group with a level of love and compassion that I had never experienced on a training before.

No matter what issues a participant brought to the training, they were treated with so much respect and love. I felt safe and allowed myself to really start to relax and to let go of some of the judgments I was holding towards myself. And I found so much support among my fellow participants too.

To me, mindfulness is like a light that shines on what is there inside of us that we may not be consciously aware of, but which is running our lives. With the light of awareness we can begin to make changes internally that are more in alignment with who we really are and who we really want to be. I believed that I was ready now to really see the truth of what was still going on inside of me.

During one of the retreats we were taught about the seeds of the mind in Buddhist psychology. Apparently, there are 51 mental conditions that are defined as mental states. These mental conditions are likened to being seeds in the mind and our mind to being like a garden.

'Which seeds are you watering in your mind?' we were asked. 'Are you watering faith, self-respect and equanimity?', for example, 'Or rather attachment, anger and jealousy?' We were then asked to liken ourselves to being the gardeners of our mind and we could choose which seeds we wanted to water at any one time. The idea is that we have all positive seeds and painful seeds; it's up to us what type of garden we want to grow. I was able to see more clearly the early seeds I had planted as a child and the later seeds I was choosing to water now that were more nurturing and supportive.

This model of the mind illustrated beautifully how we are all participants in our own transformation and how we can choose which way our mind develops.

This view of being able to choose what seeds we water in the mind reminded me of being back on the Dale Carnegie sales training course all those years ago and to his quote:

'Think and act positively and you will become positive.'

I realised that even though I had had the initial realisation that I had choice all those years previously, it had taken commitment and perseverance to keep making the choices that would empower me the most. It hadn't been easy to do, and I had fallen back into watering the seeds of pain and suffering on many occasions, despite my best intentions.

'Clear intention, commitment and perseverance are key to sustained change.'

So often in the personal development world I had seen and heard 'experts' proclaiming how they had 'the answer' to living in joy and happiness and how easy that process could be. 'You just need to choose it,' they would declare. They were right, of course, you do need to choose it, but adding the word 'just' makes it seem easy and effortless and that was anything but what I had experienced on a personal level. And I had judged myself so harshly as a result.

For me, the process had been:

1. Initial personal awakening and realising that I had choice

2. Setting clear intention around what life I wanted to create for myself

3. Committing myself to creating that life

4. Failing to consistently create that life

5. Beating myself up for being a failure

6. Steeling myself for one more attempt

7. Recommitting to the process

8. Repeating steps 2-7 again and again and again

This process had been exhausting.

I think that if I had known just how long and challenging the journey was likely to be I might have been able to accept the setbacks I experienced as being a natural part of the process a lot earlier. Instead, and believing that this should all have been a lot easier and quicker than it was for me, the process became a source of suffering in and of itself. I felt like a constant failure and it had reinforced my beliefs that there was something inherently wrong with me. It was also another form of punishment.

'There is something wrong with me. I deserve to be punished.'

These beliefs had played out in many different ways in my life.

Scientists used to believe that a person's brain did not change after childhood and that it was hardwired and fixed by the time we became adults. We have all heard the saying 'you can't teach an old dog new tricks.'

Advances in science in the past 10 years have proven that our brains can adapt and change throughout our lives and so the old dog apparently can change and learn new tricks, but only if they want to and choose to and commit to doing so!

Our brains, neuroscientists have discovered, are like plastic and so they have coined the term 'neuroplasticity' for the way the brain adapts and grows. This is the ability we possess to be able to rewire our brains. How exciting is that? We do possess the power to rewire our brains and to create our own inner peace and happiness. This is no longer just the talk of Buddhist monks; this is being proven as a fact by neuroscience.

I loved how mindfulness was supporting me with the tools I needed to be able to rewire my own brain and to keep watering those seeds of positivity.

Over the course of the retreats I was able to develop much greater compassion towards those deeper parts of myself that I had rejected for so long.

'Our feelings can feel real but aren't necessarily true.'

One of our retreat facilitators told us this quote from an amazing lady called Tara Brach who has written several books including 'Radical Acceptance[62]'. In one of her many YouTube talks Tara explains that feelings can feel real, but that they aren't necessarily actually true.

An example of this were the feelings of worthlessness I had felt for so long that felt very real to me, but I began to question whether it was true that I actually was worthless in reality?

Just as I had learned years earlier that 'just because you have always believed it to be true doesn't mean that it is' I now learned that some of the really intense feelings I was feeling felt so real to me, but they didn't have a basis in factual truth. Beliefs and feelings were inextricably linked. Some feelings masked deeper levels of pain. Anger and resentment, I learned, can mask deeper levels of shame and hurt. In order to avoid feeling shame (feeling that your whole self is wrong) it is safer to feel anger or resentment instead. The way to heal is to find a way to feel the shame and to hold it with kindness and compassion.

I am so grateful that I found the mindfulness training at this time in my life. I felt like the teachers, the teachings and my fellow participants held me through this transitional phase in my life.

I was developing the compassionate part of me who I had first connected with during my 3 weeks in silence at Nilambe. I was able to connect more and more from this compassionate place in me with the traumatised teenager inside.

I left the course at the end of the year feeling that I had created some very firm foundations that I could now build upon. I was no more on shaky ground. There was still an element of fear, but I could hold myself in a stronger, more loving and centred space than before.

Having received so much compassion from Sean and on the mindfulness training I realised the transformative effect that it had had on me. Whilst I had previously felt judged by others I had not been able to feel safe enough to open up on a deeper level. And whilst I had judged myself it had definitely not been possible. Just as my previous revelation in Nilambe during my 3-week silent retreat, I now deepened my understanding that developing compassion towards myself would be key to my personal happiness.

'Self-compassion is key to personal happiness.'

Through this awareness, I also developed more understanding and compassion towards my parents. I had travelled to Sweden a few years before to train with an organisation called Familylab International[63]. This organisation is based on the great work of Jesper Juul[64]. Jesper is a Danish family therapist and author of several books on parenting to a general audience. In his book *Your Competent Child*[65] (1995, in English 2001) he argues that today's families are at an exciting crossroads because the destructive values — obedience, physical and emotional violence, and conformity — that governed traditional hierarchical families are being transformed and replaced with personal responsibility, personal integrity, authenticity and equal dignity.

Jesper claims that he has seldom met parents who did not love their children. But there are a lot fewer who could convert that love into what the child experiences as loving behaviour. I really resonated with this aspect of his teachings from my own experience. I had wanted to experience love in a different way than my parents had given to me as a child, but they had loved me nonetheless and in their own way. I knew that now. And with that understanding I accepted that they both loved me the only way they knew how.

Through studying with Familylab and reading Jesper's books I had committed to living my life with the four values underpinning his work. I was taking personal responsibility for how I felt and not blaming anyone else, I was learning how to differentiate what was me being in my personal integrity and what wasn't, I was expressing myself authentically and I was also holding other people in a space of equal dignity (my favourite explanation of equal dignity is that everyone has the right to be seen, heard and to feel that they matter).

In her Harvard University Commencement Speech in May 2013, Oprah

Winfrey said that: 'The single most important lesson I learned in 25 years talking every single day to people, was that there's a common denominator in our human experience. The common denominator I found in every single interview is *we want to be validated.* We want to be understood. I've done over 35,000 interviews in my career… They all want to know: *'Was that okay? Did you hear me? Did you see me? Did what I said mean anything to you?'*

I realised that as a child I had really wanted to be seen, to be heard and to feel that I mattered. Instead I had felt invisible most of the time. As children take whatever happens in their world to be about them (unless they are told otherwise), I had thought that I just wasn't good enough, that I just didn't really matter. As an adult now, I could see that the key adults in my life as I grew up had their own emotional pain that impacted their behaviour towards me. And that that was not a reflection on who I was, but more a reflection on who they were and what they were going through at the time.

Initially I felt very challenged around asserting my personal boundaries. As a child (with my step-dad), it had often been unsafe for me to push back if my personal boundaries were being overstepped and so I felt nervous when trying this out. Prior to this, and in compromising my own personal integrity for the sake of someone else's happiness, I would often struggle to say how I really felt about something (for fear of rejection or reprisal). Now I really was facing this fear and choosing to assert my integrity anyway.

I remember clearly one day I was working with Ray, Gordon and Dave on researching the youth project I mentioned earlier. We had all met through our shared intention of wanting to support young people. It was initially Dave's drive and passion around this that had brought us together, and we were researching different ways that we could potentially work together. One day we were all on a skype call and the guys were talking about a project that they all wanted to do. 'I really don't want to do this' my internal voice said. In the past I would have tried to please others rather than admit that I didn't want to do something. I could feel lots of thoughts coming up in my mind around this and how uncomfortable they were making me feel. I didn't want to upset the guys or face their rejection and so my initial (and habitual) thoughts were around what I could say that would still keep them happy but not commit me too much to the project.

In an instant I saw how that would play out. I would not say that I didn't want to do it, then they would take that as a 'yes' from me. I would find myself embroiled in a project that I didn't want to do, would not be motivated around, would actually feel resentful towards them for, and would end up in me feeling angry and having to leave at some point. I knew this pattern very well. Not asserting my integrity and personal boundaries would lead me down a path of suffering.

This day I decided to take a risk. Ray, Gordon and Dave had all done the Familylab training too (in fact Ray was the one who had discovered Familylab and had very generously hosted the training at his summer house in Sweden) and since our return to the UK I had been delivering the values into the nurseries and primary schools that Gordon's family owned, with great success. Part-way into the conversation I clumsily blurted out 'I don't want to do this'. There was silence. Internally I felt a bit pf panic, what would they say now, what would they do? Would they reject me? After what was probably only a few seconds but felt like an eternity Ray replied 'Oh, OK. Well, that is clear then', and the others agreed.

No drama. No fuss. I had said the truth of how I felt, and the world had not collapsed. I had not been rejected and I had, in fact, felt really empowered! 'Can it really be that simple?' I mused. 'I can just say how I really feel and that is OK?' It had taken a lot of courage to speak up when it felt so risky to me to do so. And yet it was so simple to tell the truth of how I felt, and for it be really heard by the others. Simple, but not necessarily easy.

'If all else fails, try telling the truth' – Jesper Juul.

This is one of my all-time favourite quotes. All we need to do is to tell the truth of how we feel! And yet, for many of us, this can feel incredibly scary and risky if we did not feel safe to do this growing up. We may feel we have lost the ability to tune into how we really feel. Internally our alarm bells can go off if we feel we are at risk of rejection or harm from the other and so we feel we need to compromise who we are to try and stay safe.

Neuroscientists have proven that we are all hard wired for connection. In his book Social[66] scientist Matthew Lieberman states that when we experience social pain (criticism or rejection for example) the feeling is as real as physical pain. He continues that our need to connect is as fundamental as our need for food and water, which is why it can feel so risky and so scary when we try and assert our integrity if we have not been taught that this is OK growing up. The pain feels very real to us and it can feel as though we are risking our very survival by speaking up. No wonder so many of us continue to 'play it small' as I had done over the years.

I was no longer prepared to reject myself. I knew now that saying a 'no' to someone else was saying a 'yes' to myself and that I was worth it, even if I did not fully believe it yet. I knew that everyone has inherent worthiness and that I was no different to anyone else.

On a deeper level, I committed to taking personal responsibility for how I felt, knowing more about my integrity and the cost of not expressing it.

Understanding now that not living in my integrity would never end well, I chose to live life in alignment with it as much as I could.

In parallel to being in my integrity was being in equal dignity with other people. I could not go around telling everyone else how I felt, without also allowing them the dignity of doing the same. This didn't mean that I had to agree with what they were saying, just that I respected their right to do so and to hear them without judgment. I no longer cried if I felt angry about something (as I had done as a child), instead I could express myself by taking responsibility for my anger and, in not blaming the other person for it, opened up a space in which we could move forwards. And this whole process felt much safer for me.

I was living without the masks that I had worn so much during my life. Each mask had been put on to try to fit in with a particular person or group of people. My desperation to belong and to 'fit in' had meant that I had 'fitted out' with myself. My cousin Kath said to me one day 'You have spent your whole life trying to fit in and now you are choosing not to!'. Choosing not to have to fit in with other people meant that I was fitting in with myself, and it was a great feeling.

My experience has been that the more that I embody these the values of personal responsibility, personal integrity, authenticity and equal dignity, the more the key relationships in my life have gone from strength to strength. Over time, Mum and I have been able to be honest with each other. I have told her how I felt growing up and she has listened to me. She has even attended some of my courses that are based on these four values and has applied them in her own life. I have also heard more about what she was going through herself when I was young, allowing me to develop more compassion towards her. As a result, we have now become a lot closer. I can always rely on her if I need support and this is very important to me.

I have also been able to give support to her and that has been a great feeling. I admire the strength and resilience Mum has developed throughout her life to face her own life's challenges and to keep going through it all. I know now that she has always loved me, even if this was shown in ways I could not understand as a child.

My anger and blame towards Mum for not being there when I felt I needed her as a teenager for a long time prevented me from seeing that she was also very giving and loving in other ways. She worked hard to provide a roof over my head, she did the food shopping and cooked meals for us and did all the washing and ironing. She also came to all my school plays and parent's evenings, lent me her car when I was old enough to drive, moved my stuff to University and much more. I had been so stuck in my anger towards her that I had not been grateful for these things at all. I realised that it had not been possible for Mum to express herself authentically when she herself was growing up and she also felt it very difficult to assert her own personal boundaries, which is one of the reasons why she had put up with the control from Robert for so long. And she had loved him, even if that was something I could not understand.

Things were always going to be more complicated with my dad. Out of all of his daughters I have spent the least amount of time with him growing up and so, as I said earlier, we missed out on the deeper level of understanding that can come through that process. As a result, we have often had painful misunderstandings and difficult conversations between us over the years. But we have also had moments of love and connection, which I have treasured dearly.

And I do want to recognise and acknowledge all that he has given to me; from the travel trips abroad, to staying in his flat in Spain, to Grandma Ida and of course all of my sisters. And how he has also tried to make things right between us, like the time that he flew out to Paris when I was living there, even if neither of us was really ready for that conversation at that time. I love him with all my heart, and my greatest wish is that he knows that is true and that he is happy in the life that he has created now.

In developing more self-compassion, I have been able to accept the idea that my extended family (when I was growing up) acted in the way that they did more through lack of awareness, than through anything malicious and I have been able to let go of a lot of judgments I was holding towards them. As the popular maxim runs, *'You can't understand someone until you've walked a mile in their shoes'*. I came to understand that although I had been holding unforgiveness towards key adults in my life for them not understanding my own situation growing up, I also had not known theirs. I had no idea what they had been going through or what beliefs were underpinning their opinions at the time. I am sure now that most of their intentions had been well-meaning, even if they had felt inappropriate and uncaring to me at the time.

In looking into my own suffering, and in discovering that my harsh judgments towards myself were unfounded, I was finding it increasingly more difficult to hold blame towards anyone else.

We all have the capacity to appear differently at different times to different people. I could see this in my own journey. One of my uncles told me as an adult that he had perceived me as a moody and difficult child. My experience as a child had been one of feeling traumatised and rejected. Both views are valid, but focusing on which one would help me to develop compassion towards myself? And towards him?

We all see life from different perspectives. All perspectives are valid at the time to the person who is seeing them. A lot of problems occur in the world when someone makes their perspective 'the right one' and the other person's wrong. The person who has been made to feel wrong then feels they have to defend or to fight back, to justify their position. And so the cycle of fighting begins. In families some feuds can last for generations. And often they are based on misunderstandings and misperceptions. It is really sad.

I had taken on other people's perceptions of me to be true for such a long time. I had taken my step-dad's anger to be about me, when it was really about him, it was his anger that I was feeling and assuming it was about me. Over the years I had given most of my focus and attention to those people who did not like me and who I perceived to be rejecting me, believing that if I could just do something more, or be someone better then I could persuade them to like me. I tried to please these people, but it just never worked, and I would end up feeling bad. I understand now that it was because I was compromising my own integrity to try to make things right for them. I would walk away feeling terrible about myself and wondering what I had done wrong when I had tried to make everything right. I created a lot of suffering for myself in this way. This was particularly true with my step-parent relationships.

My favourite quote from the Harry Potter films is from J.K. Rowling's book *Harry Potter and the Order of the Phoenix*[67]. I loved this quote so much that I had to watch the film on DVD and pause the screen to write it down. Harry's godfather Sirius Black says to him:

'We've all got both light and dark inside us. What matters is the part we choose to act on. That's who we really are.'

I think that the way we focus on the light that Sirius mentions is through living and being in our integrity (and in understanding what that really means for us). I have dark and light aspects within me, and so does everyone else. That is the nature of the human spirit. It is who I am choosing to be and what I am choosing to act on that makes the difference.

'I have choice. I choose to live in my integrity.'

The words from Dale Carnegie echoed in my mind. I can choose who I want to be. I loved the values from Familylab so much that I integrated them with some coaching, personal development insights, NLP and mindfulness into something I call Connected Communication. I run training courses in schools, in the corporate world and in open courses to which anyone can attend if they wish to live life in their own integrity. The more I deliver the content to other people, the more I embody the connected communication approach myself and the more I align myself with my own integrity.

One day, out of the blue. I had the startling realisation that 'I am the one I have been waiting for.'

'*I* am the one I have been waiting for.'

All my life I had been waiting for someone to come along and sweep me off my feet and to make everything all right for me. I had wanted someone to come and rescue me and to take me away from all the pain and suffering I had felt. Initially I had wanted my parents to protect me, then my sister, then boyfriends and friends and yet no-one could ever seem to give me the love and attention that I craved, and lasting relief from the pain I felt inside. And the longer this rescuer had taken to appear in my life, the more isolated, alone and feeling depressed I had become.

Now I knew that the one I had been waiting for had been here the whole time!

➢ I am the one who is strong and courageous

➢ I am the one who is in control of my experience

➢ I am the one who is choosing to love and accept all aspects of myself

➢ I am the one who is committed to my own happiness and

peace of mind

➤ I am the one who has a passion to make a positive difference in the world

➤ I am the one who can give me what I need

➤ I am the one I have been waiting for

I felt so empowered with these realisations. My own happiness and inner peace were mine to create and they didn't have to depend on the input of anyone else. I didn't have to let the opinions and judgments of anyone else affect my own sense of self-worth. A good friend around this time gave me a Q-Tip (which are used to clean people's ears).

'**Q-Tip, Quit Taking It Personally**', she said. 'Keep this as a reminder'. I carry it around in my phone case to this day, to remind myself not to take anything personally. I knew that I had been keeping myself feeling small for a long time, thinking that if I stepped up to share my story I would receive a lot of judgment and accusation from certain people in my life. I had focused so much attention on this that I had lost sight of why I wanted to share my story in the first place, to share my learnings in the hopes that it might help someone else struggling in their own life to find inner peace and happiness.

With a renewed sense of vigour, I felt that it was now time to leave my safeguarding roles and return to the work that I found most fulfilling; empowering people who know that their potential is far greater than their current reality.

CHAPTER 14
The Visibility

"I hope you have not been leading a double life, pretending to be wicked and being good all the time. That would be hypocrisy."

Oscar Wilde[68]

The vision returned of me standing on a stage in front of hundreds of people that I had first seen 10 years previously whilst lying on my back with a slipped disc. The vision that had seemed so far away and so dreamlike back then was feeling more possible now than ever before.

I realised now that the vision was about more than me standing on a stage and speaking to people. The vision was really about having a bigger platform on which to share my life's journey and the key lessons I had learned along the way. It was about sharing what I had learned with as many people as possible, so that no-one else would have to suffer unnecessarily, as I believed I had. And so that people could fulfil their true potential and not to play small anymore, as I had done.

Feeling the time was right to step up and create my vision, I joined the Professional Speaking Association[69] (PSA) in London. I loved the energy of this group of professional speakers. I felt welcome and accepted from the first visit I made. After only a couple of months I took the plunge and gave my first speech to the London group – it went OK – I managed to remember all the words at least but I felt that there was another level in my speaking that I could go to that I had not yet reached. I was proud of myself for taking this bold step.

'I will feel the fear and do it anyway.'

I had read a book by Susan Jeffers called *Feel the Fear and Do It Anyway*[70]. In this book, Susan says that we all feel fear and that a lot of the time we have a misperception that other people who are more successful don't feel fear. We then wait to do what we want to do, thinking 'when I am no longer afraid I will try that', but that day rarely comes. Successful people have learned to push through their fear, to 'feel the fear and do it anyway'. I had committed to taking her advice.

About a month later I found out very last minute that there was a 'Speaker Factor' competition at the PSA. This was a competition for anyone who was in their first year of membership. The entrants had to deliver a five-minute speech and were judged on the following criteria; stagecraft, script, delivery and bookability of the speech. By the time I heard about the competition there wasn't much time to prepare my speech before I entered but, as I would only have to speak for five minutes, I decided to gather all the courage I could muster and enter the competition to speak about my life story.

There were 13 other entrants in the competition, and some were professional speakers who had been speaking for a while and so I had no expectations of anything other than taking part and speaking publicly about my story and the lessons I have learned through it. I loved listening to the other speeches and learned a lot through the different ways they presented in their five-minute slots.

I was incredibly nervous about sharing my story in front of peers who spoke professionally for a career, to the point of nearly throwing up in the toilets just before it was my turn to speak. This was taking fear to a whole new level! Eventually my name was called, and I walked shaking onto the stage and gave my speech, 'It's the thoughts that count'. Once again, I remembered all the words and felt relieved when it was over.

I felt incredibly vulnerable on the stage sharing the most painful parts of my life so openly. But I also felt liberated that I had been able to do it.

Afterwards people came up to acknowledge me for having been through and overcome so much. I wasn't expecting to receive so much care and support from the group – it was lovely. After lunch all the speakers received feedback from the judges and I was grateful for the feedback I received which would help to make my speech even better.

When the time came to announce the winner, I was excited to see who was going to win and be the representative for London PSA at the national semi-finals of the competition at the annual conference in a few months' time.

'And the winner is... Lis Cashin for her speech entitled, "It's the thoughts that count!"' I was genuinely shocked and stunned and burst into tears. My fellow PSA members rose to their feet to give me a standing ovation as I went on stage to receive my winner's certificate. What an incredible feeling that was! I felt really seen, heard and validated in a very public arena.

'Sharing my vulnerability connects me to people.'

I was finally able to let other people see me, hear me and validate me as I had got to the stage where I was able to see, hear and validate myself. It does seem ironic that some of the things we want so dearly from others can only come once we have given them to ourselves...and then we don't need them from others but we are more likely to get them anyway!

And then reality dawned... I would have to give my speech again at the national semi-finals in a few months in front of even more professional speakers! The vision was another step closer...

Having done so well with delivering my speech, the book about my life journey came back into my awareness. People were asking me if I had ever thought about writing a book about my experiences. The time felt right to revisit my writing and to finish the book at last.

Just as going travelling had been a thought that kept repeating earlier in my life, so writing a book about my life story and lessons learned and speaking about them publicly had become the next thoughts that would keep repeating and would in fact continue to do so over the next few years. They became the 'things I will regret not doing' in my life if I didn't achieve them, just as travelling had been earlier on in my life. I knew that I had to do them in order to feel at peace with myself. My inner guidance system (as Esther Hicks had taught) was set to destination 'published book and public speaker' and that was undoubtedly the direction into which my life was now heading.

Getting my speech ready for the Speaker Factor semi-finals I was very lucky to have the support of some fantastic speakers from the London group.

Cassie heard my speech in the first round and recorded a 5-minute motivational audio recording that I was to listen to everyday up to the finals. In this recording I visualised myself on stage delivering the speech and how I would feel and the impact the speech could make. Pearl (the president of the PSA at that time) gave me some performance coaching; Michael, Philip and Claire helped my speech and writing to have even more impact.

Lots of other members also wanted to give me feedback. I felt a little overwhelmed by all the different advice I was being given and over time my speech felt like it was going off-track and was being delivered in a way that was not authentic to me.

At one point, I had to stop and really re-visit what it was that I wanted to say and how I wanted to say it. I had initially entered the competition to just have the opportunity to share my story and now it was becoming a speech in a competition and it wasn't feeling right to me. Having something so tragic being judged as part of a competition wasn't sitting right with me and I questioned my judgment around putting myself in this position. But I accepted that I had and that now the London region were counting on me to do the very best I could to represent them in the semi-finals.

It became a fantastic learning in how to speak in my integrity in a way that feels authentic to me. I realised that delivering my speech authentically was the most important factor and so it was that that I focused on during my preparation for the final rounds.

Talking about The Accident and the key lessons learned in just five minutes wasn't easy. Each time I spoke I would remember The Accident and what happened and how I felt. During one session where I was being supported to make my speech delivery even better the person working with me kept taking me right to the point of the accident and to feel all the feelings that I had felt back then. They kept telling me to go back again and again and again. I was feeling re-traumatised but felt I had to keep going in order to be professional and to represent London in the competition.

Arriving at the PSA conference in a hotel in Birmingham where I was to speak in the semi-finals felt quite daunting. To be surrounded by my peers and fellow professional speakers (some of whom have created very successful careers for themselves in speaking) I felt my nerves rising. Reality struck; I was going to have to speak in front of all of these professional speakers.

The semi-finals were in the afternoon of the Friday that I arrived. This was in a smaller conference room that held around 75 people. There were 12 of us speaking in the semi-finals. I was the last speaker so had to sit through listening to all of my fellow speakers' fantastic speeches. Eventually it was my turn to speak and I managed to make it all the way through without fault, which was such a relief.

I was really surprised (and delighted) once again to make it through the semi-finals and into the final round of the competition the next day. The finals were to be held in the main conference room (which was much larger and held around 200 people) and there were 5 of us who would speak this time.

Getting ready for the final round with my great speaker friends, Cassie and Jo-Dee, I realised that once more I had a choice. I could choose to really step into my authentic adult self on stage and speak from my personal integrity or I could speak from the place of still feeling like a traumatised teenager.

I made a conscious decision to step into my personal power in my adult authentic self.

I walked onto the stage still shaking inside but trying to feel as confident as I could, whilst fully acknowledging myself for everything that I had courageously overcome in my life to get me to this place.

The speech started well and at one point I turned to talk to the 13-year-old me and I acknowledge her for the courage and resilience she showed at that time, and also my gratitude to her and Sammy for all the lessons I have learned through our journey together since that day. I really felt every word that I said and believed that I delivered it in the way I wanted to. When I finished my speech I got a standing ovation from some of my peers in the crowd.

This was a particularly special moment in my life.

The courage it had taken for me to stand on that stage and to reveal myself to the audience was huge. Sharing my vulnerability with others had once more created a deeper connection with them.

So did I win the competition?

No, I didn't win. But I did feel as though I had won a big personal victory. I had been courageous, made a stand for myself and my personal integrity and I had also acknowledged myself in a very public way.

And my dream of standing on an even bigger stage was edging closer.

Following on from my success at the PSA final I began to share my story with more people and was booked to speak at different events.

Linda Aspey, a fellow speaker at the PSA who had seen me speak at the final introduced me to an incredible man named Gian Power. Gian was setting up a new organisation called TLC Lions[711]. Gian describes TLC as 'igniting emotional engagement through story-telling to help the inclusion and diversity and wellbeing agenda.'

Gian is an entrepreneur with an inspiring vision and a powerful story of his own after his father went missing, presumed murdered, in India in 2015. By joining TLC, I felt that I had come home to a community of inspirational individuals who had all overcome challenges they had faced in their own lives.

I was excited to see how I could contribute to and learn from this group and, by sharing my story into the corporate wellbeing space, to help organisations develop workplaces that are emotionally engaging, honest and real places to be; where teams feel connected and inspired to achieve more.

And yet at the same time I was still feeling re-traumatised from the process of reliving The Accident through my PSA speaking journey. I wondered how I could ever build a speaking career when speaking about what had happened still felt so traumatic. I didn't want to keep putting myself through the pain of that. I wondered if I should let it all drop now and take my life in a different direction, but I knew that the persistent thoughts I had been having around writing my book and speaking on a larger stage would not allow me to have any kind of peace until I had achieved them.

One day, I was with my friend Penny's daughter, Hannah Power. Hannah is an amazing young lady and as a part of her entrepreneurial business she has created her own jewellery range Sederhana Designs[722]. She gives £30 of every necklace sold to RASASC: The Rape and Sexual Abuse Support Centre to enable them to give more support to rape survivors.

Hannah had been through a very traumatic experience herself the year before we met up and she had been going through some treatment for Post-Traumatic Stress Disorder (PTSD). Although the details of our individual traumas had been very different, we had a lot of similarities in our symptoms and experience since our traumas had occurred.

I was listening to the support that she had received and how much it had supported her own recovery. I had heard about PTSD in the few years previously and had originally thought that it was something that only soldiers experienced. Having had my therapy sessions with Merry and talking about some of my symptoms I had asked her if she thought that I might be suffering with PTSD. She recommended that I read the book *The Body Keeps the Score*[733] by Bessel A Van Der Kolk. Just reading the first chapter, my whole life since The Accident started to make sense.

The book describes how people who have been through trauma often feel out of control and are afraid that there is something wrong with them and that they are beyond redemption. Trauma can have a very big impact on the body, it says, and those who have experienced trauma can have a reduced feeling of being alive. It talks about the hypervigilance that traumatised individuals can suffer which affects their ability to spontaneously engage in their daily lives. It also states that traumatised people so often keep repeating the same problems and have a lot of trouble learning from experience because the trauma has made actual changes in the brain.

The relief I felt from reading all of this was immeasurable. I felt that I was reading a lot of my life story through the words on each page. *Could PTSD explain the way I has been feeling and why I was still struggling to move on from those feelings completely, even after all these years?*

I realised that the rage I had felt, and not been able to resolve during my earlier therapy with Marie, was in fact part of my PTSD symptoms. As was the difficulty sleeping, the reckless behaviour and taking drugs, the emotional flashbacks, feelings of depression or numbness at times, feeling irritated, jumpy and unable to concentrate for long periods of time, the feelings of shame and guilt and the belief that I was inherently bad and inability to sustain feeling positive emotions. The detachment from others and how I felt like I was living in a glass box and the rest of the world was on the outside of the box. It all now made complete sense. These were all things associated with PTSD.

Merry was not qualified to make a formal diagnosis or to treat PTSD and so I decided to go to my GP and ask for a formal assessment. When I went into his surgery, sat down in his consulting room and started to share my story I immediately felt a lot of compassion from him. He said that he was shocked that no other doctor had ever thought to send me for a PTSD diagnosis, he apologised on behalf of the medical profession and he referred me straight away for an assessment. I felt validated in that moment and his apology meant a lot to me following my earlier difficult experiences with doctors as a teenager and young adult.

From the initial assessment I was referred to a Cognitive Behavioural Therapist (CBT) for a further assessment. After sharing my story and the symptoms I was experiencing, it was decided that I would follow a course of trauma CBT sessions to help me to deal with PTSD symptoms I was experiencing from The Accident. My therapist Emilia was absolutely perfect for me. Her energy was very soft and gentle, and she went at a pace that I could deal with. She was incredibly supportive from the beginning.

I was nervous about revisiting these painful memories. But I also knew that I had not had any specific therapeutic trauma-based support and so I held onto hope that this time might be different from the other things I had tried (even though they had each helped me in their different ways).

The first few sessions with Emilia were about learning grounding techniques and finding a safe space in my mind where I could retreat if the subsequent trauma sessions became too overwhelming. I was also given the Flashback Protocol[744] to help me to deal with the feeling flashbacks I experienced on a regular basis (a feeling flashback was when I would be triggered by something that happened in my present environment and would feel the shock and horror from the moment The Accident occurred in the past).

The first time I used the Flashback Protocol I was able to reduce the intensity of the feelings of the flashback and to get into a grounded space much more easily. Creating the safe space in my mind and using the Flashback Protocol were such simple things to do but they had a profound impact on my inner feelings of safety and security.

During these first few weeks of the trauma CBT process I began to trust Emilia, which I knew was the most important first step of the process. *"What you are experiencing"*, Emilia said *"is a normal reaction to an abnormal event."*

In the next few sessions, I had to re-experience The Accident all over again. In one session I had to re-live the whole day as if it were happening right in the moment. I walked myself through the day of The Accident from getting up in the morning to being at school and ending up at the hospital. I re-experienced the shock and horror and the full trauma of that day. It was horrendous. I realised why I had not been able to get to this level of healing before as the pain was so overwhelming I thought I was going to pass out at times, and I had to have built up enough inner strength to be able to support myself through it all. All of the other things I had done over the years had been preparing me for this.

As I progressed through the trauma and the day itself Emilia would ask me what thoughts I was thinking at that point of the day, what I was feeling inside and what beliefs I was creating. I was able to witness the creation of the very destructive thoughts and beliefs that had been running my life since that day. These were, that:

1. Part of me might have done it on purpose and there was something inherently wrong with me

2. I was going to be in a lot of trouble for having done something wrong (as I was always blamed for everything already by step-dad)

3. Everyone was going to hate and reject me for what I had done

4. I was going to die as a punishment for what had happened

5. Something terrible was going to happen to me

6. I was going crazy

7. I was evil and deserved to be punished

Once we had established that these were my thoughts and beliefs created at the time The Accident happened, we spent the next few sessions exploring each one in more detail to assess and question their validity.

In starting to unpick these thoughts and beliefs Emilia would very gently start to question me about their validity. When we got to 'I am evil and deserve to be punished' she asked me how long I had been upset about The Accident. When I responded that it was 35-years she asked me,

'Would an evil person be upset for that long over what had happened?'

Something inside me felt uncomfortable and started to shift. The part that had been holding on to this belief that someday I would discover that I really was evil started to loosen its grip on me. 'I've worked with murderers in the past,' she continued 'and very often they will kill someone and then go and make a cup of tea or go about their lives, without showing any emotion or remorse for what they had done, which doesn't sound like what happened to you at all. Would you agree?'

This made sense to me. An evil person would probably just have killed Sammy and then carried on with their life regardless, they would not have been devastated like I had been or been so concerned that Sammy would be OK and tried so hard to get her help immediately after it had happened.

For the first time since The Accident had happened I had the absolute feeling that I was not evil.

I had desperately wanted to believe it before but had never been able to actually *feel* it. Now going back and processing it all with Emilia, there was no evidence that I could find to back up this belief. I had been searching inside myself all of these years, terrified that I would find an evil part of me. And I could not find one. It wasn't there. I had *not* wanted The Accident to happen, some part of me had not created it on purpose. It was a complete accident.

'I am NOT evil. It was an accident.'

A longed-for hope before this moment, it now felt unquestionably true.

We then explored the other thoughts and beliefs I had created at the time. We started to work through them one by one, firstly to find the evidence against them since it had happened and secondly to find a more balanced view.

For each one, I realised that there was either very little or no evidence to prove that any part of it was true, and I had a stack of evidence to disprove it. Bit by bit, belief by belief, we dismantled the internal belief structures that had been the destructive driving force of my life to this point. Although I had been able to change some of my beliefs in previous years, I had never been able to get to these core beliefs before, which is why I had kept yo-yo'oing between feeling better and then worse again. Nothing else had been able to stick before as the core beliefs kept pulling me back into feeling bad about myself. I had had awareness that the beliefs were there before, but this was very different to fundamentally feeling that they were untrue, as I did now.

On that day back in 1983, I was an innocent child walking out onto the school field. I did exactly as I was instructed to do by the teachers, I shouted Sammy's name when I could see the javelin was heading towards her so that she could duck to miss it, I was in massive shock when it did, and I had immediately wanted someone to get help for Sammy. None of these things indicated anything about me, except that I hadn't done it on purpose and that I cared about my friend who was seriously hurt.

At one point in the process I looked at Emilia and exclaimed '*I really didn't do anything deliberately wrong!*'. I was so moved and surprised to discover that I really hadn't done anything wrong that day, and that there was nothing inherently wrong with me. All these years I had held onto destructive thoughts and beliefs because I had had no help at the time to process what had happened. I had done what children and people in trauma naturally do and that was, in the absence of any other information to the contrary, blame myself entirely.

'I didn't do anything deliberately wrong.'

Understanding that I had done nothing wrong did not detract from the responsibility I felt from having thrown the javelin that day. I had still played an integral part in what had happened to Sammy. But I knew that I had in no way done anything to deliberately hurt her and that was a wonderful feeling of release from the guilt and shame I had still been carrying all this time.

I remembered the insights that I had gained during my 3-week silent meditation retreat in Sri Lanka and how true they were. I really had suffered enough, in fact there was no need for me to have suffered at all, except to come to terms with the tragic accident that had happened that day and to grieve for the loss of a friend. I had not been able to sustain the happiness and inner peace I had felt at the end of that retreat as, although I had had awareness of the destructive beliefs I had created, I hadn't been able to get to the heart of them and to question their validity in a safe space, as I was able to do here now with Emilia.

Emilia said that I had been a victim too that day on the sports field and I had never even considered this as a possibility before. I realised that both Sammy and I had had a right to be safe at school and for the school to have put appropriate safety measures in place during the sports day.

Thinking back I had been so young, just a child when it happened. A child who already felt so sad and lonely. I wished that I could turn back the years to give her what she really needed back then; the loving support to process the shock and bewilderment of such a horrific event. But then I realised that I could give it to her now, from the place of my own compassionate adult, 'the one I have been waiting for':

- 'I have done nothing deliberately wrong

- There is nothing inherently wrong with me'

And with this knowledge came freedom, the ultimate freedom to be me without restriction, and without needing permission:

- 'I can be happy now

- I can create a successful life for myself'

I knew that the yo-yoing I had experienced up to this point of wanting so badly to create a happy and successful life for myself and feeling like a failure when I couldn't achieve it was coming to an end. The process from now on would be:

1. *Setting clear intention around what life I wanted to create for myself*

2. *Committing myself to creating that life*

3. *CREATING THAT LIFE!*

I could feel this to be true. What had seemed virtually impossible up to this point now felt entirely possible. It was incredible to realise that my internal beliefs had acted like barriers to my happiness. What power they had held over me up to this point!

I had done nothing deliberately wrong. Having viewed the world for so long through the lens of my destructive beliefs, it felt very strange to be saying this and knowing it to be true. I felt joy bubbling up with this knowledge.

I felt that I was finally able to reveal the 'good' me inside, the one that I had connected with as a child and had felt was who I really was, but had rejected all this time. Someone said to me 'con men usually hide from people how cunning and manipulative they are, but you have been hiding your light all this time. It's time to shine now.'

I didn't want to hide anymore. I wanted to shine my light brightly. I was reminded of a beautiful quote I had read:

"*Our deepest fear is not that we are inadequate. Our deepest fear is that we are powerful beyond measure. It is our light, not our darkness that most frightens us. We ask ourselves, 'Who am I to be brilliant, gorgeous, talented, fabulous?' Actually, who are you not to be? You are a child of God. Your playing small does not serve the world. There is nothing enlightened about shrinking so that other people won't feel insecure around you. We are all meant to shine, as children do. We were born to make manifest the glory of God that is within us. It's not just in some of us; it's in everyone. And as we let our own light shine, we unconsciously give other people permission to do the same. As we are liberated from our own fear, our presence automatically liberates others.*"
- Marianne Williamson, A Return to Love: Reflections on the Principles of A Course in Miracles[75]

It was time to shine now.

CHAPTER 15
The Freedom

"Turn your wounds into wisdom."

Oprah Winfrey[76]

Around this time I was introduced to an American lady Judy Ban Greenman who facilitates the BodyBrainFreedom[77]® Process. My lovely friend Jude had been on one of Judy's retreats in Granada in Spain and had been a student on Judy's year-long training programme. I had seen the effects that the training had had on Jude (she was much more relaxed, confident and at ease with herself) and I was curious to learn more.

Judy's process involved sessions to teach you 'how to change neural pathways through movement to improve and optimise your body's own internal healing process'. I knew that my nervous system had struggled under the weight of living with PTSD all these years and I was curious to see whether BodyBrainFreedom® could help it to settle down. I had worked through the mental and emotional aspects of living with PTSD and now wanted to work with the trauma that was still being held in my body on a physical and neurological level.

Years earlier when I had been doing the work study programme at Esalen, I had had the amazing and transformative sessions with Jules. His sessions were also based on Cortical Field Re-Education[78]®, which I discovered was a part of the BodyBrainFreedom® process. When I had returned from the US I had tried unsuccessfully to find a practitioner in the UK who did this type of work. I had told my friend Jude about how powerful I had found Jules's session. When she experienced a similar response with Judy Ban Greenman, Jude couldn't wait to tell me all about it. I marvelled at the synchronicity of life once more.

When Jude then organised for Judy to deliver a two-day BodyBrainFreedom® course in the UK I was excited to attend. The weekend was great, and I came away with a feeling of lightness and my body felt much more aligned and at ease. Not long after the weekend course I was invited to attend Judy's longer course which was a retreat in Majorca, Spain with another fabulous facilitator, Kora Dierichs[79], who is from Germany. I knew from my previous learning about the mind-body connection that healing would need to take place on all levels within me, and not just in my mind and emotional levels.

What I loved about Judy's work was how gentle the process was. Nothing was forced, and the majority of time was spent lying down on a yoga mat doing very gentle and incredibly slow movements with the body. In the slowing down, my body got to feel safe and could release emotions it had been holding onto and I felt there was a real experience of letting go. I remembered how it used to drive me mad when people would say to me 'you just need to let go' when I had no sense at all of what that really meant. I had had some experience during my silent retreat in Sri Lanka of the mind letting go. Now on this retreat I could feel my body finally learning to let go and it felt wonderful. I felt very relaxed.

In one session, there was some deeply held rage surfacing in me. I tried to observe it, not to judge it and then I requested to have a one-to-one session with Judy to see if I could process what was going on around it. In our session suddenly I had an image of my step-dad appear in my mind. I felt deeply held rage towards him resurfacing, just as it had done during my retreat in Sri Lanka.

This time, and in a safe space, I let the raging teenager within me verbally express what she had not been able to express in person at the time it had happened, or out loud during my silent meditation retreat at Nilambe. She really went for it! She was shouting and screaming at Robert for a good few minutes. Then I felt the grief behind the rage like a wave washing over me. The rage had been masking the grief and shame that I was feeling underneath and had been too afraid to feel, until now. I realised how suppressed and oppressed I still felt on some level from being controlled so much by him as a teenager. I was still allowing Robert to control me inside my mind, even though he had been physically gone from my life for over 20 years.

I remembered hearing a story of how elephants are trained: Apparently, elephants initially have a strong rope tied around their legs and the rope is then attached to a secure pole. The elephants naturally try to walk away and are stopped by the rope. They pull and push and twist and turn and eventually figure out that they just aren't strong enough to break free of their shackles, so they stop resisting and just stay where they are.

The next time the elephants are tied up they try to break away once again, pulling on the rope to see if they can go free. When they work out that once again it is futile and that they are stuck, they stop pulling and settle down and stay where they are.

The same thing happens over and over until eventually, when the rope is put over their legs but is no longer tied to the pole, they no longer pull and push and try to break free because they believe it is futile. That is why you can sometimes walk by a circus and see giant elephants standing passively with a rope tied around their legs that isn't attached to anything at all.

The elephant becomes so accustomed to being held back by the rope, that just the rope itself keeps the animal in check. They don't know how powerful they really are. If only they realised that by the time they have grown up, even a rope 'secured' to a pole can no longer restrain them. Then they would know what true freedom is. But they don't.

And that is how I still felt inside my mind.

I had tried and tried so hard to assert my personal integrity as a child and had felt it being squashed time and time again. In the end I had had to suppress my inner rage at having my personal boundaries constantly overstepped and I had given up even trying to push back. It just seemed pointless even trying any more. And this is why in my subsequent romantic relationships I had allowed myself to be controlled once more.

Now as an adult I was free and powerful but had not allowed myself to realise it. I was metaphorically still tied to the rope on some level, like the elephants.

In the moment of this realisation, I recommitted to myself that I was taking my personal power back, that I would not need anyone else's permission to be myself and that I was going now to create the life that I longed to live.

'I am taking my personal power back. I give myself permission to be myself'

I was reminded of the phrase from Theodore Roosevelt's speech 'Citizenship in a Republic[80]' that Dr. Brene Brown wrote about in her fantastic book *Daring Greatly: How the Courage to Be Vulnerable Transforms the Way We Live, Love, Parent and Lead*[81]. In this quote Roosevelt says 'It is not the critic who counts... The credit belongs to the man who is actually in the arena, whose face is marred by dust and sweat and blood; who strives valiantly... who at best knows in the end the triumph of high achievement, and who at worst, if he fails, at least fails while daring greatly...'

Dr. Brene Brown herself added "I want to be in the arena. I want to be brave with my life. And when we make the choice to dare greatly, we sign up to get our asses kicked. We can choose courage or we can choose comfort, but we can't have both. Not at the same time."

I really felt like 'the man in the arena' who dares greatly. I was no longer concerned with the opinions of those people who shouted criticism from the side-lines, whilst trapped in their own fear. I wanted to be around other people who were also willing to be 'in the arena', who were willing to fight for their happiness and peace of mind as I had done.

After the session, I went to lie by the pool as it was a lovely May afternoon and the sky was blue and the sun was shining. As usual I was listening to music on my headphones. Some of the dance tunes that I used to love when I was raving years ago came onto my playlist. As usual when I hear music with a strong beat my feet started tapping and I wanted to get up and dance. I wanted to hear the music with more volume and so asked the other women by the pool if they minded having music on by the pool, but they said that they preferred silence, which I respected.

But my feet wanted to dance! I was sunbathing topless and I thought 'I can't just get up and dance here' (I didn't want to subject my fellow sunbathers to that sight!) But this desire to dance wouldn't go away, in fact it was getting stronger and stronger and then suddenly I felt compelled to get up, wrap my sarong around me and run over to a piece of grass and dance. I really went for it! I felt so joyful, so alive in that moment. I was dancing because I WANTED TO DANCE. And no-one could stop me. I didn't need anyone's permission. I was dancing, and I felt so free.

The 'spell' had been broken.

I wondered what else might be possible if I just did whatever I felt compelled to do in the moment, with no fear of judgment or rejection?

That night over dinner, I told the other women (some of whom, unbeknown to me, had seen me dancing that afternoon) that I was going to go down to the yoga studio fifteen minutes earlier than our evening session was due to start and that I was going to put on some music and I was going to dance. I extended an invitation to anyone else who would care to join me.

Proclaiming to the group what I was going to do felt like a stretch out of my comfort zone. Although I was going to go and dance alone I also hoped that maybe one or two others would come and join me.

When the time came I put on one of my favourite dance tunes just as Susanne was walking into the yoga studio. She immediately joined in the dancing! We had great fun dancing together.

Then slowly one by one the others flowed down to the studio in order to join the evening session. Hesitant at first, they began to join in with the dancing. Then some were asking me for requests 'Can you play Abba Dancing Queen' was the first. And so it was that we all danced, with numerous song requests and the dancing became the evening session itself.

At the end of the evening we sat in a circle to debrief the day. Many of the women admitted that they never usually dance as they feel too self-conscious. And yet somehow the atmosphere we had all created together invited them into the dance. I felt like I was giving a gift back to myself of allowing myself to dance, without needing to take drugs in order to do so. I wondered how I could create more dancing spaces like this in my life?

Judy asked me what I had learned from this experience. 'Just flippin' do it' I said.

'No more procrastination, no more keeping myself small to please other people. Just get on with it!'

Coming back from Majorca I became very focused around finishing this book, now that I felt the ending I wanted to write had been lived. My intuition had been correct nine years earlier when I had written the first draft, that I then had to live the next part before I would be able to complete it.

I now wanted to live the fullness of life in every single moment. I had finally done it, I had broken free.

A couple of weeks later I was at a music festival with my sister, brother-in-law and their friends James and Rachel. We had such a good laugh throughout the weekend, and I danced for the whole two days. On the Sunday night the closing act was called 'Hacienda Classical'. Graeme Park[82] and Mike Pickering[83], who were DJs at the legendary Hacienda nightclub in Manchester when I had been raving there in the 1990s are the brains behind Hacienda Classical, which is a unique collaboration with Manchester Camerata to reinvent iconic dance tunes as classical compositions.

Graeme and Mike provide the bassline and beats for the tunes, and the Manchester Camerata play the orchestral parts. Along with some backing singers who sing the famous lyrics to the songs, the whole thing together is incredible to hear and to see. I made my way right to the front of the stage and I danced non-stop throughout the music set list. I was completely transported back to my raving days and I felt on a high by the end, but this time around I had taken no drugs at all and yet I felt just as ecstatic, if not more so, than the first time around. I was shining my light so brightly I felt I was going to burst! Another full circle had been reached.

My strongest intention back in the days when I had been taking drugs was that I could find a way to feel that good without them. I had felt blissful when I had had my reiki session with Adinda in India and I had moments of bliss in my time spent at Nilambe. Now here I felt ecstatic dancing to some of my favourite clubbing tunes, with no drugs in my system at all. I felt so happy and so free.

Some very good friends of mine Steve and Liz have a daughter who calls me Aunty Lis. Ella is the most beautiful girl and she just melts my heart. One day I was due to go to see Steve and Ella and in the morning Ella proclaimed to Steve unprompted "It's Lis Cashin day!". I felt so uplifted to be greeted by this when I arrived. Another day I was playing with Ella in her sandpit and she needed more water bringing. "Shall I go and get some more?" I asked Ella. "Yes Aunty Lis, JUST DO IT!" she said with such energy and enthusiasm (aged 2) that I felt compelled to go and get the water. So aged 3 years old Ella has now become my life coach!

I am genuinely excited to see how my life now progresses. My biggest investment in my life has been in me, and what a return on investment that has given, and continues to give. I am worth a lot of money! I have redefined what success means to me and created very firm foundations in my life that I can now build upon. I wake up most mornings with an inner smile, knowing that there is nothing now that can stop me from creating the life I have always wanted to live. I feel motivated and inspired to share what I have learned with those who are ready to hear what I have to say.

I am speaking on a professional stage and am loving it more and more. I don't think it will be long before my vision of standing on an even bigger stage and sharing my story becomes a reality, which is very exciting.

For the past few years I have been working as a consultant, speaker and trainer in the area of mental health and wellbeing. I love going into organisations and getting people talking about mental health to help to challenge the stigma that still exists. I work with organisations to create mentally healthy cultures. These organisations invest in their people; everyone feels a sense of belonging, are really clear on the value that they bring to the organisation, relationships are built on trust and mental health and wellbeing support is not only clearly signposted but is fully utilised by those who need it.

I also work with women who know in their hearts that their potential is far greater than their current reality. I have created a community for these women called 'She Who Shines' to empower them to step up, be seen and to make a positive difference in the world.

I was originally going to call my book 'The whole of me' as it's been a journey to wholeness, of retrieving all those parts of me that have felt stuck and rejected. It's been understanding that all levels - mental, emotional, physical and spiritual - need to be in balance for me to feel in balance. I spend time every day making choices that support my wellbeing; I practise mindfulness and attend regular mindfulness retreats, I go to the gym twice a week, I supplement my diet with ayurvedic herbs, I eat as healthily as I can, I walk in nature, I surround myself with positive people, I do work that I love, I dance, I trust myself, I spend quality time with friends and family and I laugh as much as I can.

I used to have a notion that life should always be great and blamed myself if something went wrong. Now I know that life ebbs and flows, and things just happen. My part in the dynamic is how I view and respond to what is happening. Happiness is therefore within my control and is not dependent on life circumstances. I'm not perfect and I have days where I feel out of balance. But I have the tools and the resources to get me back on track again.

Belief systems, I have come to realise, are like belief 'goggles' through which we see the world. Remember - you can always choose a different lens for your own belief 'goggles' and learn to see the world in a more supportive and empowering way.

What happened with Sammy that day is not something I will ever forget, and nor do I want to. Sammy was a friend and although she physically died that day, I have felt her spirit with me ever since, guiding me, encouraging me, supporting me to go on, particularly in those darker moments. I don't believe that either Sammy or her parents would have wanted me to suffer over what happened, and I am so glad that I have now found a way to let go of suffering and to use what I have learned through my life's journey to help other people to stop suffering and to live happier and more fulfilling lives. In sharing what I have learned and in making a positive difference in the world I now feel this is the best way to honour Sammy's memory.

My journey has involved me having a lot of hope, faith and trust. I have not known that I would eventually end up in the place where I am now until I arrived here, but I have hoped that it would happen, and I had faith and trusted that it would too. It felt true and I trusted that feeling.

I know that on continuing my journey through life, life will happen as it always does. I cannot control what happens to me but what will help me to create a happy and fulfilling life is knowing that **THIS IS ME:**

1. I have choice

2. I am strong

3. I trust myself

4. I am grateful

5. I am perfectly imperfect

6. I love and accept myself

7. I am enough

Do you sense that your potential is far greater than your current reality? If so, this book is your call to action! You have within you everything you need to create the life you want. And this is my parting message to you:

'Commit to your happiness, you are worth it. Give yourself permission to be you. Create your life 'on purpose' and be grateful for what you have. Spend time getting to know yourself. Meditate. Take responsibility for how you feel and the choices you make. Stand up for what you believe in and say a resounding YES to yourself. Speak your truth, even when your voice shakes. Surround yourself with empowering people who can hold you to becoming the greatest version of yourself. Be in the arena; be brave, be bold, take positive risks! Be kinder to yourself and soften into your vulnerability. Create clear and strong personal boundaries. Remember that you are enough. Laugh. Dance. Be playful. Trust yourself. Forge your own path. Do it! Do it now…*You are the one you have been waiting for*. Shine your light so brightly it lights up the world.'

Epilogue

*"Owning our story can be hard but not nearly as difficult as
spending our lives running from it. Embracing our vulnerabilities
is risky but not nearly as dangerous as giving up on love and
belonging and joy—the experiences that make us the most
vulnerable. Only when we are brave enough to explore the
darkness will we discover the infinite power of our light."*

Dr. Brene Brown[84]

Looking back and reflecting on my life through the writing of this book was initially like seeing a big jigsaw puzzle with many scattered pieces. It was as though I had to go and find all the missing pieces and try and see where they fit together into the bigger picture before I could see it all more clearly.

Now I can step back and see the whole picture. Everything now fits together.

To get from where I was as a child to where I am now seems nothing short of miraculous. But it didn't happen instantaneously, it has taken many years and much perseverance. I have kept taking the next step and the next step, deconstructing and then re-building my life, walking in faith and trust.

I have learned that the power of the human spirit is immense and that the things that cause us the most pain can be the catalyst for, and hold the keys to, our personal freedom.

Everything is a matter of perspective. As a child, things seemed very black and white to me. With awareness I began to see different perspectives around what had happened to me, the role the adults in my life played, and the way I viewed myself.

The midwife when I was born said that I was 'bloody minded'. Although as a child I took this to be a criticism and therefore negative, looking back I can see that there have been times when I have had to be very determined to keep going in life. Maybe there was some truth in what she said. Maybe an element of bloody mindedness has got me through to where I am today. There are always positive ways and negative ways of looking at things and it's what we choose to focus on that determines how we feel.

Along with this came the discovery of the impact of using the word 'also'. I used to think in terms of absolutes 'I am worthless', and the midwife had proclaimed that I was 'just' bloody minded as a baby, as though that was all I was. Now I know that I can believe I am many things at the same time. I can believe that I am worthless, whilst ALSO believing I am kind and worthy of love and belonging. We can, paradoxically, have different belief systems running at the same time. This really helps me if I am ever feeling low to remember that, although I am feeling bad I am ALSO many other things, including a woman who is making a positive difference in the world.

I can see now that those people who bullied me as a child, were coming from a place of low self-esteem themselves. Emotionally balanced and happy people have no need to make other people feel bad in order to make themselves feel better. This realisation has helped me to develop compassion (and to let go of my anger) towards them.

There were glimpses of who I would become when I was a child. I loved to write and to act, and now I am a professional speaker and author. I took great comfort from reading the words of Desiderata when I was feeling low (Go Placidly amid the noise and the haste and remember what peace there may be in silence), and now I am a qualified mindfulness practitioner.

As you have read, my personal growth journey has not been linear in any sense. It has been full of many twists and turns, ups and downs. At times it has felt as though I was going around in circles, at other times going backwards, but all the time I realise now moving upwards in a spiral to get to where I am today.

Asking the bigger questions in life, such as 'what is the meaning of life' and 'what is the purpose of my life' set in motion a process of discovery for me, leading to what some people refer to as a 'spiritual awakening'. From this point on I have felt connected to something much greater than myself, a universal creative intelligence, of which I am an integral part. I have come to understand that when I follow my intuitive whispers and trust in a bigger picture to life, I marvel at the synchronicities and support that life brings to me.

I used to let other people control me, until I re-discovered my integrity and started to lead my own life in the way that I wanted to live it. My biggest commitment to myself has been to live life in my integrity and not to compromise who I am to please someone else. I am learning to trust myself. The more I live from my integrity the greater the trust becomes.

My belief now is that I don't need to die to go to hell. I have experienced 'hell on earth', through the thoughts and beliefs I created in response to the trauma and abuse I experienced growing up (and in the subsequent rejection of myself) along with living with undiagnosed PTSD for over 30 years and the stress that this put on me mentally, emotionally, physically and spiritually.

Having lived with mental health challenges for a large part of my life I am now passionate about challenging the stigma around mental ill health and am delighted that there is a real focus around this in the schools and organisations that I work with. I want to get to a place where no-one feels that they have to suffer in silence, as I did, and where there is much more awareness and support around mental health.

If you are struggling with your mental health, then talk to someone you trust. You don't need to know what is wrong with you in order to get help, just that you recognise that something isn't right. If you see someone else who is struggling, then let them know that 'I am here for you', as and when they are ready to talk. If someone you know has been through trauma or abuse it is important that they understand that a) there is nothing wrong with them and b) that what they are experiencing is a normal reaction to an abnormal event.

We all have mental health and it's important that we all come to understand that and learn how to take care of our mental health, just as we do our physical health. If you work for an organisation that is looking to build a more inclusive culture around mental health and wellbeing, then do connect with me via my website to have a chat around how I can support you to achieve that.[85]

Purpose has become a driving force in my life. I have a strong sense of direction. I have created a life with positive meaning. I truly believe that whatever cards life deals us, we can always re-shuffle the pack and deal again. We always have choice; not necessarily over what has happened to us but in how we choose to define ourselves by it now. Within us lies the power to reclaim our integrity, to stand up tall and to create amazing lives filled with passion, purpose and meaning.

I now understand the power of intention and realise how much I have created in my life through having a strong intention about it first (peace of mind and happiness, feeling free, making a positive difference in the world, etc.) What are your intentions for your own life? Pay attention to your thoughts because whatever you are focusing on with strong intention is what you will create in your life.

I hope that in reading about the discoveries I have made along my own 'hell of a path to happiness' you have been able to reflect and be inspired and perhaps taken comfort from some of the words. I hope that you now know that wherever you are is perfectly ok, that YOU are ok. There is nothing wrong with you. Your potential is far greater than your current reality and fulfilling that potential begins with accepting yourself and your current reality, just as you are.

If you are a woman and would like to join my growing community of women empowering women you can join my mailing list at www.liscashin.com or you can find the She Who Shines group on Facebook: https://www.facebook.com/groups/shewhoshines/. I would love to see you there!

Be courageous as you take your next step and I will leave you with the wise words of Christopher Robin to Winnie the Pooh:

"You are braver than you believe, stronger than you seem, and smarter than you think.[86]"

Until the next time…

Appendix

Organisations in the UK

Please don't suffer in silence. If you are struggling with your mental health then reach out to someone – a friend, colleague or relative who you trust. The following are additional suggestions of where you can seek professional help:

1. Visit your GP

2. IAPT services through NHS Choices: https://www.england.nhs.uk/mental-health/adults/iapt/

3. To find a private therapist:

   BACP: http://www.bacp.co.uk/

   UKCP: https://www.psychotherapy.org.uk/find-a-therapist

4. Phone lines:

   ➢ Mind Info Line: 0300 123 3393

   ➢ Mind Legal Advice Line: 0300 466 6463

   ➢ Citizens Advice Bureau: 0300 023 1231

   ➢ NHS Stressline: 0300 123 2000

   ➢ Anxiety UK. helpline: 0844 477 5774

- ➤ The National Association for People Abused in Childhood (NAPAC): 0808 801 0331

- ➤ Victim Support: 0808 168 9111

- ➤ ASSIST trauma care helpline: 0178 856 0800

- ➤ Samaritans: 116 123

- ➤ Relate: 0300 100 1234

- ➤ Young Minds: 0808 802 5544

Bibliography

1 Dying to Be Me: My Journey from Cancer, to Near Death, to True Healing, https://anitamoorjani.com/

2 https://www.enidblytonsociety.co.uk/malory-towers.php

3 https://www.amazon.co.uk/Wickedest-Witch-World-Knight-Books/dp/0340197854

4 https://www.amazon.co.uk/gp/bookseries/B00JQP1Y1Y/ref=dp_st_1681370077

5 http://mwkworks.com/desiderata.html

6 https://www.dwightdeisenhower.com/

7 Mistral's Kiss, https://www.laurellkhamilton.com/

8 http://robinwilliams.com/

9 https://www.nelsonmandela.org/

10 https://www.dalecarnegie.co.uk/

11 http://www.rumi.net/

12 https://www.tolkien.co.uk/

13 https://www.amazon.co.uk/Old-Souls-Scientific-Evidence-Search/dp/0684851938

14 http://www.brianweiss.com/about-the-books/many-lives-many-masters/

15 https://www.reiki.org/faq/historyofreiki.html

16 http://mwkworks.com/desiderata.html

17 https://www.thesanctuarythailand.com/

18 https://www.lonelyplanet.com/

19 https://www.louisehay.com/

20 https://juliacameronlive.com/the-artists-way/

21 https://www.purenlp.com/

22 https://www.amazon.com/Healing-Angels-Doreen-Virtue/dp/140190422X

23 https://coldplay.com/song/yellow/

24 https://coldplay.com/release/a-rush-of-blood-to-the-head/

25 https://www.eckharttolle.com/power-of-now-excerpt/

26 https://www.osho.com/iosho/library/read-book/online-library-definition-character-sannyasin-6f1f705b-34e?p=e72da640067c4a7ea88bffdeaeb1bdc1

27 https://harrypotter.bloomsbury.com/uk/

28 http://www.aboutbuddha.org/

29 https://www.alternatives.org.uk/

30 http://marydaniels.co.uk/

31 http://spinalbreath.com/

32 http://www.essence-process.com/

33 https://brenebrown.com/

34 http://www.byronkatie.com/

35 https://thework.com/

36 https://www.abraham-hicks.com/book-excerpt-ask-and-it-is-given-chapter-16/

37 https://www.thesecret.tv/products/the-secret-book/

38 https://www.hki.org/helen-kellers-life-and-legacy#.XKI16ZhKhPY

39 https://www.parmarth.org/

40 https://www.parmarth.org/pujyaswamiji/

41 https://www.sadhviji.org/

42 https://www.dhamma.org/en/index

43 https://www.dhamma.org/en/about/goenka

44 https://www.sriaurobindoashram.org/mother/

45 Radical Acceptance: Embracing Your Life With the Heart of a Buddha
https://www.tarabrach.com/store/

46 https://www.nilambe.net/

47 https://www.ekrfoundation.org/

48 https://www.viktorfrankl.org/

49 https://www.britannica.com/biography/Johann-Wolfgang-von-Goethe

50 https://www.esalen.org/

51 https://www.integralwaytaichi.com/

52 (http://www.feldenkrais.co.uk/what.html)

53 (https://taichiforhealthinstitute.org/what-is-tai-chi/)

54 https://www.cfrhealing.com/

55 http://dari-rulai-temple.org/master-yu/

56 http://www.centeroftheheart.com/philosophy-global-vision

57 http://www.atlantisgym.co.uk/gym.php

58 http://annemcintyre.com/about/ayurveda/

59 http://www.byronkatie.com/

60 https://homeshare.org/

61 https://youthmindfulness.org/

62 https://www.tarabrach.com/store/

63 http://www.family-lab.com/

64 http://www.jesperjuul.com/

65 http://www.jesperjuul.com/bibliography/books/item/your-competent-child

66 https://www.amazon.co.uk/Social-Why-brains-wired-connect/dp/0199645043

67 https://bloomsbury.com/uk/harry-potter-and-the-order-of-the-phoenix-9781408855690/

68 https://www.cmgww.com/historic/wilde/

69 https://www.thepsa.co.uk/

70 http://www.susanjeffers.com

71 https://www.tlclions.com/

72 https://sederhanadesigns.com/

73 https://besselvanderkolk.net/the-body-keeps-the-score.html

74 https://books.wwnorton.com/books/detail.aspx?id=9137

75 https://marianne.com/a-return-to-love/

76 http://www.oprah.com/index.html

77 https://www.bodybrainfreedom.com/the-work

78 https://www.cfrhealing.com/

79 https://www.kora-yoga.com/about/

80 https://theodoreroosevelt.org/content.aspx?sl=1175358451

81 https://brenebrown.com/

82 https://www.thisisgraemepark.com/

83 https://heathersmall-mpeople.com/mike-pickering-biography

84 The Gifts of Imperfection, https://brenebrown.com/books-audio/

85 www.liscashin.com

86 https://www.imdb.com/title/tt0119918/

CPSIA information can be obtained
at www.ICGtesting.com
Printed in the USA
LVHW081759120619
621003LV00016B/991/P